Langage Cleir Illumynate

Scottish Cultural Review of Language and Literature

Volume 10

Series Editors
Rhona Brown
University of Glasgow

John Corbett
University of Glasgow

Sarah Dunnigan
University of Edinburgh

James McGonigal
University of Glasgow

Production Editor
Ronnie Young
University of Glasgow

SCROLL

The Scottish Cultural Review of Language and Literature publishes new work in Scottish Studies, with a focus on analysis and reinterpretation of the literature and languages of Scotland, and the cultural contexts that have shaped them.

Further information on our editorial and production procedures can be found at www.rodopi.nl

Langage Cleir Illumynate

Scottish Poetry
from Barbour to Drummond,
1375-1630

Edited by

Nicola Royan

Rodopi

Amsterdam - New York, NY 2007

Cover image:
William Brassey Hole, *Processional Frieze*, 1898.
© Scottish National Portrait Gallery

The image depicts both William Drummond and John Barbour

Cover design: Gavin Miller and Pier Post

The paper on which this book is printed meets the requirements of "ISO
9706: 1994, Information and documentation - Paper for documents -
Requirements for permanence".

ISBN: 978-90-420-2319-2
©Editions Rodopi B.V., Amsterdam - New York, NY 2007
Printed in The Netherlands

Contents

Contributors

David W. Atkinson is Professor of English Language and Literature at Carleton University, Ottawa. He has published widely on sixteenth and seventeenth-century literature, including *The Selected Sermons of Zachary Boyd* for the Scottish Text Society.

R. James Goldstein, Professor of English at Auburn University, is the author of *The Matter of Scotland: Historical Narrative in Medieval Scotland* (Nebraska UP, 1993), the chapter on Scottish writing in *The Cambridge History of Medieval English Literature*, and articles on Henryson, Lyndsay, Chaucer, and Langland.

Rosemary Greentree is a visiting research fellow at the University of Adelaide, South Australia. She has recently published a bibliography of criticism of the Middle English lyrics, and has also written on Robert Henryson's works, particularly the *Moral Fables*.

Katherine McClune is a tutor at St Hilda's College, Oxford. Her thesis focused on the work of John Stewart of Baldynneis, and his significance as a poet at the court of James VI.

J. Derrick McClure is a Senior Lecturer in English at the University of Aberdeen, Chairman of the Forum for Research in the Languages of Scotland and Ulster, editor of *Scottish Language* and author of numerous publications on a wide range of Scottish linguistic and literary topics. His recent work has concentrated on translations in Scottish literature and Middle Scots poetic prosody.

Sally Mapstone is Reader in Older Scots Literature, University of Oxford. Her many publications include *Scots and their Books in the Middle Ages and Renaissance* (Oxford, 1996) and (ed.) *Older Scots Literature* (Edinburgh, 2005). She is President of the Scottish Text Society.

Joanna Martin is a Darby Fellow in English at Lincoln College, Oxford. Her research interests cover Older Scots and late Middle English writing. She has just completed a book on medieval Scottish poetry, and is about to take up a lectureship at the University of Nottingham.

Nicole Meier was educated at the Universities of Bonn, Aberdeen and Edinburgh. She teaches Old English, Middle English and Scots at the Department of English, Bonn University, Germany, and is working at the Medieval Studies Centre at Bonn University. She has written on Scottish Ballads, Alfred and Hoccleve and is currently preparing an edition of Walter Kennedy's poetry.

Nicola Royan is a lecturer in medieval and early modern literature in the School of English Studies at the University of Nottingham. She is Editorial Secretary of the Scottish Text Society.

Thomas Rutledge is a lecturer in English at the University of East Anglia. His research interests are in the medieval reception of classical literature and in the impact of humanism in late-medieval and early-modern Scotland.

Michael R.G. Spiller is Honorary Senior Lecturer in English and Cultural History at the University of Aberdeen, and now lives in Edinburgh. His publications include *The Development of the Sonnet* (1992), *The Sonnet Sequence: a Study of its Strategies* (1997) and *Early Modern Sonneteers: from Wyatt to Milton* (2001).

Andrew Taylor teaches in the English Department at the University of Ottawa. He is the author of *Textual Situations: Three Medieval Manuscripts and Their Readers* and one of the co-editors of the anthology *The Idea of the Vernacular*. His research concentrates on the history of reading and of minstrel performance in the later Middle Ages.

Acknowledgments

The final volume of proceedings from the 9th International Conference on Medieval and Renaissance Language and Literature, held at the University of St Andrews in 1999, this collection has had a difficult journey to publication, having lost an editor and a publisher, and having gained en route two essays, by Thomas Rutledge and Katherine McClune, and an afterword, by Sally Mapstone. As the editor, therefore, I have even more thanks owing than usual. Firstly, I must express my gratitude to the original contributors, who have been amazingly patient with me as I sought a publisher, and funding, and additional contributors. They have always given the impression that they believed I would bring the whole thing off, and I am very grateful for their confidence and their support. I must also thank the newcomers to the collection: Katherine McClune, Thomas Rutledge and Sally Mapstone. I also owe a large debt to Joanne Norman, who volunteered to act as co-editor for this volume, but was forced to withdraw at a late stage as a result of family illness. Before her withdrawal, however, she offered careful and detailed readings of the essays then submitted, and I have drawn heavily on her recommendations. I regret that this volume was not completed before her own premature death.

John Tuckwell originally agreed to publish this collection, but on his retirement, an alternative publisher had to be found. I am delighted that the Scottish Cultural Review of Language and Literature, in the persons of Rhona Brown, John Corbett, Sarah Dunnigan, and James McGonigal, stepped into the breach and enabled this collection to see the light of day. I am also very grateful to the reader of the proposal: I hope that we have met all the challenges set down in the report. Ronnie Young has been an exemplary typesetter, and many thanks must also go to him. Money is far more of an issue in academic publishing than I had ever imagined: particular thanks are therefore due to Professor Douglas Dunn, the School of English and St Andrews Scottish Studies Institute, who hosted the original conference, and to the Department of Scottish Literature, University of Glasgow under the headship of Professor Douglas Gifford, and to the Quick Response Fund, University of Nottingham, for subsidies along the way.

I have also always been fortunate in my colleagues, wherever I have worked: in this context, particular mention must go to Frances Mullan, Douglas Dunn, Rhiannon Purdie, Ian Johnson, Theo van

Heijnsbergen, Judith Jesch and Thorlac Turville-Petre. I was married eight weeks before the conference from which this volume originated: my final thanks go to my husband, Derek, who has endured the vicissitudes of this collection for far too long.

Introduction

Nicola Royan

Keywords: John Barbour; John Bellenden; criticism; court; Gavin Douglas; William Drummond; William Dunbar; Robert Henryson; James I; James VI; Walter Kennedy; David Lyndsay; national identity; poetry; Scottishness; John Stewart of Baldynneis.

That the Scots of the fifteenth and sixteenth centuries apparently pre-ferred verse to prose in their vernacular writing has been noted before (Lyall 1988). This collection, therefore, can be said to represent those preferences in writing and reading throughout early Scottish literature. For although the attractions of prose are beginning to creep in, through John Bellenden's translations of Livy's *Ab urbe condita* and Hector Boece's *Scotorum Historia*, and James VI's *Reulis and Cautelis,* this is a volume about poetry, in its many forms and genres. Each of the essays discusses important and familiar Scottish texts, by the stalwarts of the discipline, such as Barbour, Dunbar, Lyndsay, Drummond; each offers a different and often new perspective on its material. The approaches range from detailed examinations of particular poems, to historical-contextual accounts of poetic influence, to a psychoanalytic reading of *Squyer Meldrum*; thus most critical schools are represented in this collection. Indirectly, it also charts a history of Scottish writing from John Barbour's *Bruce* to William Drummond's *Flowres of Sion,* through the dominance of romance and chivalric values, the influence of Chaucer, the rise of humanism, the uncertainties of the Reformation and the developments of early modern literature. The period covered is one of the richest in Scottish literature, and in defiance of conven-tional periodisation, usually based on English patterns, attempts to divide it into medieval and early modern are only ever partially suc-cessful. Instead continuity takes priority over difference, and across the collection, these essays speak to one another, whether addressing formal or thematic or contextual matters. This is of course most obvi-ous when reading both essays on Lyndsay, or both on Drummond, but also applies across both time and writer, suggesting parallels between Barbour and Lyndsay, Henryson and Stewart of Baldynneis, Dunbar and Drummond.

John Barbour stands at the head of most narratives of Scottish literature, and this collection is no different. In "From Heraldry to History", Andrew Taylor examines again the difficult problem of Barbour's sources. He negotiates the opposing positions of the most recent editors, between the rebuttal of possible oral material and the positing of a finished heraldic text, to suggest the possible influence on Barbour of heraldic narrative, a particular kind of story-telling (McDiarmid and Stevenson eds 1985: I: 38–44; Duncan 1997: 14–30). His account points out the shared styles of narrative in Froissart and other chroniclers, including some of the Wars of Independence, and explores the nature of such heroic narrative and the purposes to which it may have been put in a chivalric society. He argues that oral reports of battles, once shaped into narratives, were specifically to encourage new knights in their military duties; as well as reorienting our understanding of Barbour's relationship to his sources, his approach might suggest another way in which the *Bruce* contributes to an advice tradition for nobles as well as for kings.

Joanna Martin's essay, "The Translation of Fortune: James I's *Kingis Quair* and the Rereading of Lancastrian Poetry" addresses questions similar to Taylor's. Firstly, her essay is also concerned with the depiction of right conduct among the ruling classes, albeit presented in a very different manner. While Taylor presents heraldic narrative as a form based on plot and open to some reshaping in terms of language and context, Martin compares James's portrayal of kingship with those of John Gower and Thomas Hoccleve, and explores the sophisticated interplay, both poetical and political, between them. James I does not incorporate a widely-circulating narrative into his poem, but rather consciously attempts to render English styles of advice material appropriate for a Scottish king in a Scottish context. Both essays reiterate the clear connections between Scottish and English culture, and both refute straightforward imitation. Barbour's work, however, clearly participates more freely in a shared understanding of knighthood and noble behaviour; James, Martin argues, is a careful reader of English poetry as well as of English government, using a variety of subject positions to explore his situation and to differentiate it from that of the Lancastrian kings and their poets. Her argument marks a new point on the trajectory from acknowledging a "so-called stylistic debt to Chaucerianism" (p.59) to examining creative tensions between the Scots and the English writers.

The *Moral Fables* of Robert Henryson are also concerned with moral government; in her essay, "'That he in brutal beist is transformate': The Translation of Man's Deeds to Those of Beasts", Rosemary Greentree considers the presentation of personal rather than political morality. Through paying close attention to the detail of the poems, she contrasts Henryson's use of the fabular form and particularly his treatment of the fox with that of Dunbar's "This hyndir nicht", pointing out the careful construction of tone and atmosphere in all the poems. Whereas Henryson puts human nature into beast form for a more effective moral lesson, Greentree argues that Dunbar rather emphasises the bestial in human behaviour, foregrounding the fox's consumption of the lamb through sexual desire. Although she argues that the specific satirical nature of Dunbar's work has lessened its impact over time, the effect of the Dunfermline setting of "This hyndir nicht", a setting associated with Henryson by Dunbar himself, together with the traditional identification of Dunbar's fox with James IV, we might speculate that Dunbar's poem is more serious in moral intent than an initial reading would suggest.

Rather than considering the immediate poetic context, like Greentree, Nicole Meier seeks to place *The Flyting of Dunbar and Kennedy* in a European tradition. She looks specifically at parallels for flyting and poetic competition in Old French and in Scots Gaelic, and concludes that while flyting may appear to be a distinctive Scottish form by the sixteenth century, it may not be an entirely Scottish invention. There are some analogies in the Old French tradition, and even though Dunbar presents Celtic identity as an insult, Meier argues that certain features of *The Flyting* have clear parallels in Gaelic equivalents. Not only then does her paper refute any insularity in Scottish literature, even when the poet is using the densest vernacular, but she also problematises further the relationship between Scots and Gaelic culture at the end of the fifteenth century. For as well as pointing out generic parallels between Gaelic satire and Scots flyting, Meier traces resemblances in fields of insult, suggesting either that the vocabulary of insult does not vary greatly between languages, or else – more contentiously – that Dunbar may have shared with Kennedy, a Gaelic speaker, some knowledge of Gaelic forms. There is no doubt that the interface between Scots and Gaelic requires further investigation: while such tantalising documents such as the *Book of the Dean of Lismore*, used convincingly by Meier, may suggest an absorption of

Scots literature by Gaelic readers, hostility to Gaelic culture often seems more prevalent on the Scots side, notwithstanding James IV's alleged fluency in the language (Bawcutt 1992: 20–21; Macdougall 1997: 284–85).

Thomas Rutledge's essay, "Gavin Douglas and John Bellenden: Poetic Relations and Political Affiliations", outlines a more certain influence. John Bellenden's closeness to the Douglas affinity is evident in both in his probable employment by the Earl of Angus and his greater support for the Douglases in his translation of the *Scotorum Historia*. Rutledge argues that such affinities are also literary, and that in his *Proheme,* Bellenden deliberately presents himself as Douglas's literary successor as well as a supporter of the Douglas kin. The parallels between a translator of the early books of Livy and a translator of the *Aeneid* are obvious: both have a concern to bring the best of classical Latin writing into the vernacular for wider circulation. In addition, reading back from Bellenden's undertaking to translate the first books of Livy, it is possible to suggest that both Douglas and Bellenden have an interest in foundational history and its influence on national identity. As the first translator of the *Scotorum Historia*, Bellenden was clearly familiar with the Scottish origin myth and also with the use Boece made of Livy in describing early Scottish history; Douglas too is on record as championing this myth. However, Rutledge's interest lies more with the particular issues of literary succession and loyal service. He argues that the *Proheme* is a programmatic poem, outlining Bellenden's literary agenda, on the model of *The Palis of Honoure*; in choosing Douglas as a literary model, though, Bellenden makes a potentially lethal statement of allegiance to an out-of-favour kin (Cameron 1998: 9–51, 329–30). Rutledge's essay therefore complicates our understanding of the court culture of James V, where it was clearly possibly for someone with Bellenden's well-known affinities both to retain and advertise those links and yet to be rewarded.

Together with service, affinity and comradeship, exemplified here by Bellenden, are perhaps the hardest of late medieval and early modern emotions to comprehend. This might be the reason why Sir David Lyndsay's poems, *Squyer Meldrum* and *The Testament of Squyer Meldrum* have proved so problematic to recent critics, producing only three discussions of any note (Hadley Williams 2000; Edington 1994; Riddy 1974). While paying tribute to previous work on the poems, R. James Goldstein takes a radically different approach, drawing on Freudian and Lacanian theory to examine "the work of mourning" present in Lyndsay's works. The result is a highly complex and suggestive piece of criticism. For Goldstein argues that *Squyer Meldrum* attempts to define normative masculinity within the chivalric code, specifically that Meldrum finds his identity through warfare before he finds it through heterosexual love. One might compare this definition of masculinity with that expressed by Barbour, as outlined by Taylor in his essay. Both Barbour's source and *Squyer Meldrum* might be considered heraldic narratives, not least because of Lyndsay's own position as Lyon King of Arms. The similarities can be extended, however. Both deal with warfare as a means of establishing masculine identity; more crucially, both require the narrative of warfare to prove that identity, as Goldstein points out. Both operate around desperate bravery, whether Giles de Argentan in the face of English defeat, or Meldrum in the face of attack by his lady's relatives. While it is clear that Lyndsay is less comfortable with the chivalric code than Barbour, nonetheless Meldrum is something of a masculine model, regardless of the relative weight given to the charitable self-sacrifice compared to the martial glory.

Goldstein also discusses more briefly Lyndsay's political grief at the loss of an adult male ruler, and, building on previous work, he argues that this is a central theme in all Lyndsay's poetry. The desire for strong and moral kingship and the need to define it are also key to Martin's reading of the *Kingis Quair* and its Lancastrian analogues. Discussions of kingship run deep in early Scottish literature, yet it is interesting that, in Martin's and Goldstein's arguments, both James I and Lyndsay use the policing of erotic desire as a metaphor for government. Clearly the different situations of Lyndsay and James produce different presentations of this metaphor, but perhaps the most striking difference is the tone of the poets. As Martin argues, in comparison to Gower and Hoccleve, James hopes to restructure kingship in his own person for a Scottish situation: the poem has a degree of political confidence. Lyndsay, in contrast, is without that hope, particularly in his later poems, for a modern reader a fitting comment on the irony of James I's death as well as on that of James V.

J. Derrick McClure's discussion of Lyndsay's metre in "Lyndsay's Dramatic use of Prosody in *Ane Satyre of the Thrie*

Estaitis" could not seem further from Goldstein's psychoanalysis. As
McClure himself points out, the technical aspect of Lyndsay's writing
is not often discussed (see McGavin 1993 as an exception) yet without
his feel for form and rhythm, Lyndsay's greatest works would be
much the less. Through his detailed analysis, McClure argues that
Lyndsay developed his competency in metre over his poetic career,
and that *Ane Satire of the Thrie Estaitis* and *Squyer Meldrum*
demonstrate his growing sophistication in handling prosody. In
particular, in *Ane Satyre*, he was able to manipulate his verse forms
for dramatic effect, while at the same time retaining the sound of the
everyday. Underlying McClure's argument is the acknowledgement
that Lyndsay did not approach the metrical skill or complexity evident
in works by Douglas and Dunbar; equally important, however, is the
probability that Lyndsay never aspired to such intricacy, since he
wrote vastly different works from either of his immediate predecessors. Nevertheless, his use of metrical variety strengthens the messages of *Ane Satyre*, whether by underscoring Rex Humanitas's
succumbing to the courtiers' blandishments and Sensualitie's appeal,
or by blurring the difference between the audience and the Puir Man.
The combination in Lyndsay's writing of a homespun style and what
appears as a common-sense morality have been said to underpin his
very popular appeal; McClure unpicks that style and demonstrates
how it works.

James VI's opinion of Lyndsay's verse style is not on record:
*Ane Schort Treatise Conteining Some Reulis and Cautelis to be
Observit and Eschewit in Scottis Poesie* is programmatic rather than
reflective of past practice. Nevertheless, in "The Scottish Sonnet,
James VI and John Stewart of Baldynneis", Katherine McClune traces
an outline of moral concern which, she argues, can be found in the
Kingis Quair, the work of James VI's ancestor and Gavin Douglas's
Prologues to the *Eneados*, as well as in his own. In his treatise, James
validates reason over passion as a guiding feature for poetry; when
this is put into practice, argues McClune, this produces a peculiarly
Scottish form of the sonnet. She explores the expression of James's
views in his own poetry, and, more particularly, its influence on the
writing of John Stewart of Baldynneis. Usually considered in Alexander Montgomerie's shadow, Stewart is one of the most interesting
poets at the court of James VI, not least because of his apparent
engagement with James VI's theories. Like Rutledge's analysis of

Bellenden's poem, which raises questions about the court of James V, McClune's exploration of Stewart's work, particularly in the context of the *Reulis and Cautelis* suggests that further examination of the cultural world of the court of James VI is necessary. McClune thus responds implicitly to questions raised in Bawcutt (1997) by examining the detail of a text rather than making general assumptions about courtly order.

The last papers in the volume represent the growing scholarly interest in the literature of the late sixteenth and seventeenth centuries. Both essays are traditional enough to discuss the work of William Drummond of Hawthornden: both explore the commonest criticism of Drummond, that his work is derivative. Through a detailed examination of *The Flowres of Sion*, David Atkinson argues that despite the imitative appearance of his work, Drummond nevertheless conveys individual voice and a personal theology. Atkinson's argument is based on a detailed reading of the text and its treatment of standard themes such as the *memento mori*, and it gives full play to Drummond's poetic skill. Atkinson also points out the sectarian ambivalence in Drummond's religious verse, noting that while the poems on the life of Christ suggest a Catholic bias, there are also occasional references to faith as a gift from God, known as a cornerstone of Protestant theology. As Atkinson points out, this ambivalence may have been shared by many of Drummond's contemporary Scots, a view confirmed by other recent scholarship; while *The Flowres of Sion* may be only "a moving, if not entirely original expression of seventeenth-century religiosity" (201), it might nevertheless reflect particular Scottish experience.

Like Atkinson, Michael Spiller does not make dramatic claims for Drummond's poetic abilities, but rather approaches the question of Drummond's derivativeness from another perspective: he suggests that Drummond was consciously attempting to "out-Petrarch" Petrarch in English and to emulate Philip Sidney, specifically in the arrangement and content of his own sonnet sequence. As evidence, Spiller deploys Drummond's own notes on Petrarchanism and also the commissioned resetting of the sonnet sequence by the printer Andro Hart between 1614 and 1616. Drummond's understanding of Petrarch is not limited to the sonnet form or to the familiar tropes, but is concerned with what Spiller calls the essence of Petrarch, the construction and ordering of his sequences, their overall effect as well as the communication of the sonnets' contents. Spiller's article builds from a comparison of one of Drummond's sonnets with its Petrarchan model to a consideration of the sequence patterns as a whole, and ultimately, it encourages a re-examination of Petrarch's reception into English and Scottish writing, acknowledging that what seems essential to us today may not have appear so in the early seventeenth century; with its view of Drummond, the essay reaffirms his status as a critic and a poet who sites himself in a European, as well as a British and a Scottish context.

Editors and publishers often fear that collections of conference proceedings are rag-bag volumes of essays whose only connection is the original location in time and space of their delivery. It is certainly possible to argue that diversity is one of this collection's strengths: its essays not only cover a wide range of material, but they are also the work of scholars at the beginning and at the high points of their careers. Notably, only two contributors are based in Scotland: it is perhaps a sad truth that there is a greater and better supported interest in early Scottish literature outwith the national boundaries. Equally true, however, is the positive view that the study of early Scottish literature is producing fine blooms, notwithstanding threats of frost and savage pruning, and this collection displays the flowers of Scottish literary studies, just like previous proceedings of these triennial conferences (a full list is included in the bibliography). Moreover, as the cursory examination of the papers above demonstrates, there are clear links between individual papers; in addition, two over-arching themes can be found. The first concerns the audience within the realm, the second the situation of Scottish literature within a wider context.

Some recent criticism has emphasised the absence of court literature in Scotland and noted the greater importance of magnatial and lairdly patrons in the composition and reception of literature in the late medieval period (Mapstone 1991). The evidence for this is compelling: named patrons tend to be noble or lairdly, such as Archibald Douglas, Earl of Moray for *The Buke of the Howlat* or Sir William Wallace of Craigie and Sir James Liddale for *The Wallace*; it is hard to identify any court poet in the court records prior to Dunbar and Lyndsay (Barbour's place seems slightly different). However, in this collection, the relationship between poet and sovereign is an important, even a central one. Two of the essays discuss work written by kings; we have no contemporary response to the *Kingis Quair*, but McClune's essay makes clear that James VI's work was read carefully by some of his subjects. *The Kingis Quair* is not only by a king, but also about a king, and while that particular intimacy between author and subject is rare, several other writers have a king at the centre of their work. This is most obvious with Barbour's *Bruce*. Although Taylor's essay is primarily concerned with the role of Giles D'Argentan, Robert I gains part of his glory in the poem and elsewhere – for instance, in *Scotichronicon* (Watt et al. 1987–98: 7: 51–7) – from being the most knightly, therefore the best of the Scots. This is a different view of kingship from the *Kingis Quair*, but just as significant for Barbour's original audience. As Greentree notes, James IV is a more shadowy presence in "This hyndir nicht", there by traditional association rather than direct reference. Bannatyne, from whom the association derives, is not always the most reliable of literary gossips, yet his view of the poem has affected its reading for so long that it is impossible to ignore. Part of its appeal must lie in the image it presents of James IV's court, where a poet can indulge in gossip and oblique criticism of the sovereign, and yet not suffer harshly for it. As such, the association might be seen as a piece of nostalgia on Bannatyne's part, for a realm with an adult male monarch, strong and confident enough to accept criticism. A more convincing picture of intimacy between king and poet is presented repeatedly by David Lyndsay, for whom, Goldstein argues, the relationship with his sovereign was the defining feature of his life. The conclusion of Goldstein's argument, that James V is present in all Lyndsay's writing, even when absent, is the ultimate expression of the importance of the king figure in political and personal life.

Lyndsay's early poetry was often about the king, as well as written to and for him. For the other writers discussed in this collection, even when the king is not the subject, he is often an implied reader. Barbour praises Robert I for his grandson; Dunbar sought a royal audience for his poems, whether or not James IV is the fox of "This hyndir nicht". The context of Bellenden's *Proheme* and the *Proloug* to his translation of Livy means that Bellenden, like his model Gavin Douglas, expected a royal audience. In both cases, poetry is used as a means of indirectly asserting a political position, in Douglas's case, as a member of one of the most powerful magnate families, and in Bellenden's case, his affinity with the same family.

Bellenden's statement must rank as the more courageous, given the behaviour of the Douglases in the decade prior to his writing. Both Dunbar and Stewart clearly expect their sovereigns to be a part of their audience, albeit in rather different circumstances. In fact, of all the writers discussed, only two, Henryson and Drummond, appear indifferent to royal opinion, even though they remain concerned with the sovereignty of the self as well as the duties of the royal sovereign. Drummond's political sensibilities come to the fore in his *History of Scotland from the year 1423 until the year 1542*, printed posthumously in 1655; Henryson's are most acute in the central fables in his cycle. Apparently also independent of any other patrons, their poetry nevertheless circulated widely; without seeking a royal audience, they may still have gained one.

The second feature recurrent throughout the collection is the examination of Scottish responses to literatures in other languages. The most obvious interaction with English writing is considered in four essays (Taylor, Martin, McClune and Spiller), although Martin's discussion of James I's absorption of the English Chaucerians is the most detailed. More significant to this collection is the influence of non-English literature, whether that be Gaelic, French, Italian or Latin. Respect for and interest in these literatures does not, however, imply any form of cultural cringe. For Drummond, as for Douglas and Bellenden, the importation of the best of foreign literature into their own vernacular was an important part of their motivation, but it did not imply that their own tradition was impoverished. Indeed, the essays by Greentree and Atkinson confine their remarks to Scottish poems in a Scottish context: this focused attention to detail brings out the richness of the poems under discussion, and a wider context is not missed. While Henryson, Dunbar and Drummond, however, can in other essays fit with other literary paradigms, other writers, notably, as McClune points out, the sonneteers at James VI's court and James himself, have to be presented as being at odds with the practice on the continent and in England.

The original intention of this volume was to showcase the strength of this discipline, demonstrating the wide range of critical approaches used to explore the most familiar of texts, to display in fact the "Makars at the Millennium". The adventures of this volume have rather swept away that brave, if dated intention, but as it turns out, the collection still achieves that goal and more, it asseverates something just as important, namely the existence of a peculiarly Scottish tradition, one that is outward-looking, self-confident and self-reflexive.

Bibliography

Aitken, A.J., Matthew P. McDiarmid and Derick S. Thompson (eds). 1977. *Bards and Makars: Scottish Language and Literature Medieval and Renaissance.* Glasgow: Glasgow University Press.

Bawcutt, Priscilla. 1992. *Dunbar the Makar.* Oxford: Clarendon Press.

—. 2001. "James VI's Castalian Band: a Modern Myth" in *SHR* 80: 251–59.

Blanchot, Jean-Jacques and Claude Graf (eds). 1979. *Actes du Colloque de langue et de literature écossaises.* Strasbourg: Institut d'etudes anglaises de Strasbourg et l'Association des médiévistes anglicistes de l'enseignement supérieur.

Caie, Graham, R.J. Lyall, Sally Mapstone and Kenneth Simpson (eds). 2001. *The European Sun: Proceedings of the Seventh International Conference on Medieval and Renaissance Scottish Language and Literature.* East Linton: Tuckwell Press.

Cameron, Jamie. 1998. *James V: the Personal Rule 1528–1542.* East Linton: Tuckwell Press.

Duncan, A.A.M. (ed.) 1997. *The Bruce.* Edinburgh: Canongate.

Edington, Carol. 1994. *Court and Culture in Renaissance Scotland: Sir David Lindsay of the Mount (1486–1555).* East Linton: Tuckwell Press.

Hadley Williams, Janet. (ed.) 2000. *Sir David Lyndsay: Selected Poems.* Glasgow: Association for Scottish Literary Studies.

Johnson, Ian and Nicola Royan (eds). 2002. *Forum for Modern Language Studies 38.2 Special Issue: Scottish Texts, European Contexts.* Oxford: Oxford University Press.

Lyall, R.J. and Felicity Riddy (eds). 1981. *Proceedings of the Third International Conference on Scottish Language and Literature (Medieval and Renaissance).* Stirling and Glasgow: Universities of Stirling and Glasgow.

—. 1988. "Vernacular Prose before the Reformation" in Jack, R.D.S. (ed.) *The History of Scottish Literature Vol. 1: Origins to 1660.* Aberdeen: AUP. 163–82.

McClure, J. Derrick and Michael R.G. Spiller (eds). 1989. *Bryght Lanternis: Essays on the Language and Literature of Medieval and Renaissance Scotland.* Aberdeen: Aberdeen University Press.

MacDonald, Alasdair A. and Kees Dekker (eds). 2005. *Rhetoric, royalty, and reality: essays on the literary culture of medieval and early modern Scotland.* Leuven: Peeters.

Macdougall, Norman. 1997. *James IV.* East Linton: Tuckwell Press.

McDiarmid, Matthew P. and J.A.C. Stevenson (eds). 1980–1985. *Barbour's Bruce* [Scottish Text Society 4th Series no. 12, 13, 15.]. 3 vols. Edinburgh: Scottish Text Society.

McGavin, John J. 1993. "The Dramatic Prosody of Sir David Lindsay" in Jack, R.D.S. and Kevin McGinley (eds) *Of Lion and of Unicorn: Essays on Anglo-Scottish Relations in Honour of Professor John MacQueen.* Edinburgh: Quadriga. 39–66.

Mapstone, Sally. 1991. "Was there a court literature in fifteenth-century Scotland?" in *SSL* 26: 410–22.

—. (ed.) 2005. *Older Scots Literature.* Edinburgh: Birlinn.

Riddy, Felicity. 1974. "*Squyer Meldrum* and the Romance of Chivalry" in *Yearbook of English Studies* 14: 26–36.

Roy, G. Ross and Patrick Scott (ed.) 1991. *Studies in Scottish Literature 26: Proceedings of the Seventh International Conference on Medieval and Renaissance Scottish Language and Literature*. Columbia: University of South Carolina.

Strauss, Dietrich and Horst W Drescher (eds). 1986. *Scottish Language and Literature, Medieval and Renaissance Fourth International Conference 1984 Proceedings*. Frankfurt am Main: Peter Lang.

Van Heijnsbergen, Theo and Nicola Royan (eds). 2002. *Literature, Letters and the Canonical in Early Modern Scotland*. East Linton: Tuckwell Press.

Watt, D.E.R. et al. (eds). 1987–98. *Walter Bower: Scotichronicon*. 9 vols. Aberdeen and Edinburgh: Aberdeen University Press and Mercat Press.

From Heraldry to History: The Death of Giles D'Argentan

Andrew Taylor

John Barbour's sources for the *Bruce* have always attracted much discussion. This essay considers the contribution of heraldic narrative, whether written or oral, focusing on the example of Giles D'Argentan. It concludes that such narratives may indeed be more significant for the *Bruce* and other chivalric romances than previously thought.
Keywords: Giles D'Argentan; Bannockburn; John Barbour; Walter Bower; *Bruce*; Edward Bruce; chivalry; Edward II; Jean Froissart; Thomas Gray; Gib Harper; heralds; heraldic narrative; Otterburn; Robert le Roy; *Scalachronica*; *Scotichronicon*.

At a certain point, neither family pride, nor loyalty to one's comrades or king, nor years of indoctrination in chivalric values can withstand the basic human instinct to escape danger, and once the first man flees the others soon follow. So it was at Bannockburn. After several hours, the battle turned against the English. According to John Barbour's account in his *Bruce*, when King Edward saw that the enemy's army had grown so brave that his own men lacked the strength to withstand and had begun to flee, he himself was so greatly discouraged ("abaysyt sa gretumly") that he and five hundred of his men took to flight in a great rush ("in-till a frusch") (McDiarmid and Stevenson 1981: 3: 61; further references to Barbour's *Bruce* will be to this edition, and will take the form of book and line numbers). Barbour adds, in fairness, that he has heard some men say that the king was led away against his will, before turning to one man who refused to withdraw:

And quhen Schyr Gylis ye Argente
Saw ye king yus and his menȝe
Schap yaim to fley sa spedyly,
He come rycht to ye king in hy
And said "Schyr, sen it is sua
Yat ȝe yusgat ȝour gat will ga
Hawys gud day for agayne will I,
Ȝeyt fled I neuer sekyrly
And I cheys her to bid and dey
Yan for to lyve schamly and fley".
Hys bridill but mar abad

He turnyt and agayne he rade
And on Eduuard ye Bruys rout
Yat was sa sturdy and sa stout
As drede off nakyn thing had he
He prikyt cryand "ye Argente",
And yai with speris swa him met
And swa fele speris on him set
Yat he and hors war chargyt swa
Yat bathe till ye erd gan ga
And in yat place yar slane wes he. (XIII: 299–319)

Then Barbour provides his final assessment, and inscribes d'Argentan into history as the third best knight of his day:

Off hys deid wes rycht gret pite,
He wes ye thrid best knycht perfay
Yat men wyst lywand in his day,
He did mony a fayr iourne.
On Saryzynys thre deren3eys faucht he
And in-till ilk deren3e off ya
He wencussyt Saryzynys twa.
His gret worschip tuk yar ending. (XIII: 320–27)

Argentan's bravery was rewarded with fame, for his defiant charge became a standard part of the medieval account of Bannockburn. The way this story took shape and circulated testifies to the strength of an oral tradition in which heralds, minstrels, and the knights themselves collaborated, burying fear and panic beneath dramatic accounts of conspicuous bravery.

In their edition of the *Bruce*, Matthew McDiarmid and James Stevenson suggest that Barbour's source for the account of Sir Giles d'Argenté or d'Argentan was a lost chronicle of the English minstrel and king of heralds, Robert le Roy (McDiarmid and Stevenson 1985: I: 38). McDiarmid and Stevenson take the suggestion from Walter Bower, who in his *Scotichronicon* of ca. 1440 also calls Argentan one of the three best knights of his day, and attributes this remark to Edward's herald, "king Robert", and also mentions that Argentan defeated two Saracens in each of two encounters (Watt et al. 1987–98: 7: 50–57).

Bower refers to Argentan twice: first in his account of the battle itself, where he singles out his death for particular mention but says little else, and then again in Book XII, where he tells how an English herald praised Robert the Bruce.

Almost always empty pleasure and delight for the unbridled spirit accompanies royal feasts. For while the body is set free in the pleasures of eating, the heart is made dissolute through empty enjoyment. This happened one day to the king of England Edward de Caernarfon, who, when he was holding a great feast for the magnates and army commanders of his land, while the wine was glistening in the bowls and had gladdened the hearts of the guests, as a way of amusing himself he asked his herald called Robert the King [of Arms] – a man who was undoubtedly discreet and intelligent, who had besides been nominated and appointed king of all the heralds of England *(tocius Anglie propterea hirellorum rege nominato et effecto)* – who in his judgment were the three knights then living who were the most tested and worthy fighters. (Watt et al. 1987–98: 7: 51)

The herald, with bowed head and bended knee, answered him respectfully that in his judgment they were the emperor Henry, Giles d'Argentan, who fought three times against the Saracens and killed two each time, and Robert the Bruce, "a fighter of invincible courage according to the common popular estimation" ("quantus fuerit invicte virtutis bellator juxta commune et populare judicium") (Watt et al. 1987–98: 7: 52). The knights were furious, and shouted loudly that no Scot, let alone Bruce, should ever be compared to them. Le Roy defended his claim, insisting that indeed Robert the Bruce should be rated the highest of the three, since Henry could always draw on large forces and Argentan was not experienced in controlling a large army or as the commander of many troops ("non tamen rector in multitudine vel multorum fuisse expertus est gubernacione") (Watt et al. 1987–98: 7: 54). He insisted that he would defend his judgment on his own body, as any herald should, but Bower, having described this thrilling episode at some length, tells us no more and we do not know if anyone took up le Roy's challenge. Bower, an Augustinian canon writing over a century after the battle, offers an account that is in many ways highly implausible – no herald would call Bruce "king" in Edward's presence – and conventional; it is an *exemplum* illustrating the Biblical theme of the foolish king humbled. Edward's feast echoes those of Belshazzar, where Daniel prophesies the king's doom, and of Herod, as portrayed on the medieval stage, where the drunken king is visited by Death (Daniel 5.1; cf. Spector 1991: 1: 192–97). There are echoes of folk tales as well, specifically the theme of the rash question. Edward is in effect asking "who is the bravest of them all".

With good reason, the editors of the *Scotichronicon* describe the
account as "a work of the imagination" (Watt et al. 1987–98: 7: 191).
But it is a work of imagination with some remarkably accurate
moments. Bower gets the name and title right, for one thing. Robert le
Roy was the king's herald and did have jurisdiction over all other
English heralds. But where did Bower hear of him? Neither Barbour
nor any of the other early accounts refer to le Roy, which is scarcely
surprising, since he was not one of the knights. Heralds were required
to keep records, however, and their own experiences might be more
likely to appear there. Was le Roy's lost chronicle the ultimate source
for Barbour's account of Argentan's charge, as McDiarmid and
Stevenson suggest, and perhaps also of Bower's account of le Roy's
provocative speech of praise?

A chronicle composed by a herald is of more than passing interest, especially if the author could be identified. In the fourteenth century, heralds were still closely associated with minstrels and such
terms as "disour" (someone who tells stories) or "gestour" (someone
who sings or tells of the deeds of knights) often seem to cover both
(Keen 1984: 125–42; Chesnutt 1987: 48–67; Taylor 1992: 38–62;
Taylor 1997: 47–72). A herald's chronicle would be something of a
missing link between oral and written traditions and between two
orders of surviving evidence for minstrel activity: pay records, from
which we may construct careers of specific performers, and texts that,
on stylistic grounds, might possibly be minstrel works. While the Low
Countries offer a few cases of identifiable minstrels with well defined
careers whose works also survive, such as Adenet le Roi, this is not
the case for England or Scotland. We have a number of works that
have often been attributed to unidentified minstrels, often as mere
supposition, such as the Middle English romances; a number of works
that might more plausibly be attributed to minstrels, such as short
poems of praise, many of them in Anglo-Norman, one good example
being the *Song of Caerlaverock* of ca.1300; and then we have a whole
ream of pay references from which we may construct careers. The few
chronicles written by heralds that do survive, such as Chandos
Herald's *Life of the Black Prince*, are part of a more elevated literary
tradition, and it would be illuminating to see how Le Roy's chronicle
compared to them.

Now Robert le Roy, also known as Robert Parvus, Robert Petit,
and Robert Little, is no fiction. He was one of the two chief heralds or

kings of heralds for both Edward I and Edward II and we know quite a lot about him from royal pay records (Bullock-Davies 1978: 159–62; Rastall 1968: 1: 31–36; Conklin 1964: 29–30). Robert first appears in 1277 when he was paid 12d. at Berwick. The record already gives him the title "king" and describes him a minstrel squire-at-arms. As Constance Bullock-Davies notes, this title was the equivalent of sergeant-at-arms, and like the other king's heralds, he was paid a sergeant's wages and received a sergeant's livery (Bullock-Davies 1978: 38–39). He appears several times in the records in the 1280s and 90s, usually designated as the king of heralds, but also as king Robert, king's trumpeter, or king Robert, the minstrel, and once as Robert, king of minstrels. Often he carries messages or presents or takes responsibility for dividing up a lump payment among his more junior colleagues, one of the chief duties of the kings of minstrels or kings of heralds, who in effect acted as a band masters. When in 1306 Edward I held a huge feast for the knighting of his son, it is King Robert and five other kings of heralds who receive the 200 marks that were to be divided among the hundred or more minstrels who performed. But le Roy definitely played music as well. In 1303 he and fifteen others are given six marks for playing before the Countess of Hereford when she was churched, and the same year he plays before the king at Dunfermline. Le Roy is seriously ill in 1316, and receives several gifts from the king. Obviously if he had praised Bruce's reputation it had not cost him the king's favour. We last hear of le Roy in 1320, organising the entertainment for a banquet for the king at Amiens. In this year his livery was valued at 33 s. and 2d, "almost a mark more than the cost of a minstrel's robe" (Conklin 1964: 30) and he rode a dappled sorrel valued at what seems the shockingly high figure of £20.

Determining Robert's professional status requires some care. His position clearly required that he follow the king on campaign. Bullock-Davies is of the opinion that "Robert's duties as a king's squire (that is, as a sergeant-at-arms) constituted the most important part of his work" and that his career as a minstrel "ran side by side" with his activities as a soldier (Bullock-Davies 1978: 160). Such would appear to have been the case with Gib Harper, the minstrel herald of Edward Bruce, who according to Barbour in one battle cleared a path for his lord with an axe (XV.181–192; XVIII. 95–98, 165–74). Given his long-standing role as a herald, however, it seems more likely that Robert le Roy's soldierly duties were confined to bearing messages, blowing signals on his trumpet, and above all observing the battle so that he could report the casualties and give due credit to the valiant.

By the fifteenth century, heralds were already more clearly distinguished from minstrels than they had been in the previous century and bore a more exalted status. In keeping with this professionalisation, heraldic jargon had become more complex and heraldic writing had developed into a fully-fledged literary genre, comprised of eyewitness accounts of major chivalric ceremonies, with dress, speeches, and blows listed in minute detail (Lester 1992: 201–12). To what extent fourteenth-century heralds had achieved the same status or level of specialisation is hard to determine. The earliest reference we have to a herald acting as an emissary is in 1333, for example, when, according to Froissart, "un hiraus d'Escoce, qui s'apelloit Dondee" came before King Edward III with a request from the lords and prelates of Scotland for a parlay (Wagner 1939: 35). Anthony Richard Wagner suggests that as late as Edward III there is no evidence that heralds were messengers of war and peace, but that from "Edward III's reign on, however, we shall see them entrusted, though sparingly at first, with military and diplomatic duties of steadily growing importance" (Wagner 1939: 33). But we should not diminish the role of the early fourteenth-century heralds nor the possibility of their keeping substantial written accounts. Fourteenth-century heralds had already acquired crucial dignities and responsibilities. As Rastall notes, "A herald represented his master, and it therefore became sacrilege to offer violence to a royal officer of arms: in the case of a King of Heralds this principle was taken a step further, and he not only wore the coat of arms of the monarch whose proxy he was but in addition was crowned and consecrated" (Rastall 1968: 1: 31–32). This practice is reflected in Barbour's account of Gib Harper, who dies wearing Edward Bruce's surcoat and whose head is presented to Edward by mistake (XVIII: 90–174). The kings of heralds were given responsibility over wide areas in which they regulated coats of arms and conducted visitations to determined who had the right to bear them, so that Bower's claim that le Roy was given responsibility for all England is more or less accurate (Rastall 1968: 1: 34). It would surely have been considered an act of extreme presumption on le Roy's part to issue a general challenge to the assembled knights, as

Bower claims he did, but Bower's suggestion that le Roy was a respected, even feared, court official, whose assessment of chivalric performance could not be corrupted, may reflect a deeper truth.

There is, unfortunately, no evidence that Robert le Roy ever composed a chronicle. The suggestion for a lost chronicle comes from a reference in the *Chronique* of Jean le Bel, where Jean refers to the "hystoire faitte par le dit Roy Robert" as his source for the account of how Robert the Bruce was hunted. In context, however, it seems clear that this "Roy Robert" is Robert the Bruce himself (Viard and Déprez eds 1904–5: 1: 111). It is likely that le Roy did keep written records of some kind, but what form they took remains an open question. Arguably, in seeking for a lost chronicle, a single written source for both the story of Argentan, McDiarmid and Stevenson have lapsed into a characteristically modern attitude, one which assumes that stability is dependent upon written texts. An alternative possibility is that certain kinds of oral tradition, in this case that of chivalric conversation, can effectively preserve a stable version of a knight's deeds.

The story of Argentan's charge was widely known. It survives not just in *Bruce* and the *Scotichronicon* but in also in two other earlier chronicles, which bear witness to conscientious reporting, although filtered through well established narrative patterns. The first chronicle is the anonymous *Vita Edwardi Secundi*, which is probably the work of a retired West Country lawyer and was composed around 1324. As N. Denholm-Young notes, the author shows a keen interest in the doings of Marcher lords, especially the Earl of Hereford, who "receives neither praise nor blame throughout", yet whose "every move is recorded almost automatically" (Denholm-Young ed. 1957: xxvii). According to the *Vita,* the Earl of Gloucester quarreled with the Earl of Hereford over who should lead the van, and seeing the Scots approaching dashed out in disorder:

Giles de Argentine, a fighting soldier and very expert in the art of war, while in command of the king's rein, watched the fate of the earl, hurried up in eager anxiety to help him, but could not. Yet he did what he could, and fell together with the earl, thinking it more honourable to perish with so great a man than to escape death by flight; for those who fall in battle for the public good are known to live in everlasting glory. (Denholm-Young ed. 1957: 53–54)

Here then we have one of the earliest detailed accounts of the battle and one which not only singles out Argentan's name but also notes that he was the king's bodyguard and that he rode to his death. The *Vita* does not mention Argentan's defiant speech, nor does it mention that he was judged the third best knight of his day. The most striking variation is that the author associates Argentan with the figure he is most interested in, the Earl of Hereford (although not in a way that reflects any credit on Hereford, whose bickering with Gloucester sets the English in disarray).

For the composition of the second source we have more information. In 1355, the border warrior Sir Thomas Gray, warden of Norham Castle on the Tweed, sallied forth to pursue a Scottish raiding party, fell into an ambush, and was captured. During the two years that he spent in Edinburgh castle he composed a history of the world, written in Anglo-Norman, the *Scalacronica*. The earlier sections of his history draw in a number of written sources, including Bede, but his account of Bannockburn appears to have been based on the experiences of his father, who was taken prisoner during one of the inconclusive skirmishes on the day before the real battle. This is Gray's version:

The English squadrons being thrown into confusion by the thrust of pikes upon the horses, began to fly. Those who were appointed to attend upon the King's rein, perceiving the disaster, led the King by the rein off the field towards the castle, and off he went, though much against the grain. As the Scottish knights, who were on foot, laid hold of the housing of the King's charger in order to stop him, he struck out so vigorously behind him with a mace that there was none whom he touched that he did not fell to the ground.

As those who had the King's rein were thus drawing him always forward, one of them, Giles de Argentin [sic], a famous knight who had lately come over sea from the wars of the Emperor Henry of Luxemburg, said to the king:

"Sire, your rein was committed to me; you are now in safety; there is your castle where your person may be safe. I am not accustomed to fly, nor am I going to begin now. I commend you to God!"

Then, setting spurs to his horse, he returned into the mellay, where he was slain. (Maxwell tr. 1907: 56–57)

As far as we can tell, these two chronicles are quite independent. The *Vita Edwardi Secundi* survives in only a single manuscript and its frank comments on the king and on the Papal Curia suggest that it was not intended to circulate widely. Denholm-Young notes that whoever wrote this work was "established or retired, or both; so he can skate on thin ice" (Denholm-Young ed. 1957: xx). Thomas Gray had access to a good library in Edinburgh castle, but it is highly unlikely that it would have contained a copy of a minor West Country chronicle. Besides, at least for Bannockburn, Thomas appears to have relied on his father's stories. Yet the versions in the two chronicles have much in common. Both Gray and the author of the *Vita Edwardi Secundi* have heard that Argentan was entrusted with the king's protection, and that he died in a reckless charge that occurred at a critical moment. Gray's story and Barbour's, written some twenty years later, are even closer. In particular, both give us the same defiant speech. In the *Bruce*, Argentan cries out "ȝeyt fled I never sekyrly / And I cheys her to bid and dey / Yan for to lyve schamly and fley" (XIII: 306–8). In the *Scalacronica* he makes the same point: "Jeo nay pas este acoustome a fuyre, ne plus auaunt ne voil ieo faire" (Stevenson ed. 1836: 143).

Since there is no evidence that Barbour had access to the *Scalacronica*, we must assume either that they are drawing on either a common written source or on a common oral tradition. McDiarmid and Stevenson are convinced Barbour drew heavily on oral sources, and take his reference to one informant, Sir Alan Cathcart, very much at face value. A. A. M. Duncan, on the other hand, is sceptical:

I have never found in the least convincing the idea that the poem was largely pro-duced from "popular lays", or from the tales of old sweats for whom Barbour bought drinks in the inns of Ayr or Edinburgh. (Duncan ed. 1997: 15)

The complexity of the narrative, which intertwines the stories of Bruce and Douglas, the accuracy of the dates, and the copious information about English matters all argue for written sources. Duncan believes these would include a lost life of Douglas, possibly kept by his herald, and "Latin verses partly preserved in Bower" which he dubs the *Verse Chronicle* (Duncan ed. 1997: 20). This lost verse chronicle or a text associated with it could have been Gray's source as well as Barbour's.

Given that there was at least one major written source that precedes Barbour's *Bruce*, and may have been more, there is no way of ruling out the possibility of a written source for Gray's account as well, even – although this may seem a rather unlikely coincidence – a written source, that was connected to the one used by Barbour. But the explanation seems unsatisfactory. As we have seen, four of the surviving accounts of the battle agree in singling out Argentan, yet they otherwise show few signs of interdependency, even though this was an age when plagiarism was no crime. It is worth considering the alternative, that an oral tradition might have been just as capable of passing on the crucial episode of Argentan's charge to the next generation. To accept this, of course, we must be prepared to accept that this oral tradition would have crossed the border, so that the stories told by an English herald would echo those told by both English and Scottish knights. Given the regular exchange of prisoners, all sharing the same chivalric code, this does not seem unlikely.

It is worth noting, to begin with, that Giles d'Argentan was a real person, who had indeed been to the crusades under Emperor Henry and did indeed die at Bannockburn. In addition to the references in the chronicles already mentioned, his name appears in the briefer accounts of the battle in the *Annales Londoniensis*, the *Annales Paulini*, the *Gesta Edwardi de Carnarvan*, and Thomas de la More's *Vita et Mors Edwardi II* (Moor ed. 1929: 19; Johnstone 1946: 116; Stubbs ed 1882–83: 1: 230–31, 276; 2: 46, 300). Argentan also left a trail in the royal records. His father, Giles d'Argentan senior, was the king's seneschal during the baron's revolt (*Calendar Close Rolls* 1908: 652). The son inherited lands in Cambridgeshire, Huntingtonshire, Hertfordshire, Essex, Norfolk, and Suffolk. Argentan was continually getting into trouble, usually for jousting, but he was always forgiven. In 1302 he is one of a number of men, including Thomas Gray, who are charged with breaking into the house of William de Mortuo Mari while he was on the king's service (*Calendar Patent Rolls* 1898: 86). This is a relatively minor incident in Argentan's provocative career, but it shows that the father of the author of the *Scalachronica* knew him personally. The same year Argentan was charged with contempt of the king and was only released from prison on the condition that he go to fight in Scotland. He went but returned prematurely, possibly bored with the protracted negotiations, and when the king summoned his host to Berwick in November Argentan was found jousting in Surrey (*Calendar Close Rolls* 1908: 531). In March of 1303 a new order for his arrest was issued, but he was pardoned in June of the following year for the harm that he had sustained at the siege of Stirling (*Calendar Patent Rolls* 1898: 121, 242). In 1307 he is one of the knights appointed to accompany Prince Edward to France (*Calendar Close Rolls* 1908: 531). In 1309, according to the *Annales Londoniensis*, he is jousting again, taking on all comers in the character of the "rex de vertbois" (Stubbs ed. 1882: I: 3–251, 157). In

1311 he departs for the Holy Land to fight with the emperor Henry (*Calendar Patent Rolls* 1894: 324). He was captured at Salonika in Greece on his way to Rhodes. Edward II wrote to the Master of the Hospital of St. John of Jerusalem, the Preceptor of the Hospital, and the *Podestà* and community of Genoa to secure Argentan's release, and when that failed, he wrote to the emperor and empress of Constantinople, their sons, Frederick, the king of Sicily, and five other nobles (*Calendar Close Rolls* 1894: 71, 76).

The record might seem paradoxical. Argentan was repeatedly in trouble, but Edward took extraordinary pains to rescue him. Why was this rapscallion so loved? Perhaps the answer lies in the way Argentan got into trouble, most often by jousting. His career would appear to resemble that of the even more distinguished William Marshall more than half a century earlier: both were knights of modest means who established a reputation as chivalric exemplars through extensive tourneying and campaigning, and consequently were appointed to the king or prince's inner circle as body guards, companions, and tutors. If anyone were bound to die on the field at Bannockburn it was Giles d'Argentan, a man whose career was based not on vast estates but on a carefully nurtured reputation for bravery. Robert le Roy, who would have ridden close by them on campaign, must have known Argentan well and would have known the kind of last words he would have wanted remembered. And like William Marshall, who was praised for his generosity to minstrels, Argentan must have known how to maintain good relations with professional memorialists such as le Roy. It would be entirely in keeping with this, that his final defiant speech should become part of chivalric oral tradition, so that two apparently independent written sources, Barbour's *Bruce* and Gray's *Scalacronica*, both reproduce it. The same pattern can be seen in the verse histories of the great households such as the Stanleys, where especially memorable speeches appear to have circulated as part of an oral tradition. When Lord Stanley hears before the battle of Bosworth that Richard III is holding his son hostage, for example, he resolves to "make him such a breakefast upon a day / as never made knight any King in Cristenye!" This phrase is repeated in both the two major ballads, *Bosworth Field* and *Lady Bessy*, and in the unpublished *Death of Richard III*, although the three works are otherwise quite distinct (Furnivall and Hales eds 1868: IV:132; Halliwell-Phillips ed. 1850: 50–96). Whether Lord Stanley ever did make this vow, his descendants and their retainers knew the line and expected it to form part of any account of the battle.

Chivalric conversation was not just idle chatter, the broken air of false rumour, blowing across the world, as Chaucer and other medieval clerks have sometimes suggested. Nor was it merely a way of filling an idle hour or cadging a drink. On the contrary, chivalric conversation was officially sanctioned as part of a squire's military formation; the Household Book of Edward IV actually lays it out as part of the daily routine (Myers ed. 1959: 128–29). The role of moral tutor and chivalric guide was regularly assigned to senior knights as a formal duty towards a particular pupil, and this role entailed passing on accounts of past battles. Telling war stories had a face-saving and therapeutic function for those who had been in battle and exercised an extreme fascination over those who had not, who desperately needed to know what it was like and whether they could endure it without shaming themselves (Taylor 1999: 169–88). Military vows and boasting, frequently the object of clerical derision, were a necessary means of getting oneself sufficiently emotionally charged to risk one's life, but this deferred aggression was governed by strict social codes. These boastings and retellings of who did what on the field were a vital part of the knights' cultural formation. Froissart's *Chronicles* actually were composed in large part from the "tales of old sweats", tales he garnered not in inns but in the outer halls of great courts. His task involved the assiduous compilation of eye-witness accounts drawn from men who were often from opposite sides but had a common understanding of how war should be told so as to transform it into an elevating record of valour (de Lettenhove ed. 1967: 11: 108; 13: 224). Two generations earlier, the task of Robert le Roy would have been essentially the same.

None of the accounts offers direct reportage. Indeed, it is their need to distort what actually happened in certain predictable ways that provides much of their structure. Retreat, whether it took the form of panic-stricken flight or just a prudent withdrawal to avoid the expenses of being captured and ransomed, was a lapse from the superhuman standards of chivalry. Somehow knights had to reconcile these self-imposed standards with the facts of life. Perfect chivalry would get you killed or captured very quickly. Ransoms were often ruinous and a king's ransom could ruin a kingdom. So Edward and his knights were only being sensible when they decided to retreat. Had Argentan not succeeded in getting the king free, he would have failed in his primary duty and Bannockburn would have been an even greater disaster for the English. Those outside the profession could afford a purer idealism. The monk of Lanercost is brutally scornful of the English retreat: "The king and Sir Hugh le Despenser [...] and Sir Henry de Beaumont [...] with many others mounted and on foot, to their perpetual shame fled like miserable wretches" (Maxwell ed. 1913: 208–9). Edward had no choice, but he must have known perfectly well the kinds of things that were being said and sung about him by "the minstrels and maidens of Scotland" and many others (Ellis ed. 1811: 420). The chivalric version of the story had to be told in very particular ways to redeem this shame. One standard feature of many of the accounts is the single combatant who shows by his suicidal defiance that courage is not dead (or, perhaps, that such pure courage is not to be demanded of all). Each retreat needs its Giles d'Argentan. I do not think we can necessarily assume that the account in the *Vita Edwardi Secundi*, in which Argentan dies trying to aid Gloucester, is necessarily closer to what actually happened than the accounts of Barbour or Bower. But it could well have been, and if so, would represent the first stage in chivalric retelling, which singles out a particular knight from the chaos of the battle and attributes his death to a deliberate act of extraordinary bravery. Barbour and Gray represent the next stage. They tell the story properly, as it should have happened, setting Argentan apart so that his deed is not lost in the general mêlée, and giving him one splendid laconic speech and then a glorious charge across an open field to certain death. That, I suspect, is not just the version that happens to be preserved by Barbour, but the version the English knights must have eventually settled on as they struggled to give their humiliation an acceptable shape.

Froissart employs similar strategies in his account of another English defeat, the Battle of Otterburn of 1388, and here too I would suggest that the written version echoes the narrative patterns employed by the knights and heralds themselves. In this case, the flight is particularly embarrassing because the English were the larger force, and Froissart is at some pains to limit the damage. First, near the beginning of the central chapter, he offers reassurance that although the English outnumbered the Scots three to one, they fought with honour, and he adds further that they were tired from their long march. Froissart then lists those knights, both Scottish and English, who distinguished themselves, before returning to the moment when the battle turned, this time attributing it not to fatigue but to the way fortune turns: "ainsi que les fortunes tournent" (de Lettenhove ed. 1967: 13: 228). Froissart manages to avoid almost any discussion of the English loss of morale or of how they began to break; we hear of the Scots who advance, not of the English who begin to drop back, a discontinuity that is typical of much military writing to this day (Keegan 1976: 36-40). Mathew Redman is the only Englishman to flee who is mentioned by name, and Froissart stresses that he does so only after his entire company has surrendered or fled, and then turns immediately to the one Englishman, Thomas Waltem or Waltham, who actually does prefer death to surrender:

At the stage where the English were losing, and while in many places people had begun to take prisoners for ransom, while others were still fighting, a young English squire, Thomas Waltham, who belonged to the Lord Percy's household, was trapped. He was a fine and brave man in arms, and showed it well, for that evening and into that night he did great feats of arms and refused ever to surrender or to flee. They told me that he had vowed at a feast in Northumberland that when the English and Scots first met in battle he would acquit himself according to the best of his ability so bravely and steadfastly that he would either be held one of the best of the two sides or leave his body on the field. Certainly they told me (for I never saw him myself, as far as I know) that he had the handsome and well-proportioned body of a brave squire and had such high prowess that before the banner of the Earl of Moray he accomplished such deeds of arms that even the Scots marveled. He was killed in combat for his bravery. They would have gladly have captured and ransomed him, if he had wished, and many knights and squires tried to, but he always said that he would not agree for he hoped to be rescued. There died Thomas Waltham in the passage of arms I have described, and there also died a most valiant Scottish squire, a cousin of the Earl of Douglas, who was called Simon of Glendinning, which caused great sorrow to those of his side. (de Lettenhove ed. 1967: 13: 228-29)

Trapped by the expectations raised by his vow, hoping still to be rescued but determined not to yield, the young squire died, emulating knights like Argentan, of whom he would certainly have heard, and in turn his story was told according to the same narrative conventions, so that it could be passed on to the next generation.

Minstrels and chroniclers both have long claimed that without them noble deeds would be forgotten but that through them these deeds can be preserved "to last ay furth in memory", as Barbour puts it. I think we can credit Robert le Roy with being one of those who preserved the story. There was no lost minstrel chronicle, if by that we mean a single, finished work, at least there is no evidence of one, and we reveal our own habits of mind when we look for one. But Robert le Roy would have observed and double-checked what happened at Bannockburn, while all the time shaping the accounts to fit the chivalric notion of truth in which war was not meaningless muddle but a clear moral record. Bower's account of le Roy's testimony before Edward may be a fiction (and certainly the testimony cannot have taken place in quite the way he describes) but in two important respects it reflects actual cultural practice. Heralds were professional memorialists, paid to rank knights and remember their deeds. And their accounts were intended to inspire or shame the knightly class to further acts of bravery.

It does appear that noble deeds were remembered with some reliability. The field of battle was under continual observation by a highly specialised group of professionals whose responsibility it was to note and remember deeds of valour. In the more controlled environment of a tournament, the heralds would record the combat with something of the accuracy of a boxing referee, noting the more powerful blows (Anglo 1965: 21–83). They would have applied these standards to the confusion of actual battle as best they could, while at the same time shaping the actions into an edifying story. Le Roy left no chronicle. He may not even have left a written record, and even if he had, few would have had a chance to read it. But he and his fellows left an oral record and this record ensured that the reputation of the third best knight of his day lasted in memory until Barbour, Gray, and others could finally entrust it to writing.

Bibliography

Anglo, Sydney. 1965. "Anglo-Burgundian Feats of Arms: Smithfield, June 1467" in *Guidhal Miscellany* 2.7: 271–83.

Bullock-Davies, C. 1978. *Multitudo menestrellorum: Minstrels at a Royal Feast*. Cardiff: University of Wales Press.

Calendar of Close Rolls, Edward I. Vol. 5: 1302–07. 1908. London: HMSO.

Calendar of Close Rolls, Edward II. Vol. 2: 1313–16. 1894. London: HMSO.

Calendar of Patent Rolls, Edward I, Vol. 4: 1301–07. 1898. London: HMSO.

Calendar of Patent Rolls, Edward II. Vol. 1: 1307–13. 1894. London: HMSO.

Calendar of Patent Rolls, Henry III. Vol. 4: 1247–58. 1908. London: HMSO.

Chesnutt, M. 1987. "Minstrel Reciters and the Enigma of Medieval Romance" in *Culture and History* 2: 48–67.

Conklin, R. 1964. *Medieval English Minstrels, 1216–1485*. PhD thesis. University of Chicago.

De Lettenhove, K. (ed.) [1867–77] 1967. *Oeuvres de Froissart: Chroniques*, 25 vols. Osnabrück: Biblio Verlag.

Denholm-Young, N. (ed.) 1957 *Vita Edwardi Secundi, monachi malmesberiensis: The Life of Edward the Second by the so-called Monk of Malmesbury*. London: Nelson.

Duncan, A. A. M. (ed.) 1997. *John Barbour: The Bruce*. Edinburgh: Canongate.

Johnstone, H. 1946. *Edward of Carnarvon, 1284–1307*. Manchester: Manchester University Press.

Ellis, H (ed.) 1811. *Robert Fabyan: The New Chronicles of England and France*. London: F.C. & J. Rivington et al.

Furnivall, F.J. and J.W. Hales (eds). 1868. *Bishop Percy's Folio Manuscript*. 4 vols. London: N Trübner.

Halliwell-Phillips, J. (ed.) 1850. *Palatine Anthology: A Collection of Ancient Poems and Ballads Relating to Lancashire and Cheshire*. London. British Library MS Harley 542, fol 31^v.

Keegan, J. 1976. *The Face of Battle*. New York: Viking Press.

Keen, M. 1984. *Chivalry*. New Haven, Conn.: Yale University Press.

Lester, G.A. 1992. "Fifteenth-Century English Heraldic Narrative" in *Yearbook of English Studies* 22: 201–12.

Maxwell, H. (trans.) 1907. *Scalachronica, The Reigns of Edward I, Edward II and Edward III, as recorded by Sir Thomas Gray*. Glasgow: James Maclehose and Sons.

—. (ed.) 1913. *The Chronicle of Lanercost, 1272–1346*. Glasgow: James Maclehose and Sons.

McDiarmid, M. P. and J.A.C. Stevenson (eds). 1980–85. *The Bruce* [Scottish Text Society 4th Series no. 12, 13, 15.]. 3 vols. Edinburgh: Scottish Text Society.

Moor, C. (ed.) 1929–32. *Knights of Edward I* [Publications of the Harleian Society 80–84.]. 5 vols. London: Harleian Society.

Myers, A.R. (ed.) 1959. *The Household of Edward IV: The Black Book and the Ordinance of 1478*. Manchester: Manchester University Press.

Rastell, R. 1968. *Secular Musicians in Late Medieval England*. 2 vols. PhD thesis. University of Manchester.

Spector, S. (ed.) 1991. *The N-Town Play: Cotton MS Vespasian D. 8* [Early English Text Society Second Series no. 11, 12.]. Oxford: Early English Text Society.

Stevenson, J. (ed.) 1836. *Scalachronica: By Sir Thomas Gray of Heton, Knight: A Chronicle of England and Scotland from A. D. MLXVI to A. D. MCCCLXII now first published from the unique manuscript.* Edinburgh: Maitland Club.

Stubbs, W. (ed.) 1882–83. *Chronicles of the Reigns of Edward I and Edward II.* 2 vols. London: Longman.

Taylor, A. 1992. "Fragmentation, Corruption and Minstrel Narration: The Question of the Middle English Romances" in *Yearbook of English Studies* 22: 38–62.

—. 1997. "Songs of Praise and Blame and the repertoire of the Gestour" in Andersen F. G., T. Pettitt and R. Schröder (eds) *The Entertainer in Medieval and Traditional Culture, A Symposium.* Odense: Odense University Press. 47–72.

—. 1999. "Chivalric Conversation and the Denial of Male Fear" in Murray, J. (ed.) *Conflicted Identities and Multiple Masculinities: Men in the Medieval West.* New York: Garland. 169–88.

Viard, J. and E. Déprez (eds). 1904–5. *Chronique de Jean le Bel.* 2 vols. Paris: Librairie Renouard.

Wagner, A.R. 1939. *Heralds and Heraldry in the Middle Ages: An Inquiry into the Growth of the Armorial Function of the Heralds.* London: H. Milford, Oxford University Press.

Watt, D.E.R. et al. (eds). 1987–98. *Walter Bower: Scotichronicon.* 9 vols. Aberdeen and Edinburgh: Aberdeen University Press and Mercat Press.

The Translations of Fortune: James I's *Kingis Quair* and the Rereading of Lancastrian Poetry

Joanna Martin

This essay considers the engagement of James I's *The Kingis Quair* with John Gower's *Confessio Amantis* and the writings of Thomas Hoccleve. It argues that in the reinterpretation of these English works, the poet negotiates the influences of Lancastrian politics and culture in order to create a positive exemplum of public stability and personal morality.
Keywords: Joan Beaufort; Boethius; Walter Bower; Geoffrey Chaucer; fortune; John Gower; Thomas Hoccleve; influence; intertextuality; James I, King of Scots; John Shirley; Kingship; House of Lancaster; love; John Lydgate; Minerva; transformation; translation; Venus; wisdom; Andrew of Wyntoun.

The *Kingis Quair* of James I of Scotland takes as its theme "how eche estate / As Fortune lykith, thame will [ay] translate" (55–56) (Norton Smith ed. 1971).[1] In reflecting upon "translacioun" in its diverse medieval senses, the *Quair* also relates how its narrating subject underwent an inner transformation, being "changit clene ryght in anothir kynd" in mind and purpose (315). It is a poem which therefore foregrounds both its public and private aspects, and the manuscript designations in Oxford, Bodleian Library, MS Arch. Selden. B. 24, made by a scribe and a later reader emphasise just this, framing the love poem as the work of a king, by the *explicit* "Quod Iacobus primus scotorum rex illustrissimus" (folio 211ʳ) (Boffey, Edwards and Barker-Benfield 1997). The *Kingis Quair* is also about influences, of which Fortune's unwelcome predilection for transposing kings and princes is just one. As Venus comments, pointing to the exemplarity of the narrator's "awin case", through "otheris influence" his "persone" "standis noght in libertee" (750–52) (Skeat ed. 1883–84: 27).[2] This essay considers these influences and translations afresh, particularly the much-neglected matter of the *Quair*'s complex engagement with John Gower's *Confessio Amantis* and with some of the writings of Thomas Hoccleve, a self-professed adherent of Gower

---

[1] All references to *The Kingis Quair* are to this edition. Line references are given in parentheses.
[2] These lines from the *Quair* are grammatically and semantically problematic. Like Skeat, I am taking "influence" as a noun.

and a contemporary of James (Martin 2002: 95–112; Summers 2003: 73–81). However, although this discussion is one of literary relations, the transference from one textual culture to another, it rejects accounts of an "anxiety of influence" emerging in the *Quair*'s self-conscious intertextuality (Fradenburg 1991: 133–34), and is less concerned with stylistic parallels, than with the ways in which literary exchange is manifested ideologically and thematically. It will be argued that the concerns of Gower and Hoccleve with exemplarity, self-reformation, and good governance were important for James's composition of the *Quair*, offering sophisticated instances in which personal history is used to examine broader institutional conditions. In particular the focus of this essay is the changing subject-position of the *Quair*'s narrator that results from the reinterpretation of these poets, and that figures James's attempts to negotiate the Lancastrian influences on his early life, finally proposing an alternative to the dangerous unpredictability of contemporary English politics.

The "influence" that Venus sees exerted on James's person alludes discreetly to the king's eighteen-year imprisonment at the courts of Henry IV and Henry V, and in related aristocratic settings (Balfour-Melville 1937: 28–105). Captured in 1406 at the age of twelve, James's involvement in the political activities of the nascent Lancastrian regime was inevitable (Spearing 2000: 123–44). The prince was of personal interest to Henry IV, who entrusted his care to important royal servants such as Lord Grey of Codenore and Archbishop Arundel. In the early 1420s James fought beside Henry V in France against the Albany/Douglas support for the Dauphin, and was also made a Knight of the Garter. Predictably James's own views on this turbulent, usurping dynasty are difficult to gauge. His surviving letters to Scotland (c.1411–12) are impatient in their inference of Albany's inactivity in relation to securing his release. Nevertheless, the young James's correspondence, although unlikely to be explicitly adversarial towards his host, also finds Henry IV "more gracious than we can say or write" (Fraser ed. 1880: 1: 286; Balfour-Melville 1922: 28–33). Even the Scots chronicler Andrew of Wyntoun conceded that Henry had received James "wiþe honeste" and "weil ay gert him tretyt be" (Amours ed. 1903–14: 6: 414). Indeed, despite an initial stringency towards the prisoner, it is likely that the rule of the youthful Henry V, with its emphasis on self-definition and the establishment of the House of Lancaster, was also to affect James's view of his own kingship, giving him what one historian has called "an education in statecraft" (Balfour-Melville 1937: 111). John Shirley's *The Dethe of the Kynge of Scotis* (c.1440s) suggests similar benefits, describing James's relationship with "Harry þe Fifte" as one of filial service rather than subjection, remarking that "in alle þing that touchid þ'onnour & þe right of þe saide Jamez, þe king of Scottis", Henry "was to him favoureable as faþer to þe sunne in alle þat touchid þaire boþe kingly estattez" (Matheson ed. 1999: 25).

The contemporary views of Abbot Bower on James's treatment by the Lancastrians are well known to be very different, and although the Abbot's presentation of Henry IV, with the blood of the Comyns running in his veins, is often ambivalent, Henry V receives virulent condemnation (Watt et al. 1987–98: 8: 37, 123– 24, 309). But despite such ideological differences, it is probable that James himself would have been aware of the difficulties experienced by the early Lancastrian kings. Indeed, his reinterpretations of Gower and Hoccleve seem to reveal an acute understanding of a troubled English political life against which Scottish rule may be redefined. In particular, by the time of the *Quair*'s composition, the fragility of Henry V's financial, domestic and foreign policies must have been apparent: England again faced minority and inter-dynastic tensions with the accession of the infant Henry VI in 1422. Bower later evoked this uncertainty when he recorded in his *Scotichronicon* – with palpable enjoyment – the lurid prognostication of an English hermit who, foreseeing the throne "alight with the flames of hell and with demons at the ready", detailed the fall of Lancaster in a description of Henry IV's successors, first "a devil; after the devil a saint; [...] after the saint a sword; and after the sword nobody" (Watt et al. 1987–98: 8: 29). The *Kingis Quair*, "Maid quhen his Maiestie wes In / Ingland" (folio 191^v), as an early sixteenth-century Selden inscription maintains, is a very kingly response to this undesirable instability, and to the consequent, and subtle interrogations of royal responsibility and current political circumstances made by these sophisticated English poets. Indeed, James's poetic record of his cultivation of wisdom and good fortune in love represents a forward-looking account of his ideals for future stability, emphasising independence from, as much as indebtedness to, English culture and policy.

That James's responses to Gower's *Confessio Amantis* might have been part of the formulation of this agenda is unsurprising given the place of the English poem in the cultural life of the early fifteenth century. The long work, an account of a lover's supplication to Venus and confession to Genius, was immensely popular at the time of James's exile. Although the poem was originally intended as an advice book for the young Richard II, most of its extant witnesses date from the fifteenth century (Grady 1995: 552–75; Doyle and Parkes 1991: 201–48). Its concern with stability and mature governance, and its desire to discuss kingship in amatory contexts, ensured its consonance for fifteenth-century readers. Yet the *Confessio* is unrelentingly political and historicised, and cannot have made wholly comfortable reading for the Lancastrian dynasty to which it had been rededicated in 1393, or for whose members and supporters it continued to be produced (Nicholson 1988: 159–80; Cooper 1874: 132).[3] The poem's lessons of enforcing the normative hierarchies of reason and sexuality, maturity and youthfulness, are as much directed at the public career as at the private affairs of the heart. Further, this didacticism is mingled with ambivalence, particularly in the poem's problematical conclusions where the narrator is unable to heed the lessons of his confessor, or the received wisdom of the Aristotelian advice to princes excursus (Book VII), in order to reconcile his love and reason. With Amans displaying traits of a whimsical, acquisitive ruler committed to the "forthringe of [his] oghne astat", and with Genius's proliferation of tales in which moral transgression is transposed into political disaster, the difficulty of enforcing prescribed systems of order inwardly or outwardly is emphasised (II.2048) (Macaulay ed. 1900).[4]

It is to these often pessimistic, or at least admonitory, political and amatory lessons, that James was especially sensitive. In particular, the subject-position adopted by the narrator of the *Kingis Quair* is shaped by the self-referential but also dysfunctional narrating personae of Gower and Hoccleve, nexuses of political apprehension and thus of misrule and instability; figures that, while not themselves princely, have a metaphorical ability to comment on royal predica-

---

[3] Oxford, Bodleian Library, MSS Bodley 902 and 294, Oxford, Christchurch College, MS 148 and Huntingdon Library, California, MS EL.26.A.17 have possible links to Henry IV and his immediate family. Margaret Beaufort possessed a "book of velom of Gower in Englisshe".

[4] All references to Gower's *Confessio Amantis* are to this edition. Book and line numbers are given in parentheses.

ments. In the *Confessio*'s first book Gower's narrating subject, the frail clerk of the prologue assumes a lover's likeness, simulating an autobiographical voice and introducing the figure of Amans as an exemplary site of moral conflict. "I am," he assures us, "miselven on of tho, / Which to this Scole [of love] am underfonge" (I.62–63).[5] This persona, which denies any ability to "setten al in evene", emerges after the prologue's revelation that temporal rulers no longer harmonise "unenvied love" with "vertu" (I.2, Prol. 116–17). In the revised – or Lancastrian – version of the poem Gower, by ceasing to claim to perform the royal charge of Richard II, and negating any hierarchised, didactic king-figure, foregrounds change and discord, privileging problematic individuals like Amans and the fictional lover-kings of the *Confessio*'s exemplary tales. Each of these, "A kingdom hath to justefie", as Genius puts it, "That is to sein his oghne dom" (VIII.2112–13).

In the *Regiment of Princes*, Hoccleve names John Gower as his "maister", and the younger poet is particularly responsive to the *Confessio*'s anxious inability to offer a stable paradigm of resolved self- or political governance (1975) (Furnivall ed. [1897] 1988).[6] In his major works, all completed before James's return to Scotland, Hoccleve's sick and uneasy narrators rebuke their youthful inability to abide by the teachings of reason and virtue, composing their texts in an almost penitential attempt to create edifying models of reform for others. These carefully constructed figures, with their strongly autobiographical dimension, offer themselves as examples of misrule, excess and weakness. Aware of subjectivity as defined by aspects of political culture beyond an individual's control, Hoccleve writes into his texts the chronology that the new regime sought to exclude – the House of Lancaster's usurping past and arguably illegitimate present, beset by rebellion, and conspiracy. In *La Male Regle* (c.1406), *Regiment of Princes* (c.1411) and a collection of prose and poetic materials known as the *Series* (c.1419–22), Hoccleve defines his narrating character, the privy-seal clerk who is preoccupied by infirmity and social and financial vulnerability, as an embodiment of early fifteenth-century precariousness. In *Regiment of Princes* the anxious "Thomas"

---

[5] This forthrightness is partly tempered by the accompanying Latin note, "Hic quasi in persona aliorum, quos amor alligat, fingens se auctor esse Amantem [...]".
[6] All references to Hoccleve's *Regiment* are to this edition. Line numbers are given in parentheses.

is found "Mvsyng vpon the restles bisynesse" of "this troubly world" (1–2). In *La Male Regle*, Hoccleve's persona, like Gower's, has also been a lover, "lust y-rootid" in his heart, precociously following his own desires, and so aligned with the unpredictability of history: as he complains, "youth is rebel / Vn-to reson & hatith her doctryne" (94, 65–66) (Furnivall ed. [1892] 1970). Hoccleve's positioning of his youthful, wayward, and amorous subject is partly conditioned by the exemplarity that is expected to reside in the king as the cure for personal anxieties and social ills. But although in the *Regiment* Thomas contrasts his dullness with the king's "estate hye & glorious", his unstable body also assumes qualities recognised as the most disturbing aspects of the political macrocosm and, indeed, of the Lancastrian monarch's own subject position (2020). It is alarming, but unsurprising, to discover that Henry V, dedicatee of the *Regiment*, suffers from the same mental restlessness as Thomas: this "book of governaunce" shall "drive forth the nyght" for an "vnresty" prince (2051, 2141). In Hoccleve's poems, as in the *Confessio Amantis*, these narratorial struggles figure the elusiveness of lasting solutions to the political problems and personal dilemmas detailed.

Like its Lancastrian precursors, the *Kingis Quair* purports to relate personal history in an attempt to formulate an understanding of a potentially treacherous world. James's narratorial figure, by turns a captive, a lover, and finally a socially integrated individual, is identified with the Scottish prince in the biographical details of stanzas twenty-one to twenty-five, and the long account of his imprisonment, that period of Lancastrian influence, is cleverly localised in time and place through clear echoes of English literary works. As in the *Confessio*, *Regiment*, and *Series*, the "buke" presented as being undertaken by the narrator records a quest for reason which, through offering James's self as paradigmatic, produces a text of some social value (91). The poem opens with James's narrating subject "in bed allone", sleepless and troubled on a winter night, trying to derive comfort from Boethius's *Consolation of Philosophy* but disturbed by the "mater" of Fortune's universality and the disparity between his experience and the model offered by the authoritative text (8, 54). While "the vertew of [Boethius's] youth" was "in his age the ground of his delytis", James retrospectively sees his youthful self, unripe and variable, as partaking of the turbulent circumstances that felled him, his internal condition reflecting, and being reflected in Fortune's domain (36–37). As Minerva later tells him, when the young lack "wit or lore" they are "in dangere and commune / With hir that clerkis clepen so Fortune" (1040, 1042–43). Many levels of allusion are evident in these opening stanzas, some of which are, of course, Chaucerian and Lydgatian. But the somatic conflation of the harsh season with the narrator's uneasy recollection of his unregulated past is strikingly reminiscent of Hoccleve's "prologue" to the *Series* set in the "broune" season following Michaelmas, where the narrator, "Syghenge sore" and "vexyd" with "thowghtfull maladye", announces his "Complaint" as a Boethian meditation on temporal uncertainty and personal misfortune (2, 18, 21) (Furnivall ed. [1892] 1970).

Beside this uneasy introspection that James shares with Hoccleve's narrator, the context of the *Quair*'s troubled opening is also very public, evoking the popular *de casibus* genre which was employed so consistently by the Lancastrian poets, and pointedly underscoring an awareness of the instability that was such a feature of recent English rule. In this, James's posture is directly evocative of the beginning of Hoccleve's *Regiment*, replete with anxiety as its narrator "Thomas" revolves in his mind the recent falls of Richard II and of many another lord: "The welthe onsure of everye creature / How lightly that ffortune it can dissolue" (16–17). In dwelling on his own comparable fall James's narrating subject is "Wery forlyin" concerned that there "is non estate nor age / Ensured – more the prince than [...] the page" (72, 60–61). Problematically, although the narrator's voice in the *Quair*'s opening stanzas is that of the adult James looking back to his "tender youth" and Fortune's enmity, this early "distresse" is not recalled from a fully resolved position (66, 68). In this James is again similar to the Lancastrian narrators of Gower and Hoccleve who rarely possess the interpretative purchase on their troubles expected of their maturity or advancing years. For example, in the *Confessio*, self-governance and understanding are not undisputed consequences of age. Amans's rueful realisation that in his "myhty youthe" he made himself into "a likenesse [...] Unto the sondri Monthes twelve" is a response to Venus's surprise revelation of his decrepitude and decision to expel him from her court, rather than a product of his own mature moral insight (2846). Thus even with a high degree of retrospection, James's thoughts are anxiously "rolling to and fro" at the contemplation of life's vicissitudes, just as the sleepless Thomas in the *Regiment* rolls "vp and doun / This worldes stormy wawes in [his] mynde" (*Quair* 64; *Regiment* 50–51). This preliminary inability to construct a simple binary of foolish youth and sagacious maturity as the structural principle of the *Quair* again gestures to an understanding of the political precariousness that produced the darkness of Gower and Hoccleve's world-view.

The indirection of the Lancastrian poems continues to be in evidence as the *Kingis Quair* struggles to make a didactic synthesis of the events it relates. Borrowing the popular Boethian tempest metaphors that become so expressive of political uncertainty for Gower and Hoccleve, signifying man's exile from the kingdom of the ruled self, James figures himself in similarly anxious and powerless contexts. For example, Hoccleve's narrator in the *Regiment of Princes* describes himself as a "þoghtful wight" and "vessel of turment", his "schip [...] well ney with dispeir y-fraght" as he tries, unsuccessfully, to absorb the conventional lessons on patience delivered by the old beggar (81, 858). The socially ostracised Thomas of the Series also compares himself to a "loste vessell" unable to speak unambiguously and with authority. In a similar manner James's first attempts to inscribe his own didactic narrative are beset with difficulties, the perils of prolixity and feeble wit seeming as insurmountable as the obstructive "wawis weltering" that faced the "feble bote" of his unguided youthful self (162, 114).

But if Hoccleve and Gower envisage solutions to misrule as elusive, James's outlook does become more determined, signalling his desire to rework the philosophical resonance of these earlier poems, and encapsulating a political statement that is afforded by his royal status and desire to mark his difference from the insecurity of the English kingship witnessed during his imprisonment, and encoded in contemporary literature. Despite its historical allusions, the *Kingis Quair* offers no explicit references to James as a king (Mapstone 1997: 53, 56). His title had been recognised at Perth in June 1406, but he remained unable to exercise any but the most superficial responsibilities of his office. As Wyntoun explained, because James was "Haldyn all agane his will",

he mycht on nakyn wys
Take ony of his insignys
As crowne, ceptoure, suerd ore ring
Syk as afferis till a king
Off kynd be rycht: ȝeit neuirþeles
Oure lege lorde and king he was (Amours ed. 1903–14: 6: 416).

Nonetheless, in the *Quair* James foregrounds himself firstly as a representative figure, and then as a socially responsible individual, a moral leader of others. A sense of agency is gradually adopted as James rewrites the exemplary mode – "Determyt furth therwith in myn entent" – using the experiences of the youth who found himself disenfranchised and subject to the influence of others (85). By writing "Sume new[e] thing", James is repeating the wishes of the *Confessio*'s narrator, who desired to "wryte of newe som matiere" (*Quair* 89; *Confessio* Prol. 6). The injunction in the *Quair*, "tell on, man, quhat thee befell", also recalls that of Venus to Gower's supplicant Amans, "I woll thou telle it on and on, / Bothe al thi thoght and al thi werk", and the Beggar's request of Thomas in the *Regiment*, to "telle oute" his heart in order to find consolation for his troubles (*Quair* 77; *Confessio* I.194–95; *Regiment* 262) (Regan 1979: 86–88).[7] But, as we shall see, James's bold revision involves asserting his difference from these prior narrators, who cannot bring their reason to their predicaments, control their desires or envisage remedies for contemporary problems.

If as a poet and king James is not initially, to borrow the words of a contemporary English preacher, "Ideo magister marinarius, oure sovereyn lord", a steer for his exemplary text and self is ultimately provided by the correct understanding of love and worldly duty (Haines 1976: 95–96). The recuperation of the ruler in James and the *Quair*'s narrative of his carefully negotiated repositioning invites comparison with Gower's exemplary "Tale of Apollonius of Tyre" in Book VIII of the *Confessio*, a story which, though frequently disturbing and ambivalent, also represents a princely lover whose sufferings eventually give way to fulfilment. The length and narrative complexity of this exemplum, with its versatile use of Boethian imagery, made it popular for fifteenth-century audiences, and it appears excerpted in miscellanies, extending the contexts through which James may have encountered the tale.[8] The episode is the *Confessio*'s final effort to make the lover understand the need for ethical governance in the personal and political realm. It relates the fortunes of a young prince

---

[7] James's "fantasye" provoked by a "bell to matyns" perhaps echoes the description of Amans's "oughne thought" of love which "semeth that a belle/ Lik to the wordes that men telle/ Answerth" (I. 1949–51).

[8] The tale appears excerpted in Cambridge University Library, MS Ff.1.6 and Oxford, Balliol College MS 354.

that seem, not unlike James's ambiguously determined "infortune" in the *Quair*, to be dictated by a baffling randomness (96). Indeed, as James ponders his fate he "can [...] noght say" whether it was "causit throu hevinly influence / Of goddis will or othir casualtee" (150–53). Prince Apollonius is "yong [...] freissh" and "lusti", but, in the manner of Book VII's *speculum principis* discourse, is also learned, generous and courageous (VIII.379). Yet, disquietingly, despite his fine qualities he remains susceptible to the workings of Fortune. Threatened by an incestuous tyrant, Antiochus, Apollonius flees his own land, is shipwrecked and is left destitute, before being rescued by the king and queen of "Pentapolim". Even after his happy marriage to King Artestrathes's daughter, Apollonius suffers yet more cruelly inexplicable misfortune and further exile before finding lasting personal stability. Indeed, we are told that this exemplary prince "Withinne himself hath litel reste" from the ever mutable Fortune (VIII. 594). His world is one of threatening political treachery, and his subsequent lack of inner tranquillity is continually figured through the Boethian metaphors of storm and shipwreck, of man, in the words of Chaucer's *Boece*, cruelly "turmented in this see of fortune" (I. Metrum 5, 54) (Benson and Robinson eds 1988: 395–496).

Problematically this arbitrariness is partly because, as Genius explains, "frele is youthe", something that James too acknowledges with his preoccupation that it is "Namly in youth" that Fortune inflicts misery on her victims (*Confessio* VIII.834; *Quair* 63). But, the complaints indulged in by Apollonius and James also signify their initial refusal to embrace the temporal agency which springs from virtue and the patient sufferance of experience. Apollonius, separated from his love and adrift from his country, "curseth and seith al the worste / Unto fortune" (VIII.1584–86). A captive in another "contree", James's direction-less *planctus* is reminiscent of that of Gower's tormented and exiled prince (167). Both princes hide their faces in darkness and despair. Apollonius lays "wepende al one" in "so derk a place" to rebuke Fortune (VIII.1605, 1641); James bewails his fate "thus allone", complaining "pitously" into the night (204, 367).

Yet, surprisingly, love facilitates the internal transformation of James and his fictional counterpart – surprisingly because in the *Confessio* love is frequently a source of volatility, especially complicating the attempts of kings and princes to reform. In the *Regiment*, part of the Beggar's advice to Thomas, and thus to Henry, is also that lawless passion causes anxiety and division: "this likerous dampnable errour / In this londe hath so large a þrede I-sponne" (1762–63). But, although Genius remarks that "the schipe of love" is most likely to lose its "rother", Apollonius represent a brief glimpse of a princely self who comes to understand and govern his affections, thus deserving his restoration to his royal estate (II.2494). The prince's recovery, which contrasts with the stasis of Amans's love, is figured as a renewal of kingship, domestic happiness, and a better understanding, if not surer control, of a contrary world. Indeed, Gower makes clear that while escaping treachery in the political macrocosm may not be possible, for "So goth the work, now wo, now wel", one can better equip oneself for its challenges through inward virtue (VIII.1738). This prospect is all the more confidently embraced by James for whom the promise of love in his youthful lady is the prelude to his growth of wisdom.

In her combination of measure, wisdom and largesse, James's lady becomes an ameliorating force in the poem, introducing attributes that befit a prince and helping James to understand the importance of true service. Joan Beaufort, instrumental in securing the king's liberty, and politically close to her husband throughout the reign, was an appropriate realisation of this portrait. But James's lady also derives her function from some of the female figures in the *Confessio*, especially Apollonius's daughter, who embodies great wisdom and helps redirect her father's irrational passions. Gower's women, distanced from intractably male, institutionalised and potentially spurious spaces of scholarship and politics, are often central in offering a glimpse of the poem's elusive ideals of stability. They frequently help create the greatest degrees of harmony, personally and socially, providing what James calls "confort and hele" for disconsolate kings and lovers (518). Indeed, by calling his lady his "souirane" James certainly foregrounds her importance in his growing governance (1267).

The dream-meetings with Venus, Minerva and Fortune increase the independence and authority of James's subject position and his identity as ruler. Venus's court, indispensable to James's tutelage for this position, draws on comparable scenes in Lydgate's *Temple of Glass*, but also perceptively invokes Book VIII of the *Confessio Amantis*, in which the swooning Amans sees a very sober Company of Elde amongst Venus's adherents. In the *Quair*'s description of Venus's palace, the "agit" lovers are paragons of constancy, "the folk that neuer change wold / In lufe, bot trewly seruit [...] / In euery age"

(578–81). Significantly, they include once war-like princes and learned poets, and, in accordance with the *Quair*'s agenda, seem to advocate virtuous love as an enriching quality for public office. Although their membership recalls the wise and royal who are seen by Amans (VIII.2666–725) they are distanced from the *Confessio*'s more problematic amorous princes and scholars, whose assertion that "the wylde loves rage" "forberth non / Age" offers Amans no resolution (VIII.2773–74). And whereas Amans's returned reason is not the result of his enduring affection or of a growth in inner virtue, but of a chance act of the gods, the opposite is the case in the *Quair*, where constancy in love represents man consciously acting according to reason, and is a source of stability to be cultivated.

To be a source of "counceill & of helpe [...]" by right of bretherhede", as Hoccleve explains in his *Regiment*, is a duty both of those who counsel a king, and of the king himself as a model of virtue (2486–87). Indeed, underplaying her own queenly role, Venus instructs James to return to the work in a didactic capacity, a role not unlike that imagined by Bower who viewed the king as a lawmaker, "schoolmaster" to himself, and guardian of his people's education (Watt et al. 1987–98: 8: 309, 313). When James "descendis doun to ground ageyne" his duty is to reform the "men that there bene resident", and reinstate the law of "trew seruis" (799 –802, 756). Venus is indeed an "Appesar of malice and violence", a "blissfull havin" in the "weltering wawis fell / Of lufis rage" (689, 696–97). Minerva subsequently extends Venus's injunction by warning James to stand "stedfast" against the "brukill sort / that feynis treuth in lufe" (918, 932–33). Consequently, the goddesses' sponsorship in the *Quair* also reinterprets the concluding instructions from Gower's Venus, who charges the poet to "make a plein reles / To love" as he turns homeward guided by "reson", and initiates his final act of praying "hierafter for the pes" (VIII.2913–14, 2919). In the *Confessio*, this new duty problematically implies the impossibility of reconciling uniquely human passions with sagacity. Left to express his wish that the world be amended "Aftir the reule of charite", the Gower/Amans persona returns to a discourse that designates romantic love as incurable (VIII.3003–5). But James's final oratory for his "brethir" is a striking refashioning of Gower's prayerful wish that "the astatz amendid were" through exemplary governance (*Quair* 1282; *Confessio* VIII.3049). Gower tentatively had Henry of Lancaster in mind when he looked even to the slimmest possibilities of the renewal of virtuous rule. James, more confidently, has himself.

In continuing to affirm James's independence from unsuitable Lancastrian precedents, Minerva teaches that an individual's virtue facilitates his agency in the world, implicitly propounding that seminal *speculum principis* lesson that mature wisdom especially befits, as Genius notes, the "king which hath to lede / The people" (VII.1711–14). In doing so she again takes further the sentiments of the *Confessio*'s "Prologue" that urged each estate to regulate its behaviour in the cultivation of stability. In teaching that man "Has in himself the chose and libertee / To cause his awin fortune" through "foreknawing" Minerva recuperates Gower's doctrine that "man is overal / His oghne cause of wel and wo" (*Quair* 1024–25, 1039; *Confessio* Prol. 546–47). Though the division that the *Confessio* sees as endemic in man seems to pre-empt any possibility of creating enduring felicity, Minerva's Boethian lesson is more open-ended suggesting that "gude wit" does generate "gude fortune" (929). Further, while Gower had seen "unenvied love", the chief of virtues for temporal rulers, become merely "love falle into discord", Minerva more optimistically sees divine love and Christian virtue as a mirror for human governance, and so the ground of the narrator's affections (Prol. 115, 121). Certainly, she shares the perspective of Hoccleve's Beggar in the *Regiment* who pronounced that "Loue on lust groundid, is not worþ a lek", urging the future Henry V to have considerations of national stability in his mind when choosing a bride (1662). But while the goddess's sentiments have often been taken to relate exclusively to marriage, just as "Honeste love", "Wel grounded" in marriage, has preoccupied critics as the *Confessio*'s resolution, Minerva's teaching has wider implications (*Confessio* VIII.1993). Love should no longer be, as in the *Confessio* man's "sor withoute salve", but "treuely gude and withoutin variance" (*Confessio* Prol. 134; *Quair* 969). But, above all, every human "labour" should be "groundit ferm and stable / In Goddis law" (*Quair* 960–61).

In conflating the amatory and political, Minerva links a lover's "trechorye" and "tresoun" to the "doubilnesse" of the public sphere, and charges James to oppose what she sees an "inconstant world" (945, 937, 946, 954). Indeed, although Bower is not without his doubts about some of the more violent strategies employed by the royal administration of the 1420s, his enduring image of James is as a defender of order in the midst of political turbulence (Watt et al. 1987–98: 8: 245; Mapstone 1998: 322). He commends James's estab-lishment of "firm peace within the kingdom", between magnates and freeholders within Scottish boundaries, as well as with old enemies without. The rhetoric of constancy and "sekernesse" as opposed to "felony" in the *Quair* noticeably accords with the tenor of some of the parliamentary business of the early years of the reign, the purpose of which was to curb the lawlessness of the preceding four years (774, 709) (Balfour-Melville 1937: 112; Brown 1994: 117). Without forcing an interpretation of such legislation, Minerva's politicised vocabulary perhaps anticipates James's ambitions for peaceable and strong rule in Scottish society; in the words of a 1424 statute, "ferme and sikkir pece [...] throu all þe Realm" and an end (as another statute hoped) to "discorde betuix the king and his pepill" and all "forthocht felony" (Thomson and Innes eds 1814–75: 2: 3, 8, 9). If Minerva is further representative of James's development of kingly status and wisdom it is noteworthy that this goddess also behaves in the manner of Hoccleve's Sapience, described in the *Regiment* as "the kynges prudence" which protects against the workings of Fortune and makes man govern himself by reason, "in þe light [...] of hir lanterne" (4747, 4764). A love of Sapience, Hoccleve teaches, "is armure / Of seurete", anchoring the prince's heart in "siker place" (4786, 4788).

James's encounter with Fortune marks his final, striking reinter-pretation of his English precursors. Fortune, calling James "be name", and addressing him "smylying [...] in game", to discover his "entent" in her presence, casts a glance backwards at Venus's amusement on beholding the old Amans, newly revealed as John Gower, in Book VIII of the *Confessio* (*Quair*, 1160, 1162). Famously calling the ashamed and speechless Amans "John", Venus beholds him, and laughs, "And axeth, as it were in game, / What love was" (VIII.2871–72). The parallel moment of derision in the *Quair*, when Fortune asks the feeble narrator "Quhat dois thou here?" is further suggestive of Gower's synthesis of the domains of the two goddesses (1161). In Gower's poem it is Venus "which kepth the blinde whel", the fall of princes being frequently the consequence of their ungoverned love (I. 2490). In the *Quair* the domain of this third goddess is verbally recon-structed as the work of James's youthful misfortune – a "weltering", "sloppar" wheel, where personal destinies fluctuate (1135–36). In the manner of the *Confessio*, where the received learning of Book VII and the poem's many exemplary tales are not sufficient to ensure personal mastery, the episode confirms that the wisdom imparted by Venus and Minerva must still be supplemented by experience, part of which will be James's steadfast affection. As James acknowledges on waking from the vision and hearing hopeful tidings of love, his "lore" increases daily, affording mastery of his wits (1265). Fortune teaches that despite his unpromising beginning, James can still "spend wele [...] the remanant of the day" (1197). He is not to give up like those he sees falling from the Goddess's wheel whose courage "to clymbe [...] was no more" (1148). The moment is strikingly like that in the final exemplar of the *Confessio*, that of Apollonius, both optimistic and fleetingly admonitory. When the mischance of the Prince of Tyre is reversed, we are told "Fortune hath sworn / to sette him upward on the wheel" (VIII.1737). James also needs help to climb on to Fortune's wheel. Significantly, as the goddess accosts him and he awakes his complaint is not immediately resolved and his spirit is briefly that Lancastrian "besy" and "vexit" being again "That neuer [is] in quiet nor in rest" (1205–6, 1213). Indeed, in the *Quair* and the *Confessio*, the improved fortunes of the exiled princes seem, momentarily, only to confirm the role of chance in their vulnerable and imperfect human existence. However, fortitude and true and patient service in love as in every other endeavour, prove indispensable in the face of political treachery. And the image of a self newly instructed in the importance of virtue, ascending on Fortune's wheel and coming to "largess" through love, is James's ultimate revision of that predominant fifteenth-century anxiety, that kings, princes, even lovers, can only anticipate their imminent destruction (1276).

It is far from certain that James's exemplarity endured in the positive way that the king had envisaged in 1424. Indeed Shirley's translation of a Latin account of James's flight from tyranny, and eventual descent into vice derives an advisory and admonitory purpose by being included in a manuscript alongside Shirley's *Les Bones Meurs* and *Governance of Kynges and Prynces*. Another manuscript in which the *Dethe* appears was probably owned by "a member of the king's council or someone very closely associated with it", and the text's most recent editor even suggests that Shirley originally compiled the work as a lesson for Henry VI (Matheson ed. 1999: 12–13).[9]

---

[9] The manuscripts are London, British Library MSS Additional 5467 and 38690.

But, in the *Kingis Quair*, it seems likely that the resolution espoused
in this exemplification of reasoned love as efficacious in an unstable
world, is permitted precisely because of James's Scottishness and his
royal status. While he shared Gower and Hoccleve's institutional positioning *vis-à-vis* Lancastrianism for eighteen years, James could
respond to their ontological and epistemological doubt with greater
confidence, and on returning to Scotland insisted continually on the
sovereignty of his majesty and the domestic order of his realm. It
seems appropriate that later fifteenth-century Scots writing, such as
the poems in Cambridge, University Library MS Kk.1.5, or Henryson's work, continues where the *Quair* left off, fostering an agenda of
social responsibility and self-improvement, and a considered response
to English poetry which goes beyond a so-called stylistic debt to
Chaucerianism. As this interpretation of the *Quair* confirms, Scots
reading English works do not conform to patterns of cultural and
political subjection, but instead seek to translate the already-written
into meaningful and intelligent approaches to Scotland's own particular afflictions and concerns.

Bibliography

Amours, F.J. (ed.) 1903–14. *The Original Chronicle of Andrew of Wyntoun* [Scottish Text Society 1st Series no. 63, 50, 53, 54, 56, 57.]. 6 vols. Edinburgh and London: William Blackwood and Sons

Balfour-Melville, E.W.M. 1922. "Five Letters of James I" in *Scottish Historical Review* 20: 28–33.

—. 1937. *James I, King of Scots*. London: Methuen &Co.

Benson, L.D. and F.N. Robinson (eds). 1988. *The Riverside Chaucer*. Oxford and Boston: Oxford University Press.

Boffey, J., A.S.G. Edwards and B. Barker-Benfield. 1997. *The Works of Geoffrey Chaucer and 'The Kingis Quair': A Facsimilie of Bodleian Library, Oxford, MS Arch. Selden. B. 24*. Cambridge: D.S. Brewer.

Brown, Michael. 1994. *James I*. Edinburgh: Canongate Academic.

Cooper, C.H. 1874. *Memoir of Margaret, Countess of Richmond and Derby*. Cambridge: Deighton Bell.

Doyle, A.I. and M.B. Parkes. 1991. "The Production of Copies of the Canterbury Tales and the Confessio Amantis in the Early Fifteenth Century" in Parkes, M.B. (ed.) *Scribes, Scripts and Readers: Studies in the Communication, Preservation and Dissemination of Medieval Texts*. London: Hambledon. 201–48.

Fradenburg, Louise O. 1991. *City, Marriage, Tournament: Arts of Rule in Late Medieval Scotland*. Madison: University of Wisconsin Press.

Fraser, William (ed.) 1880. *The Red Book of Menteith*. 2 vols. Edinburgh: privately printed.

Furnivall, F.J. and I. Gollancz (eds). [1892] 1970. *Hoccleve's Works: The Minor Poems* [Early English Text Society Extra Series no. 61, 73.]. London: K. Paul, Trench, Trübner.

Furnivall, F.J. (ed.) [1897] 1988. *Hoccleve's Works: The Regement of Princes and Fourteen Minor Poems* [Early English Text Society Extra Series no. 72.]. Millwood NY: Kraus Reprints.

Grady, Frank. 1995. "The Lancastrian Gower and the Limits of Exemplarity" in *Speculum* 70: 552–75.

Haines, R.M. 1976. "'Our Master Mariner, Our Sovereign Lord': A Contemporary Preacher's View of Henry V" in *Medieval Studies* 38: 83–96.

Macaulay, G.C. (ed.) 1900. *The English Works of John Gower* [Early English Text Society Extra Series no. 81–82.]. 2 vols. London: K. Paul, Trench, Trübner.

Mapstone, Sally. 1997. "Kingship and the *Kingis Quair*" in Cooper, Helen and Sally Mapstone (eds) *The Long Fifteenth Century*. Oxford: Clarendon Press. 51–69.

—. 1998. "Bower on Kingship" in Watt, D.E.R. et al. (eds) *Scotichronicon by Walter Bower in Latin and English*. 9: 321–38.

Martin, Joanna. 2002. *Readings of John Gower's* Confessio Amantis *in Fifteenth- and Early Sixteenth Century Scotland*. PhD thesis. University of Oxford.

Matheson, Lister M. (ed.) 1999. *Death and Dissent. Two Fifteenth-Century Chronicles. The Dethe of the Kynge of Scotis and Warkworth's Chronicle*. Woodbridge: Boydell Press.

Nicholson, P. 1988. "The Dedications of the Confessio Amantis" in *Medievalia* 10: 159–80.

Norton-Smith, J. (ed.) 1971. *James I of Scotland: The Kingis Quair* [Clarendon Medieval and Tudor Series]. Oxford: Clarendon Press.

Regan, C.L. 1979. "The *Kingis Quair*: ll. 75–83. A Possible Source" in *American Notes & Queries* 17: 86–88.

Skeat, W.W. (ed.) 1883–84. *The Kingis Quair together with A Ballad of Good Counsel by James I of Scotland* [Scottish Text Society 1st Series no. 1.]. Edinburgh and London: William Blackwood and Sons.

Spearing, A.C. 2000. "Dreams in The *Kingis Quair* and 'The Dukes Buke'" in Arn, M.J. (ed.) *Charles d'Orleans In England, 1415–40*. Woodbridge: D.S. Brewer. 123–44.

Summers, Joanna. 2003. *Late-Medieval Prison Writing and the Politics of Autobiography*. Oxford: Clarendon Press.

Watt, D.E.R et al. (eds). 1987–98. *Scotichronicon by Walter Bower in Latin and English*. 9 vols. Aberdeen and Edinburgh: Aberdeen University Press and Mercat Press.

The Flyting of Dunbar and Kennedy in Context

Nicole Meier

This essay puts *The Flyting of Dunbar and Kennedy* against two other traditions of poetic insult, the first Old French and Provençal debate poetry, and the second Gaelic satire and eulogy. In so doing, it challenges the notion of flyting as a peculiarly Scottish form but rather stresses its participation in universal patterns.
Keywords: *Book of the Dean of Lismore*; Celtic culture; William Dunbar; eulogy; flyting; Walter Kennedy; *partimen*; satire; *sirventes*; *tenson*; *trouvères*; Ulster cycle

The following lines from David Lyndsay's *The Testament of the Papyngo* are among the few instances in literary history where Dunbar and Kennedy are mentioned in the same breath, but they are praised for their aureate verses and not for their collaborative enterprise – *The Flyting*:

[Q]uho can now the workis cuntrafait
Off Kennedie, with termes aureait?
Or of Dunbar, quhilk language had at large,
As maye be sene in tyll his golden targe? (Hamer ed. 1931: I: 56)

The excerpt from Lyndsay's poem also foreshadows the fate of *The Flyting of Dunbar and Kennedy* in the following centuries. *The Flyting* was very popular in the sixteenth and seventeenth centuries and its legacy ranges from a short fictional flyting of a cobbler and a tailor in the Bannatyne Manuscript to the famous flytings of Montgomerie and Polwarth, James V and Lyndsay. In recent centuries, however, *The Flyting* has been outdone by poems such as *The Goldyn Targe* or *The Thrissil and the Rois*, has been much undervalued in scholarship and has often been criticised as bizarre, opaque and not in line with the poets' other work (See Scott 1996: 178). Yet, *The Flyting* is not a one-off: several features and themes of *The Flyting* can be found in various genres and literary traditions, as previous critics have noted. However, with Bawcutt (1992) as a notable exception, previous discussions, such as Schipper (1884), have tended to overrate direct influences without discussing the genres in detail. This essay attempts to address this lack by focusing on two particular genres: Old French and Provençal debate poetry and Celtic satire.

Medieval French and Provençal lyric poetry had an immense impact on European literature, and the forms and concepts which the troubadours of Provence and the trouvères of Northern France used were to influence many a later poet. The verse forms which are of importance to *The Flyting* are the *partimen*, the *tenson*, and the *sirventes* (these are the Provençal terms, as although the OF equivalents describe similar forms, they are later usages). Since the nineteenth century, a lively discussion about the origin, definition and mutual relationship of the *tenson* and the *partimen* has been going on (Jeanroy 1934; Selbach 1886; Knobloch 1886; Zenker 1888). The problem in defining the origin of the *tenson* and the *partimen* and their meaning stems from the various uses of the word *tenson* in the manuscripts. In one of the earliest *tenson*s, a poem by Uc Catola and Marcabru (first half of the twelfth century), the word *tenzon* does not describe a specific poetic genre, but refers to a general discussion of a controversial topic (Dejeanne 1909). The term *partimen*, however, can be found from the fourteenth century onwards. Many critics, such as Selbach and Zenker, have regarded *tenson* and *partimen* as synonyms for one literary genre. Others have described the *tenson* as the original form. Hagan points out that *tenson* and *partimen* are both based on the principle of alternating dialogue and the difference between them is not a generic but a stylistic one (Hagan 1983). Köhler examines the origin of the *tenson* and finds out that the original form is not what is later meant by *tenson* (a free exchange on a controversial issue), but the *partimen* (Köhler 1959). In this, Köhler refutes Selbach's theory that the *tenson* was influenced by the *conflictus* as well as Jeanroy's view that the *tenson* sprang from the exchange of *coblas*. He maintains that medieval dialectics as expressed in the *disputatio* or Abelard's *sic-et-non* method and various other kinds of argumentation exercises provided the basis for the Latin *conflictus* as well as for vernacular debate forms. Of great importance to the development of the *tenson* (in its general meaning) was, according to Köhler, the legal practice of the *joc-partit*, for example, the naming of umpires. The courtly rules involved therefore also determined the literary form of the *partimen*. But what is meant by the term *tenson* then? Later, the *tenson* is not the generic term for the dispute genre, but applied to a new form which owes its origin to another development in which the meaning of the word *tenson* was restricted and specified and then referred to free disputes between poets (quite often jongleurs).

The *partimen* is a poetic exchange of stanzas between poets in which a theme is proposed in the form of a dilemmatic question. The opponent was then free to choose the side he wanted to defend and the challenger was to maintain the remaining side. Usually the argument passed through four stanzas and ended with an appeal to a judge. Very often, the subject of the *partimen* is love (a *demande d'amour*). Sometimes more than two poets participated in a *partimen* which is then called *torneyamen*. The *partimen*, "Gauclem, tres joc enamoratz", between Savaric de Mauleon, a baron, patron, and troubadour, Gaucelm Faidit, a famous troubadour, and the minor poet Uc de la Baccalaria is also a *torneyamen*. It is initiated by Savaric's question as to which token of love (a look, a handshake, or a kick) is more precious. Gaucelm then sets out to maintain that a lady's look is the greatest sign of love, whereas Uc defends the handshake and Savaric the kick. After these exchanges, Savaric appeals to two judges and says: "vuoill qe fassa·l jutgamen / mo Gardacors [...] e Na Maria" (81–83); Gaucelm wants "Guillelma de Benauges" (87) to be the third judge (Mouzat ed. 1965: 425–33).

In Northern France the *partimen* is called *jeu-parti* and shows similar features. In the *jeu-parti* between Jean Bretel and Lambert Ferri, it is Ferri who propounds the antithetical question: who is nobler and more courtly – someone whose love is yet unfulfilled or someone who is already indulging in love? This later French *jeu-parti* lacks the appeal to an umpire which is characteristic of many Provençal *partimens*. This feature of the *partimen*, however, bears some relationship to *The Flyting*. *The Flyting*, of course, does not contain a dilemmatic question and does not deal with a *demande d'amour* either, but Bannatyne also appeals to his readers to judge "quha gat the war". Moreover, *The Flyting* contains several legal terms which are also reminiscent of courtly procedures, for instance "commissar" (34); "recompansing" (46); "cedull" (48) (Bawcutt ed. 1998: I: 201; all further references are taken from this edition and will be made in the form of line numbers in parentheses in the text). The debate form in general was certainly influenced by legal practices as well as other institutional exchanges. The troubadours were familiar with the law-schools of Provence which provided them with legal terminology. Reed enumerates several parallels between law and literature of which the most important is this: they seem to fulfil similar functions – to define values and identities (Reed 1990). The *partimen* discusses such values and love-conventions; in *The Flyting* values like "guid making" and poetic ability as well as social and cultural identities are at stake. Reed also mentions the analogous terminology: whereas at court the plaintiff's sergeant is called narrator and reads a "tale", arguments in the *partimen* are defended ("triatz", Gaucelm 69) and a judgement ("jutgamen", Gaucelm 92) is called for (Mouzat ed. 1965: 428-429). The features the *partimen* and *The Flyting* share are the dialogue form – although the *partimen* is a constructed debate and poets do not necessarily defend their own point of view – and the indebtedness, which can be traced in structure and terminology, to institutional exchanges like those of the law-courts. It is quite probable that Dunbar and Kennedy were acquainted with judicial procedures: Dunbar, for instance, seems to have acted as an advocate at least once, and Kennedy is called "attorney" once (Fraser 1888: II, 117-19; Donaldson 1952: no. 962; *Aisa Papers*, no. 166).

Yet, the Provençal *partimen* as well as the French *jeu-partis* are not invectives and we therefore turn to the *tenson*. The *tenson* is also an exchange between poets, but in contrast to the more systematical *partimen*, the *tenson* does not necessarily deal with love. The *tensons'* subjects are literary or personal in nature, "personalities rather than formal questions are at issue" (Reed 1990: 133). In her thesis, Hagan speaks of the literary and the insult *tenson,* where no antithetical question initiates the exchange of arguments, but a pattern of insults controls the structure of the *tenson* in which "the participants aim insults at each other, vilifying the opponent in a display of real or feigned antagonism" (Hagan 1983: 98). This already recalls various aspects of *The Flyting*. In spite of Bannatyne's classification and Dunbar's friendly lines to Kennedy in "I that in heill wes and gladnes", the reader of *The Flyting* is never sure how serious Dunbar's and Kennedy's insults are meant to be (witness his address of Kennedy as "Gud maister Walter Kennedy" in line 89 of "I that in heill wes and gladness", and Bannatyne's introduction of *The Flyting* as "The Flyting of Dumbar and Kennedie / Heir efter followis jocound and mirrie" (fol. 147)). But even more telling are the insults which characterise several *tensons* as well as *The Flyting*. Hagan remarks that the insults uttered in the *tensons* often refer to physical appearance, character traits or disreputable incidents. A typical example of these insult *tensons* is the thirteenth-century exchange between Gui de Cavaillon and Falco, a jongleur. Gui starts his invective by referring to Falco's readiness to defame people and adds that a kick would serve him right: "Falco, en dire mal / Vey qu'es trop abrivatz" (Jones 1934: 83–86, 83). He challenges Falco by saying that it puzzled him that Falco left his monastery. Falco in turn insults Gui and says that he lives but in a "paubr' ostal" (Jones 1934: 83) and that he behaved dishonourably towards his protector, the count Alphonse, and above all, lived on other peoples' expenses. This recalls Dunbar's description of Kennedy as a "longeour" (212) who has got nowhere to stay and nothing to eat during the winter and warms himself "at ane uthir auld wyvis ingle" (117) and who lives in a "laithly luge" (154). This again reminds us of Gui's charge in *cobla* v in which he tells Falco: "E s'e·l yvern coral / Es nutz ni despulhatz" (Jones 1934: 84). Gui reacts to Falco's insults by calling Falco a "jongleur" and by condemning whoever told Falco to open his mouth at all. Such an inventor of slander should be punished with a razor, he demands. As in *The Flyting*, poetic identity and poetry itself are the things at issue here. It should be remembered that Kennedy also calls Dunbar a "jugelour" (524) who is not able to produce elaborate poetry but only calumny, horrible blather and noise. Falco wishes Gui to be attached to a stake and to be burnt for his invectives; Kennedy threatens Dunbar with similar sanctions: "Do thou not thus [renounce thy rymis], bogane, thou salbe brynt / Wyth pik, fire, ter, gun puldre, or lint" (333–34).

The third literary form related to *The Flyting*, the *sirventes*, is one of the main genres of troubadour poetry. Originally, the *sirventes* had no specific form or content but was a commissioned poem. Later, the *sirventes* obtained a new function and it often criticised the ideals presented in the *canso*. Quite frequently the *sirventes* became a kind of invective which did not necessarily contain an answer to a challenge or an exchange of insults. The topic of a *sirventes* could also be poetry itself. In the *sirventes* by Bernart Marti, the author maintains that even the best troubadour poetry is not capable of expressing moral truths and can therefore only be imperfect (Rieger ed. 1980: 84–89). The incentive for this *sirventes* was a poem by Peire d'Alvernha in which he styled himself the best troubadour. This recalls Dunbar's first lines in *The Flyting* in which he tells John the Ross that Kennedy and Quintene "thame self aboif the sternis styled" (3). Marti also seeks to ridicule his opponent's boast, and stresses that only foolish poets would endeavour to produce perfect poetry and accuses Peire d'Alvernha of producing mere lies and of being "fols joglares" (Rieger ed. 1980: 86), a foolish minstrel. He condemns d'Alvernha's boasting and calls it befitting a peasant but not in accordance with courtly behaviour.

The *sirventes* "Amics Marquer, enquera non a gaire" by the Catalan troubadour Guillem de Berguedan recalls the original panegyric code of the *sirventes* but then turns out to be an inversion of a praise poem. Guillem intends to ridicule Pons the Mataplan (Rieger ed. 1980: 146–51). He is called a braggart ("gabaire"), a coward ("volpill", "coart") and a traitor ("traicher") (Rieger ed. 1980: 146–48). Guillem also wants Mataplan to be afflicted with gout blotches and threatens that he will see to it that his *sirventes* is made public. This *sirventes* and Dunbar's and Kennedy's flyting have several features in common. Both intend to degrade their opponents by ridiculing them and both threaten their rivals with sanctions. Like Guillem, Dunbar announces that he will make Kennedy's shame known "throw all cuntreis and kinrikis" (24) and "throw all Bretane" (69).

However striking these parallels between Old French and Provençal forms and *The Flyting* are, Dunbar and Kennedy's flyting cannot simply be classified as a *tenson* or a *sirventes*. Although many *tensons* and *sirventes* do make use of insults, they never solely consist of tirades of insults but very often try to establish positive values as well (religious attitudes, courtly behaviour, poetic theories). It is difficult to prove that the *tenson* or the *sirventes* had a direct influence on *The Flyting*, yet several other poems by Dunbar and Kennedy are indebted to French literary forms, such as Dunbar's elegy on Bernard Stewart ("Illuster Lodovick...") which recalls French *regretz* and *complaints* and *The Tretis of the Tua Mariit Wemen and the Wedo* ("Apon the midsummer evin...") is indebted to French *demandes d'amour* and the tradition of the *chanson de mal mariée*. Just as *The Flyting*, they make use of various elements which can be traced back to various literary traditions and genres.

In *The Flyting*, Dunbar describes flyting as "sic eloquence as thay in Erschry use" (line 107) and thus compares his own flyting with Kennedy not first and foremost to French, English or Latin models, but to a Celtic literary form. Although I do not wish to contend that urban Lowland poets writing in Scots like Dunbar looked to Celtic literature for models, it is also not realistic to maintain that the different cultural and linguistic regions of Scotland existed alongside each other without any communication or influence at all. When Pedro de Ayala visited the court of James IV in 1496, he reported that the king was able to converse in various languages, among them Gaelic (Brown 1891: 38). The king also maintained a Gaelic harpist, and although it is difficult to determine how extensive his language skills were, he was by no means as hostile to Gaelic culture as James VI, who described his Highland subjects as "barbarous" (Craigie ed. 1944: 1: 71). On both sides we find regard as well as disregard for each other's language and culture. Pupils in Aberdeen Grammar School in 1553 were reported to be allowed to speak Latin, Greek, Hebrew, French or Gaelic at school but not Scots, their vernacular (Simpson 1906: 99–102).

As far as literature is concerned, the most remarkable example of cultural contact is the sixteenth-century Gaelic manuscript, *The Book of the Dean of Lismore* (Edinburgh, National Library of Scotland MS Adv. 72.1.37). *The Book of the Dean of Lismore* is an anthology of Scottish and Irish verse compiled between 1512 and 1526 by James MacGregor, Dean of Lismore, and his brother Duncan. What makes the *Book of the Dean of Lismore* of special interest to *The Flyting* is that, as Donald Meek puts it, "[it] intermingles Gaelic culture and Scots culture" (Meek 1989a: 387). This is manifest in the contents as well as in the origin of the hand and the scribes of the manuscript. Its compilers, the MacGregors, were vassals of the Campbells, who themselves had a great interest in both Gaelic and Scots culture, and were probably bilingual. James MacGregor was not only Dean of Lismore but also vicar of Fortingall in Perthshire, on the border of the Gaelic-speaking Highlands. The Book of the Dean of Lismore is written in secretary hand, a script to which James MacGregor was accustomed as a notary public (the script usually found in Gaelic manuscripts is the *corr-litir*, lineal descendant of the Hiberno-Saxon hand of the Insular Middle Ages). What is so special about the *Book of the Dean of Lismore* is the fact that it makes use of a spelling system based on Scots. Although the *Book of the Dean of Lismore* is particularly striking in this regard, Meek (1989b) also gives examples of the use of a similar Scots-based spelling system using in manuscripts and inscriptions from the Scots-Gaelic border: for instance the Black Book of Taymouth or passages from *The Book of the Howlat*. Meek discusses possible reasons for this practice: more generally, he suggests it might result from the bilingualism of the scribes from the contact

region; for the *Book of the Dean of Lismore* in particular, he remarks
as a notary public MacGregor was familiar with the writing and
spelling conventions of the Scottish Lowlands, and, what is more, as
he was located on the border of both regions, he was certainly aware
of the different literary traditions. It should be noted that Kennedy also
came from a region which was still Gaelic speaking in the sixteenth
century (Lorimer 1949; Lorimer 1953; MacQueen 1973). Like the
MacGregors he was probably able to converse in Scots and Gaelic.

In the *Book of the Dean of Lismore* this interface is mirrored by
the contents too. The manuscript contains Gaelic bardic verse,
Ossianic ballads, love lyrics and satires, but also lines in Scots, taken,
for instance, from Henryson's *Testament of Cresseid* (Edinburgh,
National Library of Scotland MS Adv. 72.1.37, p. 92b "Luffaris be
war and tak gowd heid") and indeed two stanzas from a poem
sometimes attributed to Dunbar (incipit "The beistlie lust [...]", p.77).
As Meek puts it, the "manuscript clearly indicates language switching
(Gaelic/Scots/Latin) and probably diglossia (Gaelic/Scots)" (Meek
1989a: 395). The various examples given here strongly support the
view that in contact areas there was an interaction between Gaelic and
Scots culture and language.

The second part of my article will therefore explore the relationship between Celtic literature, especially Celtic satire, and Dunbar's
and Kennedy's *Flyting*. Celtic literature has always been associated
with satire, and satire was a means of power. This belief may have its
foundation in the relationship between satire and magic. In Early Irish
literature, the term *aér* refers to incantational satire – that is, satire
supported by magic rites – as well as to satire without the aid of
magic. The fact that Irish satire had its roots in magic, is connected
with the idea that satirists were poets as well as magicians or druids.
Therefore, Celtic satire cannot be compared to English satire; especially in early literature, it does not function as a castigation of general
moral conditions but, apart from it being a spell, curse, or enchant-
ment, it is basically personal attack, lampoon or invective. Satirists
were feared and respected in Celtic society as they were said to work
destruction with their satires. Satire was not only feared for its out-
ward effects but was also destructive to the honour of a person. The
same poets who could create a good reputation were also capable of
destroying it by their satire.

In the Middle Irish *Second Battle of Moytura*, Cairbre mac Elaine is reported to have made a satire on Bres mac Elathain, king of the Tuatha Dé Danann. As Bres was very avaricious and had insulted the poet Cairbre by not treating him as a *file*, Cairbre composed a satire on Bres who then lost his health and his position as a king. The effect satire could have on its victims is also illustrated by an example from Cormac's Glossary. Nede, who wanted to become king of Connaught, made a satire on his uncle Caier, king of Connaught, which caused three blisters to appear on Caier's face who was thus not capable of being king anymore. The fact that satire was reputed to mutilate people's faces is also described in the *Siege of Howth*. The infamous satirist Aithirne, who was feared for his satires, was refused by Luaine, which induced him to make a satire on the latter. As with Caier, three blotches could be seen on Luaine's face as the effect of Aithirne's satire.

The tales belonging to the Ulster cycle, for instance the *Scéla Mucce meic Dathó* or the *Táin Bó Cúailnge*, tell the story of the quarrels between Connaught and Ulster (Thurneysen 1935 and O'Rahilly 1976). These tales are interesting to *The Flyting* as they feature a kind of verbal duel, also called flyting by some critics, which can be compared to similar exchanges in epics such as *Beowulf* or *The Battle of Maldon* (Parks 1990: 3; Anderson 1970). Although epic flyting is carried out in a different literary context from our flyting, it shares several features with Celtic satire and Scots flyting. In his study on the *Táin*, Bernard Martin describes epic flyting as "vocal threatening which often precedes ritualised combat" (Martin 1994: 44). He regards flyting in the epic as a "generative kernel" and enumerates several features: opponents boast of their ancestors and of themselves while at the same time trying to belittle their opponents. In the *Scéla Mucce meic Dathó*, Ulster and Connaught warriors exchange boasts and insults in order to determine a victor in a battle of words, who is then allowed to carve the famous pig of Mac Dathó. The flyting exchanges in the *Táin* are mainly between Cúchulainn of Ulster and queen Medb's warriors. Martin also points out that "the semantic polarities of animal-human, feminine-masculine, immature-grown, and weak-strong all resonate with thoroughly *ad hominem* insults" (Martin 1994: 55). Of course, the *Táin* also contains various references to satirists. The satirist Redg is employed against Cúchulainn; Medb sends satirists who threaten Ferdiad with the infamous three blisters. Thus, satire was employed as a powerful weapon to enforce one's demands in various contexts. Although at some point, the magic rites accompanying satire had fallen away, the fear of the satirist had not, and satire was frequently employed as a threat.

Nevertheless, a distinction was made between just and unjust use of satire. Nede, for instance, is said to have been punished for his unjust satire. Therefore, several examples of satire can be found in legal tracts like the Brehon Laws which classify satire as a crime of the tongue, although these examples are very epigrammatical (O'Donovan et al. eds 1865–1901). Several Middle Irish treatises on versification also contain examples of Irish satire. The Book of Ballymote, compiled about 1400, for example, contains a treatise on types of satire (Atkinson ed. 1887). It is difficult to tell them apart or to find suitable examples for each kind. It will therefore suffice to point out features which might be relevant to *The Flyting*, for instance the importance of naming in Celtic satire which is expressed in several examples from the Book of Ballymote's tract. I have already mentioned the role a good reputation had and the shame and desocialisation satire causes. Above all, names are linked to genealogies and define a person's position. If one's name was attacked or mutilated, this had a serious impact on the person. In *The Flyting*, Dunbar does not exploit the possibility of attacking Kennedy's name, perhaps because Kennedy came from a wealthy and powerful aristocratic family. (He was the grandson of James Kennedy and of Mary, Countess of Angus, a daughter of Robert III, and he was thus the nephew of James Kennedy, bishop of St. Andrews. He himself also possessed estates in Carrick and Galloway (*Ailsa Papers*, no. 214)). In contrast, Kennedy ridicules Dunbar's ancestors and plays on the name Dunbar. Thus Dunbar is associated with a genealogy of traitors, his name is related to the Devil himself which leaves Dunbar an outsider, an effect similar to the one Dunbar achieves in the Edinburgh mobbing scene, where Dunbar creates a bizarre picture of Kennedy who scares the town-dwellers and is then chased out of town by boys and fishwives throwing their refuse at him (210–32).

The grammatical tracts as well as the glossaries contain several examples of Early Irish verse. I will give several instances of insult which recall the tone of *The Flyting*:

A mir do duiniu, a delb in demain
[You dwarfish man, shape of devil]. (Meyer 1919)

As in *The Flyting*, the lampooned person's physical appearance is
ridiculed, in this case short stature (cf. Kennedy: "mymmerkin", (29),
"dearch" (33)), and associated with devils and demons (cf. Kennedy:
"devill", 33 et passim). Not only the person addressed but also his
family and belongings are attacked:

A gilla duinn a Dermaig, ocata in ben donn deolaid
[Brown [haired] boy from Derry, who has a brown poor wife].

Compare this to Dunbar: "With the ane sowtaris wyfe, off blis als bar"
(155). In the Irish examples, the addressee of satire is often called
"druth", a fool:

A druith, cid tai dom airbire?
[Fool, how do you dare to revile me?]

Compare this to Kennedy: "Fantastik fule" (55). Very often, these invectives are tirades of obscure insults and recall the final lines of *The
Flyting*. Compare the verbal vigour of "Herretyk, lunatyk, purspyk,
carlingis pet / Rottin crok, dirtin dok, cry cok, or I sall quell thee"
(247–48) to

A Dallain doburthanaig digradaig,
a cammain chrinlamaig chonfathmannaig chuaranaig
a phitig phaitig phiananais
a thiaganaig etig aitig uarlamaig!

[Dallan, evil, degraded, crooked, with withered hands, shaggy as a dog, wearer of
sandals, keen on food and the bottle, pest, ugly reviling bearer of bags with cold
hands.]

But attacks do not only aim at outside or inward qualities. There are
insults which are targeted at poetic craft and/or the position of the poet
himself, for example:

A fetanaig, [...] a chleraige, a sgelaige
[Piper, vagabond minstrel/musician, story-teller].

Kennedy calls Dunbar a "jugelour" (524) and tells him to "take [...] a
fidill, or a floyte, and geste" (507) whereas Kennedy is styled "baird"
several times (for example, 17, 49, 63, 96, 120). As in medieval

France and Provence the troubadours and trouvères did not want to be associated with lower orders of poets like the jongleurs; medieval Celtic society also had its preconceptions about the position and function of different sorts of poets, distinguishing bards from *fili*, originally clerical poets. In Scots, the term "bard" was almost always used derogatorily and synonymously with strolling singer or vagabond minstrel, notably in *The Buke of the Howlat* (Bawcutt and Riddy ed. 1987: 46-84, 76-8). Furthermore, Dunbar, the court poet, dissociates himself from the "Erschry" tradition which lacks "feill of fair indyte" (109).

Yet, while discussing Celtic satire and the relationship of Gaelic and Scots literature, it is promising to compare the position of the poets in both societies to each other as they exhibit several parallel features. I will concentrate on the position of the poet in the period between 1100–1600. In this Classical Bardic period, ruling families employed an official bardic poet (*ollamh*) who had been educated at the bardic schools. Williams describes the court poets of this period as a "well-organised and highly-trained literary order" (Williams 1971: 85). The task of these court-poets was to produce official bardic verse for the noble families. The main genre of these trained professional poets was eulogy. Nevertheless, praise and shame, eulogy and satire are closely related. In the Book of Ballymote, for instance, satire and praise poetry (*aér* and *molad*) are complementary modes: while eulogy underlines or creates social position and renown, satire defames and destroys good name. The techniques at work, however, are of a very similar nature: bardic eulogy as well as satire employ exaggeration and often present a set of characteristics which do not completely correspond to reality. If one fails to recognise this relationship, as some critics of *The Flyting* have done (Baxter 1952), one is likely to take several insults of *The Flyting*, for instance Kennedy's allusion to Dunbar's short stature, for granted and use them as a quarry for biographical facts.

A good example of the complementary nature of satire and eulogy can be found in the *Book of the Dean of Lismore*. An anonymous poem "Cóir feitheamh", addressed to John Stewart, underlines the relationship of panegyric and satire (as discussed by Gilles 1986):

A Eoin Stiúbhairt a crích Raithneach
a lámh Gaoidheal as fearr buaidh,
gabh, a laoich as solta i gcagadh,
laoidh mholta agus bagar uaim.

Tángas chugad, mheic Shir Roibeirt,
a Eoin Stiúbhairt na rosg ngorm;
beir, a chleath nach mion fá mheabhair
breath, is sin do-gheabhair orm.

Más í do chomhairle bhunaidh
bheith 'gam eiteach, a fholt réidh,
a lámh thréan na nGaoidheal soinnimh,
fa séan aoir id choinnibh é.

Déar-sa riotsa, a mheic Shir Roibeirt
a Ghaoidheil nach críon fán chrodh,
fa mó an díoth dhuit mo theagmháil
ná síoth agus beagán domh.

Nárab tusa thollas oram:
Nimh na n-aoir ní an cogadh soirbh;
's fearr dhuit gach radháil ón teinidh
ná a gabháil mar eiridh oirbh. (Watson ed. 1937; 184–91).

[Thou John Stewart from the bounds of Rannoch, thou whose hand has more virtue than all the Gael, receive from me, thou warrior stout in warfare, a poem of praise and a threat withal.

I have come to thee, thou son, of Sir Robert, thou John Stewart of blue eyes: give judgement, thou pillar not slight of sense, and by it thou shall find me abide [...]

If it be thy fixed intent to make me refusal, thou of the smooth hair, then, thou mighty hand of the eager Gael, that shall be an omen of satire against thee [...]

I shall say to thee, son of Sir Robert, thou Gael who stintest not stock, it were a greater loss to thee to encounter me than to make peace and grant me somewhat.

Let it not be thou who rousest my enmity: the venom of satires is no light warfare; better for thee to be scorched by fire than to take it on thee as a burden.]
(Gillies 1986)

Satire and praise are also confronted in another poem from the *Book of the Dean of Lismore* by Giolla Críost Brúilingeach, "Dá urradh i n-iath Éireann" (Watson ed. 1937: 46–59) which compares Tomaltach MacDermot and Tómas Maguire. Tomaltach is depicted as the good chief, Tómas as the bad chief. Tómas is mean and faulty ("lom lochtach", line 469) whereas Tomaltach is valiant ("cródha", line 470). Their horses, mailcoats and weapons are compared; the contrast is epitomised in lines 533–40 when one chief (McDermot) is called strong, renowned and skilful ("láidir aithnid eólach") and the other is but a feeble helpless man ("daoi anbhfann aintreórach").

A further example from the Dean's Book bearing witness to the interrelation of praise poetry and satire, is the satiric elegy on Allan, son of Roderick, "Theast aon diabhal na nGaoidheal" (Watson ed. 1937: 134–37.) by Finlay, the Red Bard (see Gillies 2005 for a discussion of this with other mock-elegies of the sixteenth century). It is a kind of black praise, in which the author enumerates every hellish deed of Allan, who is frequently associated with hell ("ifrean", line 1237), equated with the devil, and therefore infamous for his heresy. This recalls Kennedy's charges in *The Flyting*, where Dunbar and his family are described as being in alliance with the devil and hence a family of traitors and blasphemers. Above all, Allan is styled a coward who has long since been gallows-ripe: "fada ó b'ionchrochtha Ailéin" (line 1294) whereas Dunbar is portrayed as a "widdefow" (line 101).

Another example of classical bardic satire from the *Book of the Dean of Lismore*, the poem "Dá ghabhladh dhéag inson dán" by Donnchadh Óg Albanach is discussing the type of satire called *mac bronn* in the Book of Ballymote. The *mac bronn*, or secret satire, satire *in petto*, in the Book of the Dean is one of the few examples illustrating the distinctions made in the Book of Ballymote. The text by Donnchadh Óg Albanach exhibits most of the characteristics of Celtic satire (see Greene 1945-47: 232-35 for a transcription and translation of the text). The question as to whether the *mac bronn* is a eulogy or satire ("An aor nó moladh mac bronn?") points at the closeness and relatedness of the two bardic modes of expression. In the following, the *mac bronn* (son of a womb) is compared to a pregnancy, as long as the satire is not communicated. Nevertheless, the author stresses the poisonous and harmful potential of the *mac bronn*. Once he will no longer conceal his satire, this will be fatal for the satire's victim:

Ag fadódh is-toigh fám thuinn
a-tá an aor, gion go n-abruim;
ní faoilcheas an taobh is-toigh
toircheas na n-aor is abaigh

Ní bhiad gá cheilt, sáthach sin;
tighearna uasal éigin
don toircheas is é as athair,
is mé fhoilcheas a anachain.

Scaoilfead uime m'éigean de,
an toircheas a-tá im bruinne;
léigfead fúibh toireacheas na troch
dúin ní hoircheas a fholach.

Ní choigeól Gaoidheal nó Gall,
is mairg theigéamhas tharam;
nathair neimhe daoibh an dán,
teine 'na haoir do hadádh.

[Burning under my skin is the satire, though I do not say it;
the inside is hidden no longer (for) the pregnancy of the satires is ripe.

I will not conceal it, it is enough; a certain noble lord is the father of the pregnancy –
it is I who conceal its harm.

I will unloose on him its oppression of me, this pregnancy in my breast;
I will leave to you the pregnancy of the wretch, it is not fitting for me to conceal it.

I will spare neither Gael nor Gall, woe to him who crosses me;
poetry is a poisonous serpent to you, a fire which has been kindled to a satire.]

It is interesting to note that Donnchadh Óg Albanach describes poetry, written words, as being so powerful, as this idea is also expressed by Dunbar when he describes the effects of the words he will produce "with pen and ynk" (12). Indeed, several other poems by Dunbar also recall the lines from *mac bronn,* for instance, "lat the vennim ische al out / Be war anone, for it will spout" from "Schir, ye have mony servitouris" (lines 85-86) and "I sall the venome devoid [...]" in *The Tretis of the Twa Mariit Wemen and the Wedo* (line 166). As a result, we are not sure whether Dunbar's final exclamation "I sall quell thee!" (248) is referring to physical actions or whether mere words will suffice to achieve their end.

The various examples of early and later satire from Scotland and Ireland exhibit many parallels to *The Flyting* in theme and tone. Yet, even if the targets of satiric verses are often selfishness, niggardliness, inhospitality, or failure to pay just debts, this is not exclusively a feature of Celtic satire. The animal imagery, for instance, is very similar in many traditions. In his study on the use of animal imagery in Gaelic panegyrical and invective, McCaughey suggests that "the language of invective almost universally involves (a) words referring to sex and/or excretion; (b) blasphemy and profanity; and (c) animal invective" (McCaughey 1989: 109). This language can be seen in the Celtic examples above as well as in *The Flyting*. But Dunbar is primarily associating flyting with a Gaelic tradition; it therefore suggests itself for comparison with Celtic satire. This also applies to the description of satire as related to magic. I do not contend that it is Celtic satire only which has its roots in magic, as there are examples from Arabia and Greece as well, but as Scotland and Ireland are much closer to Dunbar and even closer to Kennedy than anything else, the Scottish/Irish examples may suffice as a model.

When comparing *The Flyting* to related genres and various literary traditions – and Celtic satire and the Provençal debates and invectives are just two examples – the influence of different literary forms becomes evident. But if we want to assess *The Flyting* and its relationship with other European texts adequately, one has to acknowledge the existence of different discourse levels in Dunbar and Kennedy's poem. On the first, literal level, both poets abuse each other and desire to destroy each other. On this level, Dunbar is the dwarfish traitor and Kennedy the lean, deformed Gaelic outsider. But we know, as did the readers or the audience of *The Flyting*, that we are not meant to take these portraits literally. *The Flyting*, after all, is a poetic game, and, of course, games also determine winners and losers. But what makes *The Flyting* so difficult to categorise is the fact that it seems impossible to formulate one explicit aim. One aim, of course is mutual ridicule and debasement: sometimes *The Flyting* strikes satiric tones, sometimes it appears to be mere abuse. Furthermore, Dunbar presents himself as loathing and despising "Erschery" and "Erschemen": in "In vice most vicius he excellis" he satirises Donald Owyr, usually identified with Donald Dubh, grandson of the last Lord of the Isles; in "Off Februar the fyitene nycht", Magoun wants to see a Highland pageant, and Makfadyane and a crowd of Erschemen appear, talk Gaelic, and make such an appalling din that the Devil sends them to hell (lines 109-20). Given this self-representation, why does Dunbar engage in flyting at all and, in other poems, use it as a threat?

The answer seems to lie on a different level of the poem. I have already pointed at the importance of language and poetry in *The Flyting*. In the poets' concepts of poetry there lies the key to an understanding of *The Flyting* and its relationship to similar European genres. *The Flyting* contains various references to poetry and poets. Each poet portrays himself as the superior artist. Kennedy dismisses

Dunbar's "scaldit scowis" whereas Dunbar differentiates himself from the bard Kennedy. Dunbar is very conscious of being a poet. Being a makar implies control and adequate usage of stylistic devices. In *The Flyting*, both poets do not get carried away with their spite but they are very conscious of the language they use – which makes *The Flyting* also a grand display of rhetorical virtuosity. Thus, Dunbar and Kennedy are aware of the traditions behind the paradigm they use – they are craftsmen who can work with any sort of material, and from Dunbar's point of view even with "sic eloquence as thay in Erschry use".

Bibliography

Ailsa Papers [*Culzean Charters*]. National Archives of Scotland, Register House, Edinburgh. NAS, GD 25/1.

Anderson, Earl R. 1970. "Flyting in *the Battle of Maldon*" in *Neuphilologische Mitteilungen* 71: 197–202.

Atkinson, R. (ed.) 1887. *The Book of Ballymote*. Dublin: Royal Irish Academy.

Bawcutt, Priscilla and Felicity Riddy. 1987. *Longer Scottish Poems I: 1375–1650*. Edinburgh: Scottish Academic Press.

Bawcutt, Priscilla. 1992. *Dunbar the Makar*. Oxford: Clarendon.

—. (ed.) 1998. *The Poems of William Dunbar*. 2 vols. Glasgow: Association for Scottish Literary Studies.

Baxter, J.W. 1952. *William Dunbar – A Biographical Study*. Edinburgh: Oliver and Boyd.

Brown, P. Hume. 1891. *Early Travellers in Scotland*. Edinburgh: David Douglas.

Craigie, J. (ed.) 1944–50. *Basilikon Doron of James VI* [Scottish Text Society 3rd Series no. 16, 18.]. 2 vols. Edinburgh: William Blackwood and Sons.

Craigie, William A. et al. (eds). 1931–2002. *A Dictionary of the Older Scottish Tongue from the Twelfth Century to the End of the Seventeenth*. 12 vols. Chicago, Aberdeen and Oxford: Oxford University Press.

Dejeanne, J.M.L. (ed.) 1909. *Poésies Complètes du Troubadour Marcabru*. Toulouse.

Donaldson, Gordon (ed.) 1952. *Protocol Book of James Young 1485–1515*. Edinburgh: Scottish Record Society.

Fox, Denton and W.A. Ringler (eds). 1980. *The Bannatyne Manuscript Facsimile*. London: Scolar Press.

Fraser, W. (ed.) 1888. *Memorials of the Family of Wemyss of Wemyss*. 3 vols. Edinburgh.

Gillies, William. 1986. "The Classical Irish Poetic Tradition" in Evans, D. Ellis, John G. Griffith and E. M. Jope (eds) *Proceedings of the 7th International Congress of Celtic Studies*. Oxford: D.E. Evans. 108–20.

—. 2005. "*Gun ann ach an ceo*: 'Nothing left but their Mist' Farewell and Elegy in Gaelic Poetry" in Mapstone, Sally (ed.) *Older Scots Literature*. Edinburgh: John Donald. 370–96.

Greene, David. 1945–47. "Mac Bronn" in *Éigse* 5: 232–35.

Hagan, Patricia. 1975. *The Medieval Provençal Tenson: Contribution to the Study of the Dialogue Genre*. PhD thesis. Yale University.

Hamer, D. (ed.) 1931–36. *The Works of Sir David Lindsay* [Scottish Text Society 3rd Series no. 1, 2, 6, 8.]. 4 vols. Edinburgh and London: William Blackwood and Sons.

Jeanroy, A. 1934. *La poésie lyrique des troubadours*. Toulouse: Privat.

Jones, David L. 1934. *La Tenson Provençale*. Paris.

Knobloch, H. 1886. *Das Streitgedicht im Provenzalischen und Altfranzösischen*. Breslau.

Köhler, Erich. 1959. "Zur Entstehung des altprovenzalischen Streitgedichts" in *Zeitschrift für romanische Philologie* 75: 37–88.

Lorimer, W.L. 1949. "The Persistence of Gaelic in Galloway and Carrick" in *Scottish Gaelic Studies* 6: 115–36.

—. 1953. "The Persistence of Gaelic in Galloway and Carrick" in *Scottish Gaelic Studies* 7: 27–46.

MacDiarmid, Hugh. 1943. *Lucky Poet*. London: Methuen.

MacQueen, John. 1973. "Gaelic Speakers of Galloway and Carrick" in *Scottish Studies* 17: 17–33.

Martin, Bernard. 1994. "Flyting and Fighting in the Irish *Táin Bó Cúailnge*" in Davidson, Lorna S. et al. (eds) *The Epic in History*. Sydney: Sydney Association for Studies in Society and Culture. 43–56.

McCaughey, Terence. 1989. "Bards, Beasts and Men" in Ó Corráin, Donnchadh, Liam Breatnach and Kim McCone (eds) *Sages, Saints and Storytellers. Celtic Studies in Honour of Professor James Carney*. Maynooth: An Sagart. 102–21.

Meek, Donald E. 1989a. "The Scots-Gaelic Scribes of Late Medieval Perthshire: An Overview of the Orthography and Contents of the Book of the Dean of Lismore" in McClure, J. Derrick and Michael R.G. Spiller (eds) *Bryght Lanternis: Essays on the Language and Literature of Medieval and Renaissance Scotland*. Aberdeen: Mercat Press. 387–404.

—. 1989b. "Gàidhlig is Gaylick anns na Meadhon Aoisean" in Gillies, William (ed.) *Alba agus A'Ghàidhlig: Gaelic and Scotland*. Edinburgh: Edinburgh University Press. 131–45.

Meyer, Kuno. 1919. "Bruchstücke der älteren Lyrik Irlands" in *Abhandlungen der preussischen Akademie der Wissenschaften*. Philosophisch-Historische Klasse. Berlin. VII, 1–72.

Mouzat, Jean (ed.) 1965. *Gaucelm Faidit, Les Poèmes*. Paris: Nizet.

O'Donovan, J. et al. (eds). 1865–1901. *The Ancient Laws of Ireland*. 6 vols. Dublin.

O'Rahilly, Cecile (ed.) 1976. *Táin Bó Cúailnge, Recension I*. Dublin: Dublin Institute for Advanced Studies.

Parks, Ward. 1990. *Verbal Dueling in Heroic Narrative. The Homeric and Old English Traditions*. Princeton: Princeton University Press.

Reed, Thomas L. 1990. *Middle English Debate Poetry and the Aesthetics of Irresolution*. Columbia and London: University of Missouri Press.

Rieger, Dietmar (ed.) 1980. *Mittelalterliche Lyrik Frankreichs I – Lieder der Trobadors*. Stuttgart: Reclam.

Schipper, Jakob. 1884. *William Dunbar – Sein Leben und seine Gedichte*. Berlin.

Scott, Tom. 1966. *Dunbar – A Critical Exposition of the Poems*. London and Edinburgh: Oliver and Boyd.

Selbach, L. 1886. *Das Streitgedicht in der provenzalischen Lyrik*. Marburg.

Simpson, H. F. Morland. 1906. *Bon Record: Records and Reminiscences of Aberdeen Grammar School from the Earliest Time by Many Writers*. Edinburgh: Ballantyne Press.

Thurneysen, R. (ed.) 1935. *Scéla Mucce meic Dathó*. Dublin: Dublin Institute for Advanced Studies.

Watson, W. J. (ed.) 1937. *Scottish Verse from the Book of the Dean of Lismore*. Edinburgh : Oliver & Boyd.

Williams, J. E. Caerwyn. 1971. "The Court Poet in Medieval Ireland" in *Proceedings of the British Academy* 57: 85–135.

Zenker, R. 1888. *Die Provenzalische Tenzone*. Erlangen.

"That he in brutal beist is transformate": The Translation of Man's Deeds to Those of Beasts

Rosemary Greentree

The fable form in Older Scots literature is inextricably associated with Robert Henryson; this essay examines the possibility that William Dunbar plays on this association in "This hindir nicht in Dunfermeling", using the characteristics of Henryson's Lowrence and his victims to enrich his satiric parody.
Keywords: Aesop; George Bannatyne; beast fable; William Dunbar; exemplum; *Moral Fables*; fox; Robert Henryson; Lowrence; *moralitas*; "The Hinder nycht"; satire.

The beast tale and its near kin, the beast fable and epic, have been well known from ancient days: from oriental sources, from Aesop in many incarnations, and from stories of the fox under many aliases. Observations of animals reveal characteristics and behaviour we may label "human" when we see them in animals and "beastly" when we find them in people. These findings are so familiar that some are now the briefest of clichés, moribund metaphors used for compliments or insults, in such epithets as "eagle-eyed" or "sheepish". Recognition of these characteristics are enhanced and exploited in tales of animals, often by means of stock characters introduced to display particular aspects of humanity, which are exaggerated and ridiculed or condemned, to persuade us to look carefully at their behaviour and sometimes to change our own.

The beast fable translates human behaviour to that of animals, but of animals that speak, reason and express their feelings, widening the range of their usual conduct, which is relatively restricted in natural life. The fabulist most often tells of an encounter between animals, and occasionally involves human characters. Frequently there is an encounter between a predator and prey. In the natural world, the outcome would most likely be the death of the prey, with a minimum of interaction before the weaker creature is eaten. The fabulist's art consists in slowing down and elaborating these events: to use a term from medieval rhetoric, it consists in amplifying them. There is often scope for a natural conclusion in a fable, but the animals' behaviour becomes less natural as it becomes more human and more apt for the fabulist's purpose. The teller adjusts the tale to portray many kinds of human conduct within a relatively narrow range of animal deeds, with the further aim of engaging the audience's belief in the message behind the patent fiction of the tale. The fabulists and poets gain and manipulate our attention and responses as they tell and teach. They may also inflict collateral damage on various literary genres, by placing absurdly elevated or despicable speeches in the mouths of their characters.

The animal stories reach a peak of development in the beast fables and epics, but tend to decline when they change from works with a general didactic aim to those that use the form only for topical, satirical purposes (Varty 1967: 21–24). The beast fable and *exemplum* had a place in the hearts of teachers and preachers before Henryson and Dunbar employed the forms. Henryson's "Prologue" to his *Moral Fables* demonstrates his consciousness of translation of this kind in his references to reproof of man "be figure of ane vther thing", and to the possibility that man, "throw custum and the daylie ryte [...] in brutal beist is transformate" (7, 54–56) (Fox ed. 1981: 3, 5).[1] Works such as the *Fables*, which are written to present messages of general and lasting application, are by their nature more likely to endure than others intended only to ridicule particular individuals, since the effectiveness of the satirical poems must always depend on the audience's knowledge of the figures represented by the animal characters. Such effectiveness is short-lived, as it is for any *roman à clef*, and it loses some zest when the jokes reside in the explanations of editors rather than the hints of poets. Henryson and Dunbar differ in their realisation of the fable form. Henryson clearly divides his fables into tale and *moralitas*, and the tale often displays overt moralising whereas the *moralitas* indicates less obvious insights. His tales have their sources in the ancient fables of Aesop and more recent tales of the fox, and they present messages meant for wide application. He plays with the delicate balance of characters and characteristics, to show many human traits in a few animals' actions. The inviting technique induces his audience to give attention to the fables; they would less willingly give it to unvarnished sermons. The moral lessons are stern, but they come to an audience prepared to receive them from childhood encounters with fables. In contrast, Dunbar glances at the fable form in a tale that shows humans as beasts, with little prospect for teaching of

---

[1] All further references to Henryson's *Fables* are taken from Fox ed. 1981 and take the form of line numbers in parentheses in the text.

any kind. In looking at Henryson's and Dunbar's translations of deeds of men and beasts, I shall refer in particular to three poems of foxes: Henryson's fables of "The Cock and the Fox" and "The Fox, the Wolf, and the Husbandman" and Dunbar's poem, called "The Tod and the Lamb" by David Laing, and "The Wowing of the King quhen he wes in Dunfermeling" in the Bannatyne Manuscript (Lyall 1974: 17; Bawcutt ed. 1998: 2: 619–21). Each poem illustrates different aspects of the vulpine nature, and each shows different aspects of translation.

Of all the animal characters of beast epic and fable, the fox is probably the one with greatest appeal. His alertness, agile intelligence and creativity – characteristics that usually gain praise – make him the master trickster; he is charming, manipulative and ruthless, always ready to exploit his victims' weaknesses to make them accomplish much of their own undoing. Many authors use his adventures to display the human qualities born of the misuse of creative intelligence. They show him as a rogue of many talents, but rarely as a murderer, although a natural predator aims simply to take the life of the prey. Henryson displays the fox at the zenith of his powers, in several *Moral Fables*, often threatening life, and sometimes even taking it, but more often deceiving and humiliating his victims, proficiently and exuberantly. For instance, the fox kills a kid in "The Fox and the Wolf" and a lamb in "The Trial of the Fox". In each case, he loses his own life as punishment, but his spirit and methods persist in the deeds of other foxes: Lowrence's son, Father-war of "The Trial of the Fox", the nameless clerk of "The Sheep and the Dog", and the enduring Lowrence of "The Fox, the Wolf and the Cadger" and "The Fox, the Wolf and the Husbandman". Dunbar's presentation of the fox, in a satirical poem, depicts a less subtle performance that seems mostly to disclose the brutal exercise of unquestionable power. "The Cock and the Fox" could be a tale of beasts or of men, and shows humans as animals; "The Fox, the Wolf, and the Husbandman" shows animals acting as humans; Dunbar's poem presents humans thinly disguised as animals. In each work, the antihero of the beast fables takes opportunities to exploit weaknesses in his fellow creatures in ways that are denied even to the most cunning wild fox.

Only in "The Cock and the Fox" does Henryson present recognizably natural animal behaviour, but the elaborated tale offers many observations of the human traits represented in Chantecleir and Lowrence. We could tell a tale of the poem's events entirely in terms of the natural behaviour of its characters – one human and several animals. The tale would be plausible, but colourless, and it would tell us nothing of how we should live. We could say:

Once upon a time, in an ordered world, in which all creatures had their place and purpose, a widow lived in a hamlet. She had a small flock of hens and supported herself by spinning. One day, as a wild fox prowled in the bushes, watching the poultry, he saw a chance to hunt the cock. He captured the bird, and carried him away. The hens that were left behind clucked and fluttered in fear, and the noise they made roused the widow. She screamed and fainted, then called her dogs to pursue the fox. During the chase, the fox dropped the cock, which flew up into a tree and then back to the safety of the widow's cottage.

We could believe all of this, but we would learn little. Henryson's translation to the story of Chantecleir and Lowrence provides narrative colour, morals and lessons. He amplifies the tale, enhancing each part of it to engage our attention. In life, we could expect a natural fox to stalk the cock by slinking inconspicuously around the hencoop, always ready to spring and pounce on his prey. In the tale, Lowrence falls on his knees before Chantecleir, to offer respectful greetings and service to his giggling dupe. Lowrence demonstrates his mastery of the confidence trickster's most effective ploy – the persuasive combination of truth and preposterous flattery. His blandishments are interpreted by a willing victim who attends only to the sense he wants to hear. Many of the fox's statements are entirely true. Of course Chantecleir's father had often provided food – his hens and progeny; of course Lowrence had held the father's head when he died; of course the fox would creep after Chantecleir, ready to serve him in the same way, when that cock, dizzy from compliments and twirling on his toes, has closed his eyes. How elegantly Henryson amplifies Lowrence's approaches to Chantecleir; how accurately and sparely he records the capture: "The foxe wes war, and hint him be the throte" (480).

For the instant of the snap of the fox's jaws the story seems indeed to be a tale of a cock and a fox, but only until the hens disturb the widow. While she is swooning, their squawking and ruffled feathers are elevated to the glorious absurdity of a "disputatioun" (494). Pertok becomes a weeping heroine, temporarily distracted by her grief, but easily persuaded by her uninhibited sister Sprutok to anticipate gaiety in widowhood, while Coppok assumes the form of a stern curate who sees Lowrence's success as divine punishment for their adulterous consort. Thus the hens offer distorted glimpses of the romance, the kind of scene observed in Dunbar's *The Tretis of the Tua Mariit Wemen and the Wedo*, and "haly preiching [that] may na thing auaill" (1390). The sentimentality, hypocrisy, malice and harshness seem ridiculous rather than despicable when they are reduced to the flurry and cackling of chickens, especially when they have been made frantic by the possibility of an event that does not even happen. These would-be widows and the human widow who owns them express their emotions, and then deal with the situation – the hens by comforting themselves with thoughts of Chantecleir's replacement and the widow by calling her dogs.

Chantecleir's release gives us the pleasure of seeing a trickster tricked. The feather-headed cock makes splendid use of his own intelligence, and so fools his captor. It could seem that "falset failheis ay at the latter end" (568) is the moral of the story, a conclusion that leaves everyone at liberty to live happily ever after. Chantecleir condemns Lowrence as a murderer (576), just as the widow had done (486). He rejects the flattery that had deceived him before. Now, when the fox is on his knees, the cock flies away. But, even though Chantecleir has learned a lesson, the *moralitas* gives him no praise. Instead it exposes him as proud and presumptuous, and advises good folk to flee from the venomous sins of flattery and pride.

It is difficult to tell the story of "The Fox, the Wolf, and the Husbandman" in natural terms, because the story is so much less plausible than "The Cock and the Fox". Only the opening scene seems natural in its depiction of the husbandman and the young, untrained oxen. It is easy to imagine the man's anger and the threat to let the wolf have the animals. We recognise the motif of the reckless promise, but must wonder if a natural wolf would want to take even one creature as large as an ox. This tale translates animal behaviour to human form. The wolf represents an opportunist oppressor, recklessly greedy and eager to seize a chance that was never really offered, while the fox presents himself as a witness, and easily and unobtrusively takes charge. It is possible to imagine that a natural wolf or a fox would threaten a man, if hunger made either bold (although they are unlikely to hunt together in nature and are generally enemies in stories of the fox). In life we could expect a sensible husbandman to throw stones at the predators rather than at his own oxen, and to try to protect his hens, not give them to the fox. There is no need to allow such everyday concerns to

intrude into this "fenȝeit fabil". Any other behaviour from the characters would be disappointingly inconsistent with the humans they
represent, and would spoil both the fun and the moral teaching that
Henryson offers.

The tale becomes more preposterous, yet paradoxically it alludes
to real issues of human life. It satirises false oaths and corrupt courts
when Lowrence promotes himself from witness to "iuge amycabill"
(2310) and the two litigants swear on his tail. The fox soon reveals the
price of his friendly judgement – some of the husbandman's fat hens.
The characters back their arguments with proverbs, and often apply
them inappropriately to reveal deficiencies in such wisdom as well as
in the force of law. As in many other stories, the fox suffers no punishment, but instead has the malicious pleasure of tricking a villain
who is brutal and stupid. Lowrence entices the wolf to exchange the
oxen for the promise of a huge cheese, the reflection of the full moon
in the water of a well. The fox departs with his bribe, leaving the wolf
stranded in a bucket at the bottom of the well. The *moralitas* reveals
the wolf as a wicked oppressor of the poor, whose covetousness gains
no reward; the fox is the Fiend, tempting a good man (the husbandman); the hens, rather surprisingly, are "warkis that fra ferme faith
proceidis" (2437).

A human tale of such oppression and injustice would be a bleak
one, and the idea of working towards salvation by bribing a false
judge can only be sustained by the supple interpretation of medieval
fable. Wicked riches, the wild woods that confuse even the wolf, and
the cheese of covetousness combine to lure man into "the Deuillis net"
(2444). There must have been many sermons preached on these subjects, but they could hardly be as amusing as the animal tale, nor
promise the satisfaction of its ending. No doubt it was possible to
illustrate the sermons with examples drawn from life, to tell of powerful men who threatened and crushed the poor, and those who encouraged and deluded them, but illustrations of that kind would be both
depressing and dangerous. The ordered sphere of "The Cock and the
Fox", where man might be expected to have some authority, has now
become for a world controlled by force and fear. "The Fox, the Wolf,
and the Husbandman" tells the story in a way the audience cannot
merely endure but enjoy. Each character talks of justice, but each is
prepared to misuse the law. Such a tale can only be bearable when it

seems unrealistic because the most villainous characters are beasts, so that they and the human they threaten seem ludicrous.

The details of the tale exploit aspects of language and literature, as they mingle aspects of human and animal behaviour. Both man and fox address the wolf as "Schir" – the first because of his fear, the second as part of his manipulation. The wolf's arrogant speeches to the husbandman, whom he calls "Carll", echo the snarling of the wild beast. As he becomes more human in his actions, Lowrence laughs (2248; 2345), but the husbandman does not (2296). Each character appeals to the uncertain authority of proverbs, interpreted as he thinks expedient. The wolf, for example, warns the husbandman that it is better to give "ane plank" freely than be forced to yield "ane mart", as he demands the man's most valuable possession – his team of oxen (2270–71). The husbandman counters with a demand for a witness, since "Ane leill man is not tane at halff ane taill" (2287). Lowrence, as witness and judge, backs his demand for a bribe with several proverbs, the most apt and audacious being "Sumtymes ane hen haldis ane man in ane kow" (2324). Henryson's swiftly drawn characters invigorate motifs that often appear in literature, although not always together, as in this tale, which probably has its origin in work of Petrus Alfonsi (Fox ed. 1981: 298–99). The themes are found in various places in the *Roman de Renart*, and the rash threat is also familiar from *The Friar's Tale*, which incidentally describes the artful summoner as mad as a hare (Benson ed. 1988: 123), a simile that Henryson uses for the enraged husbandman ("The Fox, the Wolf and the Husbandman" 2242). The Middle English *Fox and the Wolf* presents the motif of the fox and wolf in the well, although that well is said to lead to paradise rather than to hell. In his description of Chantecleir in particular, Henryson seems to draw on the associations of the *Nun's Priest's Tale* in "The Cock and the Fox". However, the sparse descriptions of "The Fox, the Wolf, and the Husbandman" reveal fresh epithets such as "pennyfull" for the moon (2388), and engaging details that remind the audience that the tale is about humans, even though it tells of beasts that go to law. For instance, Lowrence plucks at the wolf's sleeve (2338), and the two creatures go "hand in hand" (2371) when they seek the great cheese, a food foreign to the wolf's natural diet, although it is a plausible addition to the tale.

Like his predecessor, Dunbar also avails himself of previous associations in his poem of "The Tod and the Lamb", and some of the

allusions recall Henryson's fables, beginning, of course, with the
opening statement that the tale was told in Dunfermline. This work
both resembles and differs from Henryson's poems. The cast of
characters alone must stir memories of the earlier poet's dealings with
these symbolic creatures – the fox, the lamb and the wolf –
particularly in references to the "wily tod" and "silly lame" (Bawcutt
ed. 1998: 1: 246, 245),[2] epithets also used by Henryson (425, 670,
2625, 2637). The refrain, of a "ferly cace", could echo references to a
"fenʒeit fabil". The sudden coming of sorrow after joy ("The Two
Mice" 290–91; "This hinder nycht" 51–52) is a theme of "The Two
Mice", and the squeaking of the lamb (and even the fox) may also
remind us of Henryson's mice who also squeak ("The Two Mice"
187, 307; "The Paddock and the Mouse" 2783). The closest resemblances of all, of course, are found in comparisons of Dunbar's poem
and an episode in Henryson's "The Trial of the Fox", in which the fox
kills and eats a lamb. When its mother accuses Lowrence of murder,
he argues that his purpose "wes with him for to haif plaid" ("The Trial
of the Fox" 1079; see also Bawcutt 1992: 304–5). Dunbar also
explains the tod's play with the lamb in terms of animal behaviour –
he "wald haif riddin hir lyk ane rame" (6).

There are, however, more differences than resemblances in the
telling. Dunbar offers no moral, and his poem only looks like a fable
(Scott 1966: 212; Lyall 1974: 18). In spite of the choice of this form,
the poet is not a moraliser here: he is much closer to the "iangleris"
(44) he affects not to join. The poem is of court life, with no hint of
the simple rural setting of the *Moral Fables*, and its actions take place
indoors. There has been speculation about the subjects of the poem,
but, although James IV seems a likely candidate for the fox, no firm
decisions have been made about the lamb or the wolf (Bawcutt ed.
1998: 2: 269–70; Kinsley ed. 1979: 313; Scott 1966: 214; Kindrick
1978: 314). Nevertheless, the poem communicates a strong impression
that it concerns particular individuals. The attention to a few details of
description convey this suspicion by seeming to imply more to a
knowing audience, as in the picture of the tod and the emphasis on the
redness and whiteness of the fox and lamb (22–23). An intimate tone
is sustained in the thread of innuendo, as in the comments on the ill-
matched duet of treble and bass (19). The lack of clarity in the wolf's

---

[2] All further references to Dunbar are taken from Bawcutt ed. 1998 and are in the
form of line numbers in parentheses in the text.

behaviour and the tod's response hints at a secret that cannot be shared completely. The refrain becomes an ironic comment on each stanza that precedes it, and also contributes to the effect of a secret conversation rather than a frank message from a moraliser, as does the sense that the observer is moving ever closer to the scene, in spite of saying that the tale was first told to him. The effect is of a tale only partly told but fully understood.

When we look at the animal behaviour and the human deeds it represents we cannot ignore the idea of the rape of the lamb, although some of Dunbar's metaphors for the fox's behaviour could apply just as well to killing and eating his victim, as Bawcutt notes (Bawcutt ed. 1998: 2: 23). Although the latter actions are clearly natural for a wild fox, the former is not. The balance of animal and human behaviour is skewed towards human beastliness that takes place behind barred doors: the obvious seduction of the unwary lamb, followed by the less distinct actions of the wolf and fox. Dunbar has cloaked his court gossip in the form of fable, and tells of people in animal disguise, even using the metaphor of a fox in a lamb's skin (57–61). The deliberate avoidance of clarity, in deeds and interpretation argues against a fable. This avoidance contributes to the impression of power that could be whispered about but not questioned. The cries of the lamb and one "allace" are more than balanced by the tone of references to the lamb as a tender morsel and the ewes as old and tough (23–25). There is none of the sympathy which is movingly conveyed in Henryson's fable of "The Wolf and the Lamb", both in the fable and in the *moralitas* (2616–776).

The three poems of foxes are of a predator who represents not a killer but in turn a swindler, a corruptor of the law and a rapist. The riches that a human swindler would take must be represented by Chantecleir's only possession, his life, but the death of a human dupe would mean the end of the swindler's income, and so a failure. Loss of the husbandman's oxen and so of his livelihood could indeed be the losses of one crushed by the demands of an unreasonable landlord supported by an unjust court. The victims of this story are first the husbandman and then the humiliated wolf. The oxen and hens (whose lives are certainly forfeited) gain only the consideration due to any farm animals, not the status of characters. The precise situation of Dunbar's characters is not easy to determine. The lamb seems certainly to be an innocent who trusted the tod, and he is very likely to represent the king. That innocent might have become a royal mistress or simply have been discarded. The wolf eludes identification, and his "hiddowis ȝowling" (57) and other actions remain unclear. The lack of clarity is the poem's most striking difference from a fable, especially from any fashioned by Henryson, who provides morals so lavishly, and there are differences in Dunbar's characterisation. He speaks of a brutal fox who hides from the wolf rather than one who relishes out-witting a stupid enemy. The balance of foxy and wolfish traits is altered, and the attitude to the lamb is equivocal. A lamb is often a symbolic victim, and Christian triumph paradoxically emphasises rather than diminishes the associations. Perhaps any tale of a lamb and a predator implies a warning to the lambkin, but the impression of a scandal that cannot be fully disclosed is stronger. Dunbar has treated the fable form as Henryson treated such genres as the romance and sermon.

Comparison of the three poems shows the range of the poets' methods and also their effectiveness in tales with enduring or brief application. The change in effectiveness and clarity also mirrors the changes in beast tales from works intended to teach all who heard them, to others designed for the satirical representation of particular individuals, told to listeners who could complete the stories.

Bibliography

Bawcutt, P. 1992. *Dunbar the Makar* Oxford: Clarendon Press.
—. (ed.) 1998. *The Poems of William Dunbar*. 2 vols. Glasgow: Association for Scottish Literary Studies.
Benson, L.D. (ed.) 1988. *The Riverside Chaucer*. Oxford: Oxford University Press.
Fox, D. (ed.) 1981. *The Poems of Robert Henryson*. Oxford: Clarendon Press.
Kindrick, R. 1978. "Monarchs and Monarchy in the Poetry of Henryson and Dunbar" in Blanchot, Jean-Jacques and Claude Graf Strasbourg (eds) *Actes de 2e colloque de langue et literature écossaises (Moyen âge et Renaissance)*. University of Strasbourg, for the Institut d'Etudes Anglaises de Strasbourg et l'Association des Medievistes anglicistes de l'Enseignement superieur. 307–25.
Kinsley, J. 1979. *The Poems of William Dunbar*. Oxford: Clarendon Press.
Lyall, R.J. 1974. "William Dunbar's Beast Fable" in *Scottish Literary Journal* 1: 17–28.
Scott, T. 1966. *Dunbar: A Critical Exposition of the Poems*. Edinburgh: Oliver and Boyd.
Varty, K. 1967. *Reynard the Fox: A Study of the Fox in Medieval English Art*. Leicester: Leicester University Press.

Gavin Douglas and John Bellenden: Poetic Relations and Political Affiliations

Thomas Rutledge

Although John Bellenden's evocations of Gavin Douglas's work have been noted by several scholars, this essay argues that such references are political as well as literary and are far more significant to the understanding of Bellenden's work than has previously been acknowledged.
Keywords: John Bellenden; *Chronicles of Scotland*; *First Five Books of Livy*; Gavin Douglas; the Douglas family; *Eneados*; humanism; James V; *Palis of Honoure*; poetry; Renaissance

The historical translations John Bellenden undertook at the beginning of the 1530s, *The Chronicles of Scotland* and *The First Five Books of Livy*, take their place among the developments of the early Scottish Renaissance with a certain cultural logic.[1] They seem to have engaged immediately with a quickening Scottish interest in the traditions of historiography given new energy and new urgency by the publication of John Mair's *Historia Maioris Britanniae tam Angliae quam Scotiae* (Mair 1521; cf. Renouard 1908: 3: 62–63), and Hector Boece's *Scotorum Historia* in the 1520s (Boece 1527; cf. Renouard 1908: 2: 195–96). They also conspicuously extend the vernacular humanism of Gavin Douglas's *Eneados* (Bawcutt 1976: 36), rendering Livy's classical history and Boece's classicising humanist historiography available to a new Scots audience (see Royan 1996; Royan 1998; Royan 2000; Royan 2002; Mason 1992; Mason 1998: 78–103; Mason 2002; Ferguson 1998: 56–59). It is elegantly emblematic that Bellenden's translation from the *Ab urbe condita* begins, as the opening chapter heading records, with precisely the material with which

---

[1] *The Chronicles of Scotland* is conventionally dated c.1531, when the work appears to have been first completed. The Pierpont Morgan manuscript was presented to James V in 1533, but Bellenden seems to have continued to work on the translation and it was printed in substantially revised form between 1536 and 1540; cf. Bellenden 1938, 1941. For the revision of the translation, see Sheppard 1941, which is a reworking of the fuller treatment in Sheppard 1936: esp. 62–68; Mapstone 1998; Royan 1998. The *Livy* is conventionally dated c.1533, but it is possible that Bellenden completed his translation of the fourth and fifth books later in the 1530s; cf. Bellenden 1900–1, 1903; Rutledge (Forthcoming): chapter 6.

the thirteen-book *Eneados* concludes: "How Eneas and antenor come
in Italy eftir the eversioun of troy; how antenor foundit Venys; and
how Eneas foundit lavyne, and was allyat with King latyne; of his
sindry aventuris and deith" (Craigie ed. 1900–1, 1903: 1: 12).[2] As
Douglas's translation marks the cultural confidence of James IV's
Scotland in 1513, a confidence, of course, which was almost immediately shattered, Bellenden's translations reflect the growing authority
and assurance of Scotland under James V's adult rule twenty years
later.

The extent to which Bellenden's translations were directly
prompted by the example of the *Eneados* has, however, remained uncertain (Bawcutt 1976: 195). Bellenden probably knew Douglas
personally. He was in service at the court in the earliest years of James
V's minority, in the period in which Douglas was most prominently
influential there. His family had strong Douglas affinities (Sheppard
1941: 420–21), and his own sympathies may be cautiously inferred
from his translation of the *Scotorum Historia* in which "his devotion
to the Douglas cause is conspicuous" (Sheppard 1941: 421–22). He
was certainly familiar with Douglas's poetry: his writing reflects the
influence of both *The Palis of Honoure* and the *Eneados*.

In particular, Priscilla Bawcutt has noted that Bellenden "clearly
imitated" *The Palis of Honoure* in his "Proheme to the Cosmographe",
the poem which opens *The Chronicles of Scotland* (Bawcutt 1976:
194–95):

Me thocht I wes in to ane plesand meid
Quhair flora maid the tendir blewmis spreid
Throw kyndlie dew and humouris nutrative.
Quhen goldin titan wt his flammis reid
Aboif the seis rasit vp hir heid
Diffounding down his heit restoretive
To every frute that natur maid on lyve.
Quhilk wes afoir in to the wintir deid
For stormis cawld and froistis penetryve. (Maitland ed. 1821: 1: vii)[3]

---

[2] Craigie ed. 1900–1, 1903: 1: 12. Unless otherwise stated, quotation of the *Livy* is
from this edition; reference is by volume and page number.

[3] Unless otherwise stated, quotation of the "Proheme" is from the first volume of this
edition; reference is by page number.

Bawcutt records the most conspicuous signs of Douglas's influence. In the spring opening of *The Palis of Honoure*, Douglas's meadow is "With Balmy dew bathit and kyndlie wet" (Charteris 1579, 13), Titan's "heit is maist restoratiue" (Charteris 1579, 43), Phoebus's beams are "nutratiue" (Charteris 1579, 48), and May is celebrated for "Diffundant grace on euerie creature" (Charteris 1579, 72).[4] The "Proheme to the Cosmographe", like *The Palis of Honoure*, is an allegorical dream poem; it is written in the intricate stanzaic form used in the first two parts of Douglas's work; and Bawcutt suggests the texture of Bellenden's verse also recalls the "run-on syntax" of Douglas's poetry (Bawcutt 1976: 195).

The parallels between the openings of the two poems, though, reward further scrutiny. We shall see that each line of Bellenden's stanza, in fact, contains clear reference to the prologue of *The Palis of Honoure* and those references highlight a consistent pattern of allusion to Douglas's writing which structures the "Proheme".

The "Proheme" also recalls *The Palis of Honoure* because it is, in part, a programmatic poem, in which Bellenden, like Douglas earlier, announces his devotion to the literary vocation. The poem rehearses a version of the Choice of Hercules in which the poet-dreamer witnesses the goddesses "Vertew" and "Delite" compete for the devotion of a young king:

Bot sone I knew thay war the Goddesses
That come in sleip to vailyeant Hercules,
Quhen he was young, and fre of every lore
To lust or honour, poverte or riches;
Quhen he contempnit lust and idilnes,
That he in virtew micht his life decore;
And werkis did of maist excellent glore.
The more incressit his panefull besines,
His hie triumphe and loving was the more. (xv)

The dreamer wakes before he has seen the king's response and his own reaction displaces and anticipates the king's as he determines to

---

[4] Quotation from *The Palis of Honoure* is taken from Bawcutt ed. 2003 throughout. Reference is given by line number and identifies the print (Copland *c*.1553; Charteris 1579) from which the quotation is taken. Following Bawcutt's reluctance to privilege either print in her parallel text edition of the poem, quotation has been taken from both prints, according to which seemed more appropriate in each instance; cf. Bawcutt 1976: 195.

begin the "panefull besines" of translating the first part of the
Scotorum Historia:

Than, throw this morall eruditioun
Quhilk come, as said is, in my visioun,
I tuke purpos, or I forthir went,
To write the story of this regioun,
With dedis of mony illuster campioun.
And, thoucht the pane apperis vehement,
To make the story to the redaris more patent,
I will begin at the discriptioun
Of Albion, in maner subsequent. (xvi)

It is extremely suggestive that Bellenden should make elaborate and
conspicuous reference to Douglas's poetry in the poem in which he
declares his own literary aspirations and introduces his own large-
scale translation. Bellenden's references to Douglas's writing, I would
suggest, in fact constitute a programmatic articulation of literary and
political affiliation.

Moreover, Bellenden makes similarly dense use of allusions to
Douglas's poetry in the "Proloug" which begins his translation from
the *Ab urbe condita*. In both prefatory poems, I would suggest,
Bellenden carefully signals his indebtedness to Douglas expressly to
situate himself as Douglas's literary successor. Bellenden adduces
Douglas's legitimating authority as he begins his own vernacular
humanist translations. It seems probable, too, that Bellenden's poetic
affiliations were also intended to place him in sympathetic relation to
Douglas's politically powerful and politically threatened family in the
precarious opening years of James V's adult rule.

Bellenden's translations, with their insistent political focus on the
central figure of the king, may, in fact, finally belie his poetic self-
positioning in relation to the Douglases and to Douglas's poetry;
nonetheless, they begin, at least, by asking to be read in relation to
Douglas's achievement in *The Palis of Honoure* and the *Eneados*.

1

The Palis of Honoure opens in "a Gardyne of plesance" (Charteris
1579, 7), set within "The tender bed and Arres honorabill / Of Flora"
(Charteris 1579, 4–5) and sporting "blisfull bewis with blomed

varyance" (Charteris 1579, 9). "Dame Flora" has "ouirfret" this "heuinly bed" (Charteris 1579, 10–11) and Douglas's dreamer sees "fragrant flouris blomand in thair seis / Ouirspred the leuis of natures Tapestreis" (Charteris 1579, 19–20). Bellenden, in his description of the "plesand meid" (vii) of the "Proheme to the Cosmographe", concentrates Douglas's series of images into a single line: "Quhair flora maid the tendir blewmis spreid" (vii). Bellenden's "kyndlie dew and humouris nutrative" recalls Douglas's "vapours hote" (Charteris 1579, 14) as well as the verse, "With Balmy dew bathit and kyndlie wet" (Charteris 1579, 13). In Douglas's prologue, "Tytan" is led out of the sea by his horse, Eous:

> Out of the sey Eous alift his heid –
> I mene the hors quhilk drawis at deuice
> The assiltrie and goldin Chair of price
> Of Tytan, quhilk at morrow semis reid. (Charteris 1579, 30–33)

Bellenden's "titan" is also "goldin" and his "flammis reid" and he, too, raises his head "aboif the seis" (vii).

In both poems, the sun brings "heit restoretive" (vii). In the "Proheme to the Cosmographe" it is welcomed by "every frute that natur maid on lyve" (vii); in *The Palis of Honoure*, by the inclusive "foulis, flouris and Rice" (Charteris 1579, 35). In Bellenden's poem, spring brings new life after the death of winter ("Quhilk wes afoir in to the wintir deid" (vii)); in Douglas's prologue, dawn brings new life after the briefer death of night ("that all the nicht lay deid" (Charteris 1579, 34)). Douglas's "Dasy" and "Maryguld" open "leuis" closed through the night "Thame to reserue fra rewmes pungitiue" (Charteris 1579, 38–39); Bellenden's "frute" recovers from winter's "stormis cawld and froistis penetryve" (vii). And Bellenden even repeats the structuring heid/reid/deid rhyme of Douglas's fourth stanza.

The concentration of references to *The Palis of Honoure* within this single stanza is most emphatic, but there are further reminiscences of Douglas's poem in the "Proheme". Bellenden reworks Douglas's opening image of Aurora at the very beginning of his poem:

> QVhen pale Aurora with face lamentable
> Hir russat mantill borderit all with sable
> Lappit about be heuinlye circumstance
> The tender bed and arres honorable
> Of Flora quene till floures amyable. (Copland c.1553, 1–5)

The frosty nicht, with hir prolixit houris,
Hir mantill quhit spred on the tender flouris. ("Proheme to the Cosmographe", v)

The "russat mantill" of "pale Aurora" becomes the "mantill quhit" of "frosty nicht". Bellenden repeats the balanced halves of Douglas's first two lines and the contrast of "nicht" and "quhit" retrieves the opposition of "pale" and "sable". Later in the "Proheme", the simile Bellenden deploys to suggest the evanescence of earthly achievement recalls Douglas's allegorical "caruell of the state of grace" which the dreamer sees tossed on the seas of "this warldis brukkyllness" in the third part of *The Palis of Honoure* (Copland c.1553, 1342–95): "As carvell ticht fast tending throw the see / Levis na prent amang the wallis hie [s] Siclik our life, without activite, / Giffis na frut, howbeit ane schado blume" (xi).

The "Proheme" also deploys important allusion to the *Eneados*. Bellenden's goddess, "Vertew", in her repudiation of the ephemeral enticements offered by her rival, rehearses many of the arguments which structure Douglas's fourth prologue. The prologue is an extended attack on "lustis inordinate" (4.Pro.182) and "brutell appetyte" (4.Pro.225; cf. Archibald 1998; Couper 2001),[5] and "Vertew", within her attack on the more general array of earthly attractions proffered by "Delite", particularly condemns those who succumb to their "lustis". Most directly, Bellenden redeploys the distinctive image of "the stonyt horß" that Douglas had taken from Virgil's third *Georgicon*:

For he that nold agains his lustis strive,
Bot leiffis as beist of knawlage sensitive,
Eildis richt fast, and deith him ouir halis.
Thairfore the mule is of ane langar live
Than stonit hors. (xiv–xv)

O Lord, quhat writis myne author of thi forß
In hys Georgikis, quhou thyne ondantyt myght
Constrenys so sum tyme the stonyt horß
That, by the sent of a meyr far of syght,
He bradis brays onon, and takis the flyght. (4.Pro.57–61)

---

[5] Unless otherwise stated, quotation of the *Eneados* is from Coldwell ed. 1957–64; reference is by book, chapter, and line number.

More generally, "Vertew" opposes "That ane, of reason most intelligent" and "This othir, of beistis following the affect" (xiv) as Douglas opposes "lust" and "lufe" (4.Pro.107) and more specifically contrasts "lufe [...] rewlyt by messure" (4.Pro.125) and "lufe inordinate" (4.Pro.128). "Vertew's" depiction of "Sardanapall" with "lustis [...] intoxicat" (xiii) recalls Douglas's coupling of "lust of wyne" and "warkis veneryane" (4.Pro.93), and her admonition to "Dant[...] the rage of youtheid furius" (xv) repeats the associations of the allegorical interpretations of Virgil's fourth book which also inform Douglas's prologue. "Vertew's" allusions may perhaps be felt to adduce the support of Douglas's earlier parallel treatment.

The "Proheme" also makes particularly striking use of reference to the thirteenth prologue. The two poems open with parallel temporal and astrological references:

Quhen silvir Diane, ful of bemis bricht,
Fra dirk eclips wes past, this othir nicht,
And in the crab, hir propir mansion, gane [...] (v)

Towart the evyn, amyd the symmyris heit,
Quhen in the Crab Appollo held hys sete [...] (13.Pro.1–2)

Bellenden's continuation of his temporal description in the opening stanza, "Quhen sterris small obscuris in our sicht, / And Lucifer left twinkland him allane" (v), is strongly reminiscent of Douglas's couplet at the close of the thirteenth prologue, "Furth quynchyng gan the starris, on be on, / That now is left bot Lucifer allon" (13.Pro.163–64). And Bellenden's account of the close of day at the end of the "Proheme", matching the emergence of "goldin titan" from the sea at its opening, again returns to Douglas's prologue:

Be than, Phebus his firy cart did wry
Fra south to west, declinand besaly
To dip his steidis in the occeane. (xv)

And fyry Phegon, his dun nychtis steid,
Dowkit hys hed sa deip in fludis gray
That Phebys rollis doun vndir hell away;
And Esperus in the west with bemys brycht
Vpspryngis, as forrydar of the nicht. (13.Pro.16–20)

It is especially suggestive that Bellenden's "Proheme" may here be seen to begin precisely where Douglas's prologues had ended, for the dense array of references to Douglas's poetry in the "Proheme" surely implies not simply admiring imitation, but the deliberate articulation of a poetic relationship.

The "Proheme" is, in part, a programmatic poem: although less straightforwardly an allegory of vocational self-definition, it is, like *The Palis of Honoure*, and "[l]ike so many dream-allegories, [...] concerned with a poet's education" (Bawcutt 1976: 52). The central allegory, of course, is presented as a contest between "Vertew" and "Delite" for the devotion of a young "crownit King" (vii):

Thir Goddesses arrayit in this wise,
As reverence and honoure list devise,
Afore this Prince, fell down apon thair kneis;
Sine dressit thaim in to thair best avise,
So far as wisdome in thair power lyis,
To do the thing that micht him best appleis,
Quhare he rejoisit in his hevinly gleis;
And him desiris, for his hie Empryis,
Ane of thaim two unto his lady cheis. (vii–viii)

The poem was almost certainly written in the very late 1520s, perhaps to mark James V's assumption of adult rule in 1528 (Sheppard 1941: 451–53; cf. Chambers et al. eds 1938, 1941: 1: xliv, where it is argued that the "Proheme" "must have been written between 1528 and 1530, when James the Fifth was in his nineteenth year"). Its political appositeness, then, is evident: Bellenden invites his own young king, as he emerges from his minority, to make a similar choice and it is clearly to the more exacting paths of "Vertew" that he is encouraged to turn.

The poem, though, is not only concerned with the king's education, for the dreamer's own choices displace and anticipate the king's. The dreamer awakes before he has seen the king respond, and, upon waking, immediately resolves to "To write the story of this regioun, / With dedis of mony illuster campioun" (xvi). His exemplary response to the freighted opposition of seductively ephemeral "Delite" and wise and moral "Vertew" is virtuously to dedicate himself to the craft of writing.

The "Proheme to the Cosmographe", then, serves more broadly to introduce Bellenden's translation of Boece's *Scotorum Historia*. The "Cosmographe and discription of Albion" is Bellenden's version of Boece's "Scotiae & aliorum locorum declaratio" and "Scotorum Regni descriptio & mores" which precede the *Scotorum Historia* in the Paris edition of 1527 (Sheppard 1941: 435–40; cf. the poet-dreamer's declaration at the close of the "Proheme": "I will begin at the discriptioun / Of Albion, in maner subsequent" (xvi)). The "Cosmographe" appears for the first time in its entirety in Davidson's edition of *The Chronicles of Scotland*, where the "Proheme" also first appears (Sheppard 1941: 451), and, although, as Sheppard notes, the "Proheme" may initially have been written as an independent poem and only belatedly "adapted to serve as an introduction" to the "Cosmographe", the "poem is not found except in association with Bellenden's version" of Boece's history (Sheppard 1941: 451–52).[6] The second stanza of the "Proheme", moreover, "expressly associates its composition" with the translation of *The Chronicles of Scotland* (Sheppard 1941: 451–52): Bellenden's dreamer emerges "to tak the recent aire", to refresh a spirit wearied by the "ardent lauboure" of his effort to "Translait the story of our progenitouris" (v–vi). The translation of *The Chronicles of Scotland*, then, is the more ambitious work for which the "poet's education" elaborated within the "Proheme" prepares Bellenden the dream-poet.

And in these terms, too, of course, the "Proheme" recalls *The Palis of Honoure*, in which Douglas more fully presents a dreamer who determines to seek the "hie felicite" of otherworldly Honour by devoting himself to the path of poetry. The allegiance Douglas articulates in *The Palis of Honoure* to the "kyngly style" of Calliope who "of nobillis fatis hes the stere" (Charteris 1579, 875–77) is also echoed in the king's presence both as the central figure within Bellenden's advisory poem, and as the first audience imagined for it. Even more than Calliope's poetry, perhaps, Bellenden's poem is doubly concerned with the deeds of a king.

Most significantly, the final part of *The Palis of Honoure* seems also to look forward to the composition of the *Eneados*. Douglas's dreamer, to fulfil his obligations to Venus, promises to translate a

---

[6] The *Treasurer's Accounts* record payments to Bellenden for the composition of his "Cronykill" from the end of 1530 to July 1533, and it seems unlikely that he had begun his translation of the *Scotorum Historia* as early as 1528. cf. Sheppard 1941: 436–8, 445–6; *Accounts of the Lord High Treasurer* 1877–1978: 5: 434; *Accounts of the Lord High Treasurer of Scotland* 1877–1978: 6: 37, 97. In 1531 or 1532, of course, James V remained a young king.

book she has given him and Douglas returns to this promise at the end of the *Eneados*: "now am I fully quyt, / As twichand Venus, of myn ald promyt / Quhilk I hir maid weil twelf ʒheris tofor, / As wytnessith my Palyce of Honour" ("Directioun", 119–22). Although the composition of the two poems was, in fact, probably separated by more than ten years, *The Palis of Honoure* seems programmatically to announce Douglas's vernacular humanist translation. The "knychtlyke style" of the *Eneados* is Douglas's next poetic performance in Calliope's "kyngly style"; the *Eneados* is the work for which the poetic education elaborated in *The Palis of Honoure* has prepared Douglas the dream-poet.

Where Douglas's dream vision anticipates a future work of translation, Bellenden's is immediately followed by his own large-scale translation and the concentration of references to Douglas's poetry within the "Proheme to the Cosmographe" is surely intended quite clearly to announce Bellenden as Douglas's literary successor. Parallels between the vernacular humanism of the *Eneados* and *The Chronicles of Scotland* are not accidental; they are carefully asserted by Bellenden as he begins his work.

It is suggestive, too, that similar reminiscences of the *Eneados* cluster in the poetic prologue with which Bellenden introduces his translation from the *Ab urbe condita*: Bellenden again uses his prologue to situate his second translation in relation to Douglas's work. Bellenden's unusual opening invocation of "Armipotent Lady Bellona serene" (1:3, 1–7) loosely recalls Douglas's account of the goddess as she is depicted on Vulcan's shield in *Eneados* 8 (8.12.71–72),[7] and perhaps also echoes the enthroned "god armypotent" of the

---

[7] It must be conceded, however, that even unrelated representations of the goddess are likely to share some similarities and there are no strong verbal parallels between Bellenden's invocation and Douglas's description. Both works place Bellona in relation to Mars: in the *Eneados*, she appears "With hir kynd cousing" (*Eneados*, 8.12.72) and, in Bellenden's *Livy*, she is "Sister of mars and ledare of his rene, / And of his batallis awfull messingere" (1:3: 3–4)). As Bawcutt 1976: 101 has shown, Douglas's curious "With hir kynd cousing" translates "consanguineo", which Ascensius prints for Virgil's "cum sanguineo". Bellenden's description, "And of his batallis awfull messingere", perhaps also recalls Douglas's "bellona of batall [...] the scharp scurgis fell" (*Eneados*, 8.12.71–2), and the final couplet of Bellenden's opening stanza distantly echoes the opening line of Douglas's *Aeneid* translation: "The horribill batellis and þe bludy harmes / To write of romanis, þe nobil men of armes" (1:3: 6–7); "The batalis and the man I wil discrive" (*Eneados*, 1.1.1).

Copland print of *The Palis of Honoure* (Copland c.1553, 1921).[8] More securely reminiscent of the *Eneados* is Bellenden's praise of the vividness of the stories he has translated:

Of awfull batallis þe crafty gouernance,
The wise array, þe manly Ieoperdie,
Ʒe may fynd here, with mony doutsum chance,
Als quyk as þai war led afore ʒoure Ee.
Ʒe may also be mony stories see
Quhat besyness may proffitt or avance
Ʒoure princely state with ferme continuance. (1: 4: 1–7)

Bellenden's lines closely recall Douglas's celebration of the visual immediacy of Virgil's poetry in the opening prologue of the *Eneados* (for a detailed account of Douglas's response to this aspect of the *Aeneid*, see Gray 2000):

Sa quyk, lusty and maist sentencyus,
Plesand, perfyte and feilabill in all degre,
As quha the mater beheld tofor thar e. (1.Pro.12–14)

Bellenden, though, assumes a significantly different set of readers' eyes. Douglas's general and plural "thar e" becomes Bellenden's specific and singular "ʒoure Ee", the eye of King James V to whom the prologue directs the following translation.

The prologue continues to celebrate the qualities of Livy's historiography:

To schaw all proffittis I wil nocht pretend
Quhilk þe first decade of þis werk dois bere,
For, þocht I spendit ane moneth to þe end,
Thare suld ʒit rest ane largeare feild til ere
Than all my pleuch mycht teill in to ane ʒere;
For in quhat sorte ʒoure hienes will delite,
Ʒe may gett stories to ʒoure appetite. (1: 4–5: 29–35)

Bellenden's *abbreuiatio* recalls Douglas's reference to Lorenzo Valla's struggles with the intractable complexity of Virgil's poem in the opening prologue of the *Eneados*:

---

[8] If Bellenden's epithet is a quotation of *The Palis of Honoure* here, it would, of course, offer considerable early support for the reading of the line recorded in Copland's text; cf. Bawcutt ed 2003: 210.

The worthy clerk hecht Lawrens of the Vaill,
Amang Latynys a gret patron sans faill,
Grantis quhen twelf ʒheris he had beyn diligent
To study Virgill, skant knew quhat he ment. (1.Pro.127–30)

Bellenden's lines also repeat the strategy of Douglas's disingenuous profession in the sixth prologue: "To wryte ʒou all his tryit and notabill vers / Almaist impossibill war" (6.Pro.121–22). Douglas's translation, of course, is precisely a rewriting of all of Virgil's "tryit and notabill vers", a proof of its possibility. Douglas cuts short his elaboration of Virgil's hidden and appropriable Christian meanings in the sixth prologue because the *Eneados* as a whole ensures those meanings are available in their entirety. Similarly, the evidence of payments in the *Treasurer's Accounts* suggests that Bellenden spent considerably more than "ane moneth to þe end", if not another "ʒere", ensuring that his translation would "schaw all proffittis" that at least the first half of "þe first decade of þis werk dois bere" (Paul et al. 1877–1978: 5: 97, 98, 206). In both works, the protestation of inability is, in fact, a declaration of ambition and an assertion of the importance of full translation. Fitting summary and selection may be impossible, but they are also unnecessary.

Finally, Bellenden's prologue concludes by reworking the nautical metaphor which structures the progression of Douglas's prologues in the *Eneados*:

For I Intend of þis difficill werk
To mak ane end, Or I my lauboure stynt,
War nocht þe passage and stremes ar sa stark
Quhare I haue salit, full of crag & clynt,
That ruddir and takillis of my schip ar tynt,
And þus my schip (qithout ʒe mak supporte)
Wil periß lang or It cum to þe porte. (1:5: 18–24)

The metaphor is not uncommon (see Bawcutt 1976: 165; and Bramble 1974: 164–66), but Bellenden's treatment recalls Douglas's third prologue. Douglas invokes the aid of Cynthia as "Rewlare of passage and ways many one, / Maistres of stremys" (3.Pro.3–4) as he attempts to navigate the "feirful stremys" (3.Pro.10) of Virgil's difficult third book. Bellenden's alliterative line ending, "crag & clynt", also echoes Douglas's "Now goith our barge, for nowder howk nor craik"

(3.Pro.39). Bellenden's lines also recall Douglas's final deployment of the metaphor in the "Exclamatioun":

Now throw the deip fast to the port I mark,
For heir is endyt the lang disparyt wark,
And Virgyll heß hys volum to me lent:
In sovir raid now ankyrrit is our bark;
We dowt na storm, our cabillys ar sa stark;
We have eschapyt full mony perrellus went:
Now God belovyt haß syk grace tyl ws sent! (1–7)

Bellenden repeats Douglas's wark/stark rhyme. While Douglas makes "fast to the porte", however, Bellenden remains far from "þe porte". Douglas's "bark" has crossed the perilous waters in which Bellenden's "schip" still flounders. Douglas's "cabillis ar sa stark"; Bellenden's "ruddir and takillis [...] are tynt" and for Bellenden it is the sea ("passage and stremes"), not the rigging, that is "stark". Bellenden displaces the confidence of Douglas's use of the metaphor to mark the beginning of his translation, rather than its completion. In the "Exclamatioun", Douglas addresses his work with satisfaction: "Go, wlgar Virgill, [...] I haue brocht thy purpoß to gud end" (37–42). In his prologue, Bellenden announces only intent, yet to be fulfilled ambition: "For I Intend of þis difficill wek / To mak ane end" (1:5:18–19). Bellenden's work again begins where Douglas's had ended. Bellenden's prefatory poetry returns both to Douglas's programmatically parallel *The Palis of Honoure* and to take the close of Douglas's poetic achievement as its own point of departure.

2

It seems probable that Bellenden's references to Douglas's poetry were also intended to have a particular political purchase. Bellenden seems to have been involved in Douglas interests, and the poem was almost certainly composed in a period of considerable tension between Archibald Douglas, sixth earl of Angus, and James V. Bellenden's literary allegiance to Gavin Douglas may figure a more practical loyalty to Douglas's family and the generalised moral advice of "Vertewe" may cloak a more partisan perspective. The translation of *The Chronicles of Scotland* which follows the "Proheme" is also

characterised by a pro-Douglas bias (Sheppard 1941: 421–22), and the
"Proheme" may be intended immediately to situate the whole work in
sympathetic association with Gavin Douglas and his family.

   Douglas was probably twenty years older than John Bellenden
and he died before Bellenden achieved significant prominence at court
and almost ten years before Bellenden seems to have begun work on
his translations. Douglas's influence, though, would have been difficult to avoid in the early years of James V's minority and the Bellen-
dens and Douglases seem to have had strong affinities and, in the
opening decades of the sixteenth century, to have moved, though with
different degrees of power, in similar circles in Edinburgh and at
court.

   John Bellenden was probably born in Lothian, possibly in
Berwickshire, in the final decade of the fifteenth century.[9] If he was
the younger brother of Sir Thomas Bellenden of Auchinoull, as is
often suggested, his parents were Patrick Bellenden and Marion
Douglas.[10] They received a grant of land in Berwickshire from Archibald Douglas, Gavin's father, in 1493, and, in 1499, Patrick obtained a
charter for the lands of Auchnolynshill in the county of Edinburgh,
from John, earl of Morton (Paul and Thomson eds 1883: 2: 420; cf.
Sheppard 1941: 420; van Heijnsbergen 1994: 192; Anderson 1877:
282; Paul 1905: 62). Patrick Bellenden was also parish clerk of the
Canongate, where his father had acquired land in the 1460s (van
Heijnsbergen 1994: 191; Paul 1905: 61). Both Patrick Bellenden and
Marion Douglas enjoyed significant court positions: Patrick was steward to Queen Margaret from 1509 until his death in 1514 and Marion
was "kepar" of the infant James V (van Heijnsbergen 1994: 191; cf.
Paul et al. 1877–1978: 4: 414, 446).

---

[9] The fullest treatment of Bellenden's life and the extant documents pertaining to him
remains Sheppard 1936; cf. Sheppard 1941. Sheppard also comprehensively surveys
and critiques the earlier, unreliable biographical traditions of Bellenden's life. I am
indebted throughout to her work. Anderson 1877: 1: 283 records the tradition that
Bellenden was "a native of the country of Haddington or Berwich"; cf. Bellenden
1822: 1: xxxvi. It is probable that Douglas was also born near Haddington, at Tantal-
lon Castle; cf. Bawcutt 1976: 4. On the basis of matriculation records at St Andrews,
Sheppard 1941: 423, concludes that the tradition that Bellenden was born *c.*1495 is
plausible.
[10] van Heijnsbergen 1994: 192, for instance, assumes that the two are brothers.
Sheppard 1941: 423 allows only that "[i]t is possible"; Paul 1905: 62 suggests "[i]t is
not unlikely that John Bellenden, the translator of Livy and Boece, was a second son
of Patrick".

On the basis of the peculiarly detailed account of the activities of Robert Bellenden, Abbot of Holyrood Abbey, c.1484–1500, in *The Chronicles of Scotland*, Sheppard suggests that John Bellenden was closely connected either to the Abbot or to the Abbey (Sheppard 1941: 422–23). Patrick Bellenden was parish clerk at Holyrood in 1486, and Robert "may have been [his] uncle or brother" (Sheppard 1941: 421). Walter Bellenden, again perhaps a brother of Patrick, was also a canon at Holyrood under Robert, and Adam Bellenden, a canon (van Heijnsbergen 1994: 191–92; van Heijnsbergen suggests that Walter Bellenden was Patrick's brother and John's uncle).

Patrick Bellenden and Marion Douglas's children continued their family's associations with the court. Their daughter, Katharine, succeeded Janet Douglas, wife of David Lyndsay, as royal seamstress (van Heijnsbergen 1994: 192). Their eldest son, Thomas Bellenden of Auchinoull, was briefly director of the Chancery in 1513 (Paul and Thomson eds 1883: 2: 420; cf. Fraser 1885: 3: 216 where Bellenden appears as a signatory witness, styled "director Cancellarie"). He also enjoyed a successful legal and administrative career under James V. Much later, in 1535, he was made an ordinary Lord of Session (van Heijnsbergen 1994: 193; Paul 1905: 63). From 10 September 1538, he was once more Director of the Chancery (Livingstone ed. 1908: 2: no.2709; Paul 1905: 63), on 27 December 1539, he was made Clerk of the Justiciary (Livingstone ed. 1908: 2: no.3239); Paul 1905: 63), and in the 1540s, he was prominently, if not unambiguously, involved in diplomatic negotiations with the English (van Heijnsbergen 1994: 193–94; Edington 1994: 49–50, 60, 167–68).

One of the documents in which Thomas Bellenden is styled "director Cancellarie" in 1513 treats the business of George Douglas, Gavin's elder brother. Thomas Bellenden and Gavin themselves are closely linked by another document witnessed for Gavin Douglas, as Bishop of Dunkeld, by Bellenden, on the fifth of November 1520 (cf. Fraser 1885: 3: 219–21). The document is a contract between Douglas and his sister-in-law, Elizabeth Auchinleck, on Elizabeth's entry into the convent at Sciennes. Thomas Bellenden was also involved in the production of the "Lambeth" copy of the *Eneados*: the manuscript's colophon records "Heir endis the buke of Virgill writtin be the hand of Iohanne mudy with master thomas bellenden of auchinoull Iustis Clerke and endit the 2 februarii anno & c xlv" (cf. Coldwell 1957–64: 1: 98–99; Douglas 1874: 1: clxxvii; Watt 1920: 139–40). Although the completion of the manuscript post-dates John Bellenden's translation of *The Chronicles of Scotland* and the *Livy* in the 1530s, it seems likely that, if John was Thomas's brother, he would have known Douglas quite closely in the second decade of the sixteenth century and the two men may have shared a fraternal interest in Douglas's literary works.

Even if John Bellenden was not the son of Patrick and the brother of Thomas of Auchinoull, he was almost certainly closely related to them and the records of his own activities in the first two decades of the sixteenth century suggest that he was moving in circles which would have brought him very close to Douglas. A John Bellenden "nationis Laudoniae", probably the translator, matriculated at St. Andrews in 1508 (Anderson ed. 1926: 201; Sheppard 1941: 423: Anderson 1877: 283; Bellenden 1822: 1: xxxvi–xxxvii), and obtained his degree in 1512 (Dunlop ed. 1964: 302; Sheppard 1941: 423. Note also Dunlop ed. 1964: 299, at which a "Johannes Ballingar" appears among those engaged in "primus actus"). Douglas was appointed an advisor to the rector of St. Andrews University in 1512 and 1513 (cf. Bawcutt 1976: 9–10). Bellenden became clerk of expenses in the king's household in 1515 and retained the role until 1522 (Sheppard 1941: 423–25; van Heijnsbergen 1994: 191; Anderson 1877: 284; Paul 1905: 62).[11] He recalls his service in the royal household within the "Proheme":

How that I wes in service with the King;
Put to his Grace in yeris tenderest,
Clerk of his Comptis, thoucht I wes inding,
With hart and hand, and every othir thing
That micht him pleis in ony maner best;
Quhill hie invy me from his service kest,
Be thaim that had the Court in governing,
As bird but plumes heryit of the nest. (vi)

Here Bellenden also records his loss of royal favour, which may have occurred in 1522, when his name drops out of the official records (Sheppard 1941: 425). Certainly he was replaced as clerk of expenses

---

[11] Sheppard and Anderson record and correct the earlier belief that Bellenden had actually been tutor to the King. Sheppard 1941: 424 adds "[i]t may be remarked that such a position in the royal household would be readily attained by a kinsman of Patrick Bellenden, late steward to the Queen".

then; his successor, Mr John Cantlie, Archdeacon of St Andrews, had assumed the position by August, 1522 (Sheppard 1941: 424). Clearly Bellenden's service as "Clerk of [...] Comptis" in the period in which Douglas was most influential at court would almost certainly have brought the two men into contact with one another.

It is possible, too, that the event which motivated Douglas's final departure for London also caused Bellenden's departure from the court: the return of Albany from France in November 1521 (this is suggested by Sheppard 1941: 425). For Sheppard, Bellenden's loss of court position ("Quhill hie invy me from his service kest, / Be thaim that had the Court in governing" (vi)) confirms his status as a "Douglas man": "the author of his dismissal was no doubt the Duke of Albany, who had returned to Scotland for the second time in November 1521, and was busy all through the succeeding year in the attempt to consolidate his position in the country" (Sheppard 1941: 425). If this is the case, as seems probable, then it suggests strongly that Bellenden and Douglas were implicated in similar factional interests; it might also be felt to corroborate association of John with Thomas Bellenden of Auchinoull whom we have seen to have been clearly involved in Douglas affairs.

It also seems probable that, after being dismissed from the royal household (and after Gavin Douglas's death), Bellenden entered the service of Gavin's nephew, Archibald, sixth Earl of Angus, as his secretary. *The Acts of the Parliament of Scotland* record a M. John Ballentyne in this position in 1528 (Thomson and Innes eds 1814–75: 2: 322–24; see also Bellenden 1938, 1941: 1: xxvii–viii). This John Bellenden is implicated in proceedings following Angus's disastrous detaining of James V at Falkland in 1528:

Quarto Septembris
In presens of þe kingis grace and Lordis and thre estatis of parliament Comperit maister Johnne ballentyne seruitour and secretar to Archibald Erle of angus And gaif in þe resonis vnderwrittin And protestit eftir þe forme and tenour Of the samin off þe quhilk the tenour followis THIR are þe resonis þat we Archibald Erle of anguß george douglas his brothir and Archibald douglas of kilspindy allegis for ws quhy we suld nocht be accusit nor compellit to ansuer at this tyme to þe presendit Summondis of tresoune maid on ws at our souererane Lordis Instance. (Thomson and Innes eds 1814–75: 2: 322)

Another entry on the same day records that John Bellenden "comperit" again to give security that Angus would appear and accept the sentence of the Parliament (Thomson and Innes eds 1814–75: 2: 324). In April, 1529, the *Registrum Secreti Sigilli* records a precept of remission for

M. Johannis Bannatyne et Willelmi Flemyng ejus servitoris, pro eorum proditoria assistentia data, prestita et exhibita Archibaldo olim Angusie Comiti, Georgio Douglas suo fratri, et Archibaldo Douglas ejus patruo et eorum complicibus, rebellibus regis, et proditoribus in suiis proditoriis factis, et pro manutenentia, fortificatione, supplemento et intercommunicatione cum dictis rebellibus; ac pro omni actione et crimine que eiis seu eorum alicui quovismodo inde imputari poterit tantum, etc. (Livingstone ed 1908: 2: no.56)

Anderson, in the nineteenth century, emphatically denied that this could be Bellenden the poet on the grounds that "this individual is stated by Hume to have been Sir John Bellenden with whom his name has so frequently been mistaken" (Anderson 1877: 284; Anderson refers to Hume of Godscroft 1644: 258–59, for whom this is "Sir John Ballandine, who was one of their dependents, & afterward Justice-Clerk"), but Sir John Bellenden of Auchinoull was only eight years old in 1528 (Sheppard 1941: 426). Sheppard argues strongly that this is the translator further involved in Douglas factional interests. She also notes "that certain of the extant letters from the Earl of Angus at this date are written in a hand which has some points of similarity to Bellenden's" and that the actions of Angus's secretary suggest that he was an "ecclesiastic, and by 1528 Bellenden was already in orders" (Sheppard 1941: 426–27). Priscilla Bawcutt, most recently, cautiously allows the possibility that Angus's secretary was Bellenden the translator (Bawcutt 1976: 194).

It was, of course, most probably in this period of political foment that much of the "Proheme to the Cosmographe" was composed and this political context may have given further purchase to Bellenden's conspicuous allusions to Douglas's poetry. The allusions may consti-tute an articulation of political as well as literary affiliation, a further manifestation of Bellenden's loyalties as a "Douglas man" in a time of considerable uncertainty. Such an articulation, moreover, would have been particularly appropriate to a man embroiled in that uncertainty as the Earl of Angus's secretary was. The "Proheme's" allusions seem to me to encourage identification of secretary and poet as the same man. And the poem's complex combination of Douglas sympathy and advi-sory purpose (marked emphatically in the doubled centrality of the figure of the "crownit King") again seems to me particularly appropriate to a man who was charged with defending the Earl of Angus's interests to a royal audience. The "Proheme's" references to Douglas's poetry, then, may also enable us to secure further this detail of Bellenden's biography.

3

The centrality of the "crownit King" to the conception of the "Proheme to the Cosmographe" may also serve to introduce an important difference between Bellenden's and Douglas's works, for, although the "Proheme" proceeds in part through open imitation of *The Palis of Honoure*, in one important aspect the two are very different poems.

In *The Palis of Honoure*, Douglas elaborates a complex and ambivalent relationship of interdependence between monarch and poet (this is more fully argued in chapter two of Rutledge, forthcoming). The poem stages the movement of the poet-dreamer away from the court music of Venus and her followers towards the greater independence of the garden of the Muses. The dreamer is afforded only a momentary and threatening glimpse of the central and dazzling "god armypotent" (Copland c.1553, 1921), and, although the poem is formally dedicated to James IV, it concludes by imagining space for itself and its author away from the "lycht" (Copland c.1553, 2167) and the scrutinising "sycht" (Copland c.1553, 2152) of the King. The interdependence of Calliope's "kyngly style" is predicated on the enabling possibilities of distance from the royal centre. The dedication of the *Eneados* to Douglas's kinsman, Henry Sinclair, in conspicuous contrast to Virgil's imagined composition of a "wark imperiall" for "the gret Octauyane, / The emperour excellent and maste souerane" (9.Pro.56–58), further sites Douglas's literary activity beyond the margins of the royal court.

In the "Proheme", on the other hand, Bellenden's "crownit King" is the subject of careful and sustained scrutiny ("With thaim I saw ane crownit King appeir, / With tendir downis rising on his beird" (vii)) and the "Proheme", like the "Proloug" to the *Livy*, presents itself directly to the "Ee" of the new Scottish king (1: 4: 4). Bellenden's dreamer opens the poem regretfully recalling his loss of court position and enviously eyes the "courtlie gallandis settand thair intentis / To sing, and play on divers instrumentis, / According to this Princis appetit" (vii). Although the "Proheme" is certainly advisory rather than propagandistic, the demands of the "Princis appetite" remain central to the conception of the poem. In *The Palis of Honoure*, by contrast, Douglas suggestively turns away from the "luf ballattis" (Copland c.1553: 498) demanded of Venus's faithful courtiers.

The focus of the "Proheme" is emblematic, for the emphases of Bellenden's translations are also consistently advisory and political. Within the *Eneados*, Douglas is certainly also aware of the political potential of the classical narrative he is retelling. He figures, as we have seen, the *Aeneid* as a "wark imperiall", intended to glorify Augustus through the deeds of his Julian ancestor. And Douglas's celebration of Aeneas ("For euery vertu belangand a nobill man / This ornate poet bettir than ony can / Payntand discryvis in person of Eneas" (1.Pro.325–27)) has been held to be the keynote of his translation, rendering it particularly available for the political and panegyrical purposes of the Renaissance (see, especially, Dearing 1952; Simpson 2002: 68–120; Coldwell ed. 1957–64: 1: 31–32; Bawcutt 1976: 84–85 provides an important corrective to this view). The dedication of the work to Henry Sinclair, however, at once radically complicates such readings; Douglas's writing insistently resists appropriation by the royal centre. The *Eneados*, in fact, much more consistently works to render available the classical narrative within a new sixteenth-century context by proposing the practices of Christian allegoresis. Douglas rather privileges the religious than the political implications of Virgil's narrative.

Bellenden, by contrast, in both the *Chronicles of Scotland* and the *Livy* insistently puts his material to political and advisory purposes. Both works repeatedly instantiate virtuous and vicious kingship and the disastrous consequences of tyranny and may therefore especially profitably be turned to the eyes of Bellenden's young king. Most strikingly, in his approach to the *Ab urbe condita*, Bellenden works to contain the cultural difference of Livy's historiography by re-inscribing the classical narrative within the terms of sixteenth-century Scottish political experience. He refashions the monarchical and the republican portions of Livy's history within the terms of Older Scots advisory literature and exploits the potentially radical republican inflection Livy's history gives to the language of tyranny, treason, and the commonweal challengingly to emphasise the responsibilities of kingship.

The "crownit king", then, remains firmly central to Bellenden's work; his translations, though, very much in keeping with his earlier sympathies to Douglas interests, offer not only advice for the education of the king, but also a more provocative warning of the consequences of royal intransigence. Bellenden's signalling of his indebtedness to Douglas in the "Proheme to the Cosmographe", then, may serve not only carefully to foreground similarities between the vernacular humanist projects of the two men, but also to enable us at once to identify fundamental differences in the approaches of their writing. If Bellenden self-consciously begins where Douglas had concluded, he proceeds to take his Scots translations in his own quite distinctive directions.

Bibliography

Anderson, J. (ed.) 1926. *Early Records of the University of St. Andrews* [Scottish History Society 3rd Series no. 8.]. Edinburgh: T. and A. Constable.

Anderson, W. 1877. *The Scottish Nation or, the Surnames, Families, Literature, Honours, and Biographical History of the People of Scotland*. 3 vols. Edinburgh and London: A. Fullarton and Co.

Archibald, E. 1989. "Gavin Douglas on love: the Prologue to *Eneados* IV" in McClure, J. Derrick and Michael Spiller (eds) *Bryght Lanternis*. Aberdeen: Aberdeen University Press.

Bawcutt, P. 1976. *Gavin Douglas: A Critical Study*. Edinburgh: Edinburgh University Press.

—. (ed.) 2003. *The Shorter Poems of Gavin Douglas* [Scottish Text Society 5th Series no. 2.]. 2nd edn. Edinburgh: Scottish Text Society.

Boece, H. 1527. *Scotorum Historia a prima gentis origine*. Paris: Iodocus Badius Ascensius.

Bramble, J. 1974. *Persius and the Programmatic Satire*. Cambridge: Cambridge University Press.

Chambers, R. et al. (eds). 1938, 1941. *The Chronicles of Scotland, Compiled by Hector Boece, Translated into Scots by John Bellenden, 1531* [Scottish Text Society 3rd Series no. 10, 15.]. 2 vols. Edinburgh and London: William Blackwood and Sons.

Coldwell, D.F.C. (ed.) 1957–64. *Virgil's Aeneid Translated into Scottish Verse by Gavin Douglas, Bishop of Dunkeld* [Scottish Text Society 3rd Series no. 30, 25, 27, 28]. 4 vols. Edinburgh and London: William Blackwood and Sons.

Couper, S. 2001. *Reason and Desire in Older Scots Poetry, c.1424–1560*. DPhil thesis. University of Oxford.

Craigie, W.A. (ed.) 1900–1, 1903. *Livy's History of Rome, The First Five Books Translated into Scots by John Bellenden, 1533* [Scottish Text Society 1st Series no. 47, 51]. 2 vols. Edinburgh and London: William Blackwood and Sons.

Dearing, B. 1952. "An Aspect of the Renaissance in Gavin Douglas's Eneados" in *PMLA* 67: 845–62.

Dunlop, A. (ed.) 1964. *Acta Facultatis Artium Universitatis S. Andree 1413–1588* [Scottish History Society 3rd Series no. 54, 55.]. 2 vols. Edinburgh: Oliver and Boyd.

Edington, C. 1994. *Court and Culture in Renaissance Scotland: Sir David Lyndsay of the Mount*. Amherst: University of Massachusetts Press.

Ferguson, W. 1998. *The Identity of the Scottish Nation: An Historic Quest*. Edinburgh: Edinburgh University Press.

Fraser, W. 1885. *The Douglas Book*. 4 vols. Edinburgh.

Gray, D. 2000. "'As quha the mater beheld tofor thar e': Douglas's Treatment of Vergil's Imagery" in Houwen, L.A.J.R. et al. (eds) *A Palace in the Wild: Essays on Vernacular Culture and Humanism in Late-Medieval and Renaissance Scotland*. Leuven: Peeters. 95–124.

Heijnsbergen, Theo van 1994. "The Interaction between Literature and History in Queen Mary's Edinburgh: The Bannatyne Manuscript and its Prosopographical Context" in MacDonald, A. et al. (eds) *The Renaissance in Scotland: Studies in Literature, Religion, History and Culture*. Leiden: Brill. 183–225.

Hume of Godscroft, D. 1644. *The History of the Houses of Douglas and Angus*. Edinburgh: Evan Tyler.

Livingstone, M. (ed.) 1908. *Registrum Secreti Sigilli Regum Scotorum: The Register of the Privy Seal of Scotland, vol.2, 1529–42*. Edinburgh: H. M. General Register House.

Mair, J. 1521. *Historia Maioris Britanniae, tam Angliae quam Scotiae*. Paris: Iodocus Badius Ascensius.

Maitland, T. (ed.) 1821. *The History and Chronicles of Scotland written in Latin by Hector Boece, Canon of Aberdeen and Translated by John Belllenden, Archdean of Moray and Canon of Ross*. 2 vols. Edinburgh: W. and C. Tait.

Mapstone, S. 1998. "Shakespeare and Scottish Kingship: a Case History" in Mapstone, Sally and Juliette Wood (eds) *The Rose and the Thistle: Essays on the Culture of Late Medieval and Renaissance Scotland*. East Linton: Tuckwell Press. 158–93.

Mason, R. 1992. "Chivalry and Citizenship: Aspects of National Identity in Renaissance Scotland" in Mason, Roger and Norman MacDougall (eds) *People and Power in Scotland: Essays in Honour of T. C. Smout*. Edinburgh: John Donald. 50–73.

—. 1998. *Kingship and the Commonweal: Political Thought in Renaissance and Reformation Scotland*. East Linton: Tuckwell Press.

—. 2002. "Civil Society and the Celts: Hector Boece, George Buchanan and the Ancient Scottish Past" in Cowan, Edward and Richard Finlay (eds) *Scottish History: The Power of the Past*. Edinburgh: Edinburgh University Press. 95–119.

Norton-Smith, J (ed.) 1981. *James I of Scotland: The Kingis Quair*. Oxford: Clarendon Press

Paul, J.B. et al. (eds). 1877–1978. *Accounts of the Lord High Treasurer of Scotland*. 13 vols. Edinburgh: H. M. General Register House.

—. and J.M. Thomson (eds). 1883. *Registrum Magni Sigilli Regum Scotorum: The Register of the Great Seal of Scotland, vol.2, 1513–1546*. Edinburgh: H. M. General Register House.

—. 1905. *The Scots Peerage, Founded on Wood's Edition of Sir Robert Douglas's Peerage of Scotland, Containing an Historical and Genealogical Account of the Nobility of that Kingdom*. Edinburgh.

Renouard, P. 1908. *Bibliographie des Impressions et des Oeuvres de Josse Badius Ascensius, Imprimeur et Humaniste, 1462–1535*. 3 vols. Paris.

Royan, N. 1996. *The Scotorum Historia of Hector Boece: A Study*. DPhil thesis. University of Oxford.

—. 1998. "The Relationship between the *Scotorum Historia* of Hector Boece and John Bellenden's *Chronicles of Scotland*" in Mapstone, Sally and Juliette Wood (eds) *The Rose and the Thistle: Essays on the Culture of Late Medieval and Renaissance Scotland*. East Linton: Tuckwell. 136–57.

—. 2000. "The Uses of Speech in Hector Boece's *Scotorum Historia*" in Houwen, L. et al. (eds) *A Palace in the Wild: Essays on Vernacular Culture and Humanism in Late-Medieval and Renaissance Scotland*. Leuven: Peeters. 75–93.

—. 2002. "National Martyrdom in Northern Humanist Historiography" in *Forum for Modern Language Studies* 38: 462–75.

Rutledge, T. (Forthcoming). *The Reception of Classical and Italian Literature in Early-Renaissance Scotland, c.1475–1535.* DPhil thesis, University of Oxford.

Sheppard, E. 1936. *Studies in the Language of Bellenden's Boece.* PhD thesis. University of London.

—. 1941. "John Bellenden" in Chambers, R. et al. (eds) *Chronicles of Scotland, Compiled by Hector Boece, Translated into Scots by John Bellenden, 1531* [Scottish Text Society 3rd Series no. 10, 15]. 2 vols. Edinburgh and London: William Blackwood and Sons. 2: 411–61.

Simpson, J. 2002. *Reform and Cultural Revolution, The Oxford English Literary History, Volume 2, 1350–1547.* Oxford: Oxford University Press.

Small, J. (ed.) 1874. *The Poetical Works of Gavin Douglas, Bishop of Dunkeld.* 4 vols. Edinburgh: William Paterson.

Thomson, T. and C. Innes (eds). 1814–75. *The Acts of the Parliaments of Scotland 1124–1707.* 12 vols. Edinburgh.

Watt, D. and Norman F. Shead (eds). 2001. *The Heads of Religious Houses in Scotland from Twelfth to Sixteenth Centuries.* Edinburgh: Scottish Record Society.

Watt, L. 1920. *Douglas's Aeneid.* Cambridge: Cambridge University Press.

Lyndsay's Dramatic Use of Prosody in *Ane Satyre of the Thrie Estaitis*

J. Derrick McClure

Previous studies of Lyndsay's poetry have tended to focus on its content, rather than its style. This essay examines in detail Lyndsay's versification, tracing its development over the poet's career.

Keywords: *Ane Satyre of the Thrie Estaitis*; humour; language stress; metre; morality; pentameter; pitch-prominence; prosody; rhyme; rhythm; Sir David Lyndsay; verse forms

John Rolland, writing almost on the eve of the assumption of active rule by Mary Queen of Scots, speaks in praise of the court poets of her father's reign:

In court that time was gude Dauid Lyndsay,
In vulgar toung he bure the bell that day
To mak meter, richt cunnyng and expart,
And maister Iohn Ballentyne suith to say
Mak him marrow to Dauid well we may.
And for the third, Maister William Stewart,
To mak in Scottis, richt weill he knew that Art,
Bischop Durie, sum tyme of Galloway,
For his plesure sum tyme wald tak thair part. (Black ed. 1932: 1–2)

In giving first place to David Lyndsay he of course anticipates the universal verdict of posterity: a fact which appears less trivial when it is recalled that he certainly knew more of Bellenden's and Durie's works, and quite possibly more of Stewart's, than have survived for later readers (on Stewart see MacDonald 1996). Nor is it only literary scholars who have awarded Lyndsay an unchallenged position among the greatest names of pre-Union Scottish literature: until recently he had the still more unusual distinction of a high and enduring place in popular affection, rivalling that of Blind Hary and excelled only by Burns.

The reasons for Lyndsay's popularity are not hard to find: obvious ones are his robust and earthy humour, his patriotism, his forthright criticism of social evils and particularly those associated with the pre-Reformation Church, the honest, sensible and eminently realistic

quality of his moral stance, and above all his courageous and energetic
championing of the rights of the common people. As with Allan
Ramsay, Lyndsay's poetic persona is a most attractive one, and is supported by what is known, has been believed, or can be deduced,
regarding the life events of the man. (To dispose of a possible red
herring: though in fact I am wholly unconvinced of either the useful-
ness or the intelligibility of theoretical approaches such as "the death
of the author" and the like, they are in any case irrelevant to this
introductory reference to *popular* attitudes to Lyndsay.) Rolland's
statement that Lyndsay "bure the bell [...] *to mak meter*", however –
assuming that the phrase means anything more than "to write poetry"
– deserves some consideration. Unlike Henryson, Douglas and above
all (of course) Dunbar, Lyndsay as metrist has not attracted a notable
amount of critical attention. That he uses a variety of metres in his
poems, and still more in his play, is of course obvious; but his actual
technique remains largely unexamined; and such comments as have
appeared since Rolland's reference are scarcely such as to endorse his
judgement: Wittig, for instance, while praising the homely realism of
Lyndsay's language (with perfect justice), notes his lack of "the aureate elegance of Dunbar or Douglas" (Wittig 1958: 91). Lyndsay's distinctive talent, Wittig suggests, is the poetic and dramatic harnessing
of the cadences, as well as the idiom and vocabulary, of everyday
speech. I propose in this chapter to examine the development of
Lyndsay's verse technique up to and including the *Satire of the Thrie
Estaitis*.

   Since I have, in recent papers on the metrical techniques of
Dunbar and Blind Hary (McClure 2001 and 2005), described my
phonetically-based approach to scansion in some detail, I will not
offer another account of it here. I request permission, however, to
introduce three terms to clarify a distinction which is certain to be
necessary in any discussion including analysis of iambic pentameter
lines.

   The definition of a line of this type is a decasyllabic line with
each even-numbered syllable stressed. However, Duration and pitch-
prominence are independent of stress, and make their own separate
contributions to the force with which any syllable strikes a listener's
ear. An iambic pentameter line may show stress *and* length *and* pitch-
prominence on all its even-numbered syllables and none of its odd-
numbered ones, or it may, while maintaining the mandatory pattern of

stresses, show no systematic correlation whatever between stress and
the other two factors: that is, pitch-prominence may occur on any of
the ten syllables, and the five stressed syllables may be long or short.
(In stress-timed languages, the duration of *unstressed* syllables in
verse is mainly a function of that of the stressed syllable in the same
foot, and is not a factor that independently affects the prosody.) The
difference is that between a line like

| The *gen-* | tyll *Ia*, | the *Merle*, | and *Tur-* | tur *trew* | (Hamer ed. 1931–36: *Testament
of the Papyngo*, 725)[1]

and one like

| **Sett** *nocht* | on *it* | Zour *hole* | fe-*li-* | ci-*tie* |. (408)

I will refer to lines of the first type as "perfect", and lines of the
second as "ordinary", iambic pentameters. (*Mutatis mutandis*, a
similar distinction could of course be made regarding lines of any
other metrical structure consisting of regular patterning of stressed and
unstressed syllables.) It should be noted that though "perfect" lines are
"*extra*ordinary" in the sense that they are statistically much the less
common of the two kinds, "ordinary" lines are of course not
"*im*perfect" in any derogatory sense: they are by definition no less
iambic pentameters than the "perfect" lines; and they are not in any
way irregular, since the patterning of duration and pitch prominence in
verse lines, unlike that of the stresses, is not prescribed.

Furthermore, it has always been permissible for a passage of
which the essential rhythm is that of the iambic pentameter to include
lines which deviate (usually within fairly rigid limits) from the "5 x a"
pattern by showing variations in the number of syllables, the
arrangement of stressed and unstressed syllables, or both: that is, lines
which are in certain specific respects *not* iambic pentameters.

---

[1] I use italics to indicate stressed syllables and bold type to indicate syllables with
pitch prominence (but note that whereas stress is either present or absent, pitch
prominence is a matter of degree). Marking of long syllables (e.g. by underlining)
would result in an unbecoming degree of typological complexity; and is in any case
unnecessary for readers who know their MSc phonology. The edition of Lyndsay used
throughout is Hamer ed. 1931–36, and references are in the form of title and line
numbers.

Examples can be found in almost any passage: a few from Lyndsay's
The Deploratioun of the Deith of Quene Magdalene are

| A-dam, | we **may** | **the wyit** | of **this** | mis-**chance** | (3)

with its trochaic inversion in the first foot,

| Thow *let* | Me-*thu*- | sa-lem *leif* | **nine** *hun*- | dreth *Zeir* | (22)

with its hypermetrical syllable in the third foot, or

| Of **Gold**, | and **perle**, | and **pre**- | cious **stonis** | **bricht** | (146)

with its monosyllabic final foot. I will call such lines "deviant" iambic
pentameters: not an unimpeachable term, since deviations of this kind
prevent them, by strict definition, from being iambic pentameters at
all; and meaningful *only* if the poem in which such lines occur
consists mainly of true iambic pentameter lines. A question of both
classification and evaluation occurs when a line deviates in more than
one or two particulars from the regular pattern: does it make sense to
describe lines like

| **Dame** Re- | **mem**-brance, | scho *said*, | **cal**-lit | am *I* | (*Dreme*, 154)

with its three trochaic inversions,

| **Pri**-ouris, | **Ab**-bottis, | and **fals** | **flatt**- | rand **freris** | (*Dreme*, 177)

with its two inversions and monosyllabic fourth foot, or

| *And* lat | **Doc**-touris | of *sic* | **hie** *mat*- |teris de-**clare** | (*Dreme*, 546)

with its two inversions and hypermetrical syllable in the last foot, as
even "deviant" iambic pentameter lines (that they are still *pentameters*
is not in doubt); and is their presence self-justifying, or should it be
regarded as a fault unless a definite literary point is made by it, in an
iambic pentameter poem?

Lyndsay's two earliest extant poems, *The Dreme* and *The
Complaynt*, are respectively in rhyme royal (except for the envoi in
nine-line stanzas) and octosyllabic couplets: Lyndsay's staples

throughout his oeuvre. The opening of *The Dreme* establishes the music of the iambic pentameter in a classically regular line:

| **Rycht *Po-*** | tent ***Prince*,** | of *hie* | Im-*pe-* | rial *blude* | (*Dreme*, 1)

where the only detail which prevents it from being "perfect", the demoted syllable in the initial foot, imparts added force to the apostrophe; and the alliteration and vowel harmony ([hiː Impiːrjəl]) provide a graceful decoration. The first stanza maintains this pattern with straightforward competence. Both "ordinary" and "deviant" lines appear, as expected – we find promotions (on*to* thy Celsitude, in seruyce *of* thyne Excellence), demotions (it be *weill* knawin, neir *ouir* blawin), trochaic inversions (*Onto* thy Grace, *for to* be schawin), and feminine endings (*knawin – schawin*) – but without coming near to upsetting the basic pattern. In the second stanza, Lyndsay's charming reminiscences of his part in the young king's upbringing are expressed in a prosodic melody of which the easy simplicity harmonises with that of the vocabulary: regular decasyllabics with alternating stressed and unstressed syllables, but with no systematic use of length contrasts (such as Dunbar uses with consummate artistry; cf. McClure 2001) nor manipulation of pitch patterns to highlight important words. In a line like

| And *in* | thy *bed* | oft *hap-* | pit *the* | full *warme* | (10)

the absence of any systematic attempt to juxtapose stress to pitch prominence (resulting in unobtrusive promotions and demotions), and the random choice of short and long syllables to bear the stress, produce a metrical pattern as artless as the action described. Almost the only phrase which calls attention to itself prosodically, "the greislie gaist of gye" with its three successive stressed syllables, which are also long and pitch-prominent, has a referent which makes this appropriate.

This impression of a competent metrist using easy and fluent iambic pentameter with no special artifice or adornment, however, soon begins to waver. Metrically infelicitous lines convey the suggestion that the task of rendering his material in verse is beginning to test his poetic skill:

| Off *an-* | tique *sto-* | ries and *deidis* | mar- | ci-*all* | (31)

with its "double iambus" (see Jespersen 1933: 264; McClure 2005);

| *And* of | ***Samp***-sone | the *su-* | per-*na-* | tu-rall ***strenth*** | (38)

with its hypermetrical syllable and awkward opening trochee with a promoted first syllable;

| *Off* the | **reid** *E-* | tin, *and* | the ***gyir*** | ***car***-lyng | (*Dreme,* 45)

in which a decidedly non-iambic pattern of pitch and stress is duplicated to give a very deviant line. None of these lines is hopelessly unmetrical – the last (as is often the case in mediaeval decasyllabics) would read perfectly well as a tetrameter – but cumulatively they suggest a lack of finesse. Lyndsay recovers, however, in the final stanza of the Epistle, in which regular "5 x a" lines predominate; and the decisive thump of the quasi-double iambus *As I best can* suggests not an accidental deviation but a firm expression of resolve. (By "quasi-double iambus" I mean a light trochee followed by a heavy iambus: a pattern much commoner, and much less of a deviation from the regular metrical pattern, than the *true* double iambus consisiting of two unstressed followed by two stressed syllables.)

In the Proloug, Lyndsay's handling of the metre at first reinforces the impression of practical, utilitarian competence. The opening line

| *In* to | the ***Ca-*** | lend-*is* | of ***Ian-*** | u-*a*-rie | (*Proloug,* 57)

scans perfectly well, and positions the stressed syllable of the last word in the correct position for the ryme with *Aquarie*, if the *-is* of *Calendis* is taken to be not the Scots plural ending, which had long ceased to be syllabic by Lyndsay's time, but the Latin ablative plural. Several lines appear which are as graceful and as classically regular as could be desired, and which are in some cases decorated with alliteration or other segment patterning:

The snaw and sleit perturbit all the air [...] (61)
Ouer all the land had spred his baner brycht [...] (70)
Thy syluer droppis ar turnit in to sleit [...] (95)
Enamalit with rosis reid and quhyte. (102)

Small details show that Lyndsay recognised the iconic value of prosodic effects: by omitting the expected unstressed syllable after the word *lang* in line 64 –

| *Ef*-ter | that *I* | the *lang* | *wyn*- |teris *nycht* |

– he augments the duration of both it and the first syllable of *wynteris*, which becomes a monosyllabic foot, in fitting concordance with the sense of the word; in

With cloke and hude I dressit me belyue,
With dowbill schone & myttanis on my handis (*Proloug*, 71–72)

the trio of trochaic words with short stressed syllables (*dressit*, *dowbill*, *myttanis*), and the shortening effect of the final plosives in *cloke* and *hude*,[2] combine to give a suggestion of abrupt and hasty movement; the emotive phrase "Pensyue in hart" (113) is underlined by the repetition of its rhythmic pattern (trochee + iambus) three times in its own and the next line, and the impression which this conveys of a slow, plodding, melancholy pace is forcefully countered by the "perfect" iambic line which follows:

| The *see* | was *furth*; | the *sand* | wes *smoith* | & *dryye* | (*Proloug*, 114)

– as if the speaker's dreary spirits had been raised by the open vista of sea and sand that suddenly presented itself; and finally the two "ordinary" lines

So with my hude my hede I happit warme
And in my cloke I fauldit boith my feit (134–35)

with their parallel grammatical structure, emphasise the comforting, reassuring nature of the actions described.

In the *Dreme* proper, however, the struggle between Lyndsay's technical skill (or at any rate his concern for metrical propriety) and his eagerness to make his didactic points becomes painfully uneven.

---

[2] The historically long vowels in those words, and also in *schone*, had probably not yet entirely lost their length (see Aitken 1977), but even with inherently long vowels a following plosive – voiced or voiceless in Scots, though in most other languages it is true only of voiceless ones – has an apocopating effect.

Deviant lines start to appear with such frequency that the iambic pentameter rhythm is in danger of being lost to sight. In such a context, a regular line, when it appears, is thrown into relief; and occasionally in this part of the poem the effect appears to be deliberate: in the two stanzas beginning at line 204, as a notable instance, where Lyndsay under the guise of a general attack on worldly prelates is patently criticising the abuses prevalent in the Scottish church of his time, the metre becomes somewhat more consistent and some forceful statements are made in lines of unimpeachable regularity:

| On *cairtis*, | on *dice*, | on *har* - | llot-*rie*, | and *huris* | [...] (207);
| And *comp*- | tit *nocht* | thair *God* | for *till* | of-*fend* |. (214)

Particularly distressing is the effect which Lindsay's metrical uncertainty often has on his rhymes.

| *By*-schope | *An*-nas, | *and* the | *trea*-tour | *Iu*-das | (218)

is a perfectly good trochaic line, but the last word has to rhyme with a stressed *was*. Other instances of rhymes between an unstressed and a stressed syllable appear: *Nero – mo* (253–55); *thousand – band* (302–4); *drye – trewlie* (440–41). In the stanza beginning at line 190, the rhyme *precheing – flecheing – techeing* sounds awkward because in only one of the lines does the pattern suggest an iambic pentameter with a feminine ending. The rhyme of *generall* with *Infernall* (319–20), to be valid, requires the latter word to be irregularly pronounced with the stress on the first syllable: the metre of the line also calls for this. Similarly, the rhyme of *confortyng* with *supportyng* (244–45) would require one or the other word to be pronounced with an abnormal stress pattern; but in this case each fits quite well into the metre of its line with its *normal* rhythm, so that either the rhyme or the metre must necessarily be sacrificed. (Later, in l. 812 "For, throw the *supporte* of Zour hie prudence", Lyndsay seems to assume a pronunciation of *supporte* with the stress on the first syllable.) The rhyme *Occararis – oppressaris – Lauboraris* (310–13) likewise calls for the stress on *oppressaris* to be artificially placed on the first syllable; but the line in which it appears is so metrically amorphous that this actually makes it more like a pentameter:

|*Theifis*, | *rei*- varis | and *pu*- | blict *o*- | pres-*saris* |.

Some lines require to be unnaturally protracted in order to make the last stressed syllable coincide metrically with its counterpart in the rhyming line:

| Lyke **wod** | **Ly**-onis, | **cair**- | *ful*-lie | **cry**-and |
| In **flam** | of **fyre** | **rycht fu**- | ri-*ous*- | lie **fry**-and | (265–66);

(where the natural reading of the first line as a tetrameter (**cair**-ful-lie | **cry**-and) would produce the rhyme a foot too soon);

| Al-**lace**, | our **panis** | ar *In*- | **suf**- |fer-*a*-byll |
| And *our* | tor-**mentis** | to **compt** | In-**nu**- | mer-*a*-byll | (300–1)

(where the rhythmically symmetrical words *insufferabyll* and *innumerabyll* require to be given different prosodic patterns). In line 325

| They **se** | bot **hor**- | ra-*byll* | **vi**- | si-*onis* |

(the rhyme words are *Scorpionis* and *derysionis*), only three syllables would be stressed in a natural reading; and to make it a pentameter (even a tetrameter would be awkward enough) places the words under an almost intolerable strain. This line, in fact, is so defective as to suggest a corrupt text, though Hamer mentions no alternative readings in the early editions.

The impression given in this section of the poem is of journeyman's verse: the poet has much to say and says it with vigour, but simply lacks the technique to say it also with poetic elegance. A factor which reinforces this impression is the repetitiveness of the rhymes: in the "Hell" section (163–334) *cummer – nummer* and *deuotion – promotioun* each appear twice, and *cair, dispair, hell, innumerabyll, panefullie, poysonabill, lamentabyll, punysioun* and *allace* are each used twice as rhyme words (the latter twice in the same stanza).

Much worse is to follow, in the catalogue of the nations of the earth, where Lyndsay seems to have given up even the pretence of a regular metrical pattern and produces lines like "The gret Ynde, and Mesopotamia" or "Pole, Hungarie, Boeme, Norica, Rethia". He recovers his touch, however, in the concluding sections of the poem. Deviant lines still appear, but in no greater numbers and rarely with a greater degree of deviation than the overall metrical pattern can readily tolerate: two interesting examples from the passage "Of the Realme of Scotland" are

| *For*-restis | *full* of | *Da*, **Ra**, | *Hartis* and | *Hyndis* | (823)

and

| **Meit**, *drynk*, | **fyre**, *clathis* | **thar** *mycht* | be *gart* | a-*bound* | (832),

where the sequences of pitch-prominent monosyllables fit neatly and with impressive effect into the predictable rhythmic patterns (trochaic in the first case, iambic in the second). A notable degree of regularity is visible at the outset of the "Complaynt of the Comoun Weill", providing it with a suitably dignified introduction: in the first stanza only two lines are "deviant", and only slightly so (921 with a hypermetrical syllable and 924 with an initial trochaic inversion), and several are "perfect". Lyndsay's skill in fitting the familiar cadences of vernacular speech into metrical form is much in evidence here, in lines such as

We saw a boustious berne cum ouir the bent [...] (919)
Allace, quod he, thow seis how it dois stand [...] (939)
I culde nocht knaw ane leill man be ane thief [...] (956)
And said to me: swyith, harlote, hy the hence [...] (971)

The final envoi in nine-line stanzas, too, is fittingly in predominantly regular lines; and the abundant rhymes on polysyllabic Latin-derived words show both greater prosodic dexterity and a more fecund vocabulary than some earlier sections of the poem.

Lyndsay's technique in this long poem is decidedly uneven; but he rarely – except in the geographical catalogue – falls below the level of competence, and often rises well above it. In the *Complaynt of Schir David Lindesay*, his handling of a very different kind of metre shows, perhaps to a greater extent, his talent for fluent and natural-sounding verse.

The tetrameter, as everybody recognises, emerges spontaneously from the basic rhythm of a stress-timed language as the pentameter does not: Lewis (1938: 30), who aptly contrasted the two as "mere nature" and "all art and spirit", remarked that "the *Kalevala* metre [most familiar in English from *Hiawatha*], if not handled with great discretion, pounds in our ear like a heart-beat". Indeed, a poem in tetrameters does not require the flexible iambics of *L'Allegro* and *Il Penseroso*, much less the relentless trochaic pulse of *Hiawatha*, to arouse an immediate empathetic response in the reader. Early Scots (and English) tetrameters do not, as a rule, show any consistently patterned arrangement of stressed and unstressed syllables – i.e. they are not appropriately described as iambic, trochaic, or any term from that set – and are not even consistently octosyllabic; though of course most individual lines *have* eight syllables and many *do* contain exclusively iambic or trochaic feet. In this respect, Barbour's *Bruce*, Wyntoun's *Cronikyl* and the *Legends of the Saints* are prosodically closer to *The Owl and the Nightingale* or *Sir Orfeo* than to, say, *Tam o' Shanter*. Yet the four-beat rhythm is as unmistakeable, and as effective in prompting the reader's physical response, as in the later and more syllabically regular poems. Simplistically, it could almost be said that while it takes a skilled manipulator of language to write in acceptable pentameters, it would take a very unskilled one *not* to write in acceptable tetrameters. To earn its writer a claim to more than basic metrical competence, therefore, a poem in tetrameters must show some degree of refinement beyond the mere fact of four beats per line.

Lyndsay's *Complaynt*, to a first glance, shows workmanlike skill rather than brilliance in its handling of the tetrameter. The rhythm is predominantly iambic and many lines are entirely regular, both "ordinary" –

| To *thame* | that *was* | **full** *far* | to *seik* | [...] (79)
| Off *eild*, | in *his* | a-*stait* | Roy-*all* | [...] (115)
| Im-*pru-* | dent-*lie*, | lyk *wit-*| les *fullis* | [...] (131)
| To *put* | the *ru-*| ther *in* | his **hand** | (146)

and "perfect" –

| I *bure* | thy **grace** | u-*pon* | my *bak* | [...] (88)
| And *als*, | my **hart** | is *woun-*| der *sair* | [...] (124)
| And *ay* | schir *flat-*| tre *bure* | the *pryce* | [...] (184)
| Bot *aye* | the **Prence** | re-*ma-* | nit *pure* | (232)

and "deviant" lines rarely go beyond permissible degrees of deviance: we find inversions in one or more of the feet –

| ***Rownd***-and | and ***rouk-***| and, *ane* | tyll *u*-ther | [...] (185)
| Off *schip*, | *mar*-chand | and *Ma-* | ri-*nall* | [...] (144)

| Be-*cause* | ane ***clips*** | ***fell*** in | the ***mone*** | [...] (120)
| ***Cast***-and | ***gal***-moundis, |with ***bendis*** | and ***beckis*** | (181)

lines with hypermetrical syllables –

| Nor *with* | my ***bre-*** | thir in ***court*** | re-***ward***-it | [...] (20)
| Sum ***gad-*** | der-it ***gold***, | sum ***con-*|* queist ***land*** | (218)

and lines with monosyllabic feet –

| I ***tak*** | the ***Quenis*** | ***grace***, | thy ***mo***-ther | (81)
| To ***Zow***, | my *lordis*, | that ***standis*** | ***by*** | (109).

However, there are clear signs that the metrical variations are not
entirely random. The poem opens cleverly by exactly repeating the
prosodic pattern of the first line in the second, and of the third – a
contrasting one – in the fourth.

Schir, I be-	***seik*** thyne	***Ex***-cel-	*lence*,
Heir my com-	***playnt*** with	***pa***-ci-	*ence*.
My ***do-***	lent ***hart***	dois *me*	con-***strane***
Off ***my***	in-***for-***	tune *to*	com-***plane***	[...]

The use of rhyme words of identical rhythmic structures further
emphasises the determined tone of this opening. The two following
lines are prosodically much less certain:

| ***Quhow***-*beit* | I ***stand*** | in ***gret*** | ***dow***-*tance* |
| ***Quhome*** I | sall ***wyte*** | of *my* | mis-***chance*** | ,

having two feet in line 5 in which the stressed syllable is the one with
the lesser degree of pitch prominence and a rhyme between a weak
and a strong syllable;[3] but this could be seen as appropriate to the
ironically questioning tone which Lyndsay here assumes. The startling
rhyme – not a common trick in Lyndsay – in lines 25–26:

---

[3] I use those as imprecise "catch-all" terms. A disyllabic word with the stress, in normal pronunciation, on the first syllable, can form an iambic foot without being grossly
mispronounced if the *pitch* pattern is retained in spite of the stress shift (for discussion
of several examples see McClure 2005); but a syllable having stress but not prominence is still "weaker" in its impact on the hearer's senses than one with both.

| Als *weill* | as *v-* | ther *men* | hes *got*-tin? |
| Than *wys* | I *to* | be *dede* | and *rot*-tin |

is nicely framed in the middle of a sequence of six regular lines, and also highlighted by the very unusual fact that the grammatical break within the couplet is stronger than that at the end of it. At the first reference to Christ in the poem, the divine name conspicuously forms a monosyllabic foot:

| Off *quhome* | **Christ** | makis *men-* | ti-*oun* | (37)

and is the only syllable in the line requiring pitch-prominence.

Later, two short passages show a notable increase in the proportion of deviant lines. The first is the famous section in which Lyndsay imagines the young king's courtiers trying to outbid each other with the charms of the girls with which they wish to tempt him. Opening with a line

| Quod *ane:* | the **Deuyll** | **stick** *me* | with ane **knyfe** | (237)

with a trisyllabic final foot and an intonational pattern which conflicts with the rhythm, it proceeds through lines with sequences of dactyls (239 and 242) and others with intonational cadences which almost override the mandatory stress patterning (241 and 246). The dialogue here is not only highly entertaining but disconcertingly realistic; but the metrical irregularity could be seen as reflecting the moral degeneracy suggested by the episode. And towards the end of the poem in Lyndsay's setting of the date for repayment of his requested loan from the King, the trick of repeating (except for a couple of details of pitch prominence) the prosodic pattern of two asymmetrical lines:

Quhen the	**Basse** and	the **Yle**	of **Maye**
Beis **sett**	v-*pon*	the **mont**	Se-*naye*;
Quhen the	**low**-mound	be-*side*	**Falk**-*land*
Beis **lyft-**	it *to*	North-**hum-**	ber-*land*	(*Complaynt* 467–70)

by highlighting the lines emphasises the fantastic nature of the events portended.

It is no doubt true that for most of this poem Lyndsay simply lets the natural rhythm of the tetrameter carry the verse along; but on

occasions his manipulation of the patterns of stress and prominence
achieves definite and attractive effects. The impression given is not of
a poet who regards the prosodic structure of his verse as a mere
vehicle for the exposition of his subject-matter, like Hary; still less (it
must be acknowledged) of a superlative technician in whose work
almost every prosodic detail is chosen for its effect, like Dunbar; but
of a skilled craftsman who recognises the aesthetic potential of
prosodic factors and sometimes, when he chooses, exploits it.

In his subsequent works, Lyndsay's technique shows a definite
development: the pentameters of *The Testament of the Papyngo* and
The Deploratioun of the Deith of Quene Magdalene flow more
regularly, with fewer impossibly bad lines and a wider range of effects
gained by adhering to or deviating from the basic pattern, than in the
Dreme. The opening lines of the *Papyngo* capture the hearer's
attention not only by consonance [ndʒ] and alliteration, and by the
unusual word "Salamonicall" (for which the OED's only attestations
are this passage and a line from Buchanan) with its five syllables
precisely fitted into the rhythmic pattern of the line, but by the
symmetrically rising intonational cadences (the successive stressed
syllables in the second, third and fourth feet must receive increasing
degrees of pitch prominence; an effect more conspicuous in the
second line, where *more* is pitch-prominent to some extent, than in the
first, where *had* is not so at all):

| Sup-*pose* | I *had* | In-*gyne* | An-*ge-* | li-*call,* |
| With *sa-* | pience *more* | than *Sa-* | la-*mo-* | ni-*call* | .

The last line of the same stanza, *Transcendith far the dull
Intellygence*, cleverly exploits the segmental patterns (repetitions of
[ɛ], [l] and [n]), as well as the rhythm and intonation, to underline the
imposing polysyllables. The only technical weakness in the stanza is
the rhyming of *memorie* (which in its context must have its normal
stress pattern) with *storie* and *glorie*: this, however, is less obtrusive
than it might have been because of the separation of the first word in
the series from the other two by a couplet adorned with the trisyllabic
rhyme *Heroicall – Rhetoricall*. (It is impossible to be certain whether
short /o/ in Lyndsay's Scots was phonetically [o] or [ɔ]: in modern
Fife dialects its reflex is certainly high-mid rather than low-mid, and
in East Fife has coalesced completely with the reflex of MSc /o:/ as a

phonetic [o]. It is at least possible that the vowels in *Heroicall* and *Rhetoricall* were alike in Lyndsay's pronunciation.) The *Complaynt* proper opens with an almost "perfect" line, *Quho clymmis to hycht, perforce his feit mon faill*. (I call this line *almost* perfect because *to* requires pitch prominence. *To hycht*, assuming this reading to be correct, means "too high", not "to height": the sense of "too" is generally expressed by *ouir* in MSc like *ower* in ModSc, but Lyndsay uses *to* elsewhere (e.g. the opening line of the *Deploratioun*) in this sense; an extraneous *t* following *ch* is of course common in mediaeval calligraphy, and "height" would not normally be used without an article.) The imposing tone imparted to the aphorism by this means, however, is immediately undercut by a line deviant not only prosodically (an inverted foot with a promoted syllable) but syntactically. The undercutting is appropriate: though Lyndsay's message is ultimately serious, there is of course a humorous irony in that the victim of life's uncertainty is a bird (introduced in a quasi-double iambus | *How* one | **fair** *bird* |: the *one*, of course, is simply the familiar MSc indefinite article *ane* with an anglicised spelling, and would not receive any stress or intonational emphasis), and this double moral vision is an enduring feature of the poem. A similar undercutting effect is visible in the "First Epystyll of the Papyngo", which commences with two grandiose lines:

| Pre-*po-* | tent **Prince**, | ***pier***-les | of ***pul-*** | chri-*tude*, |
| **Glore**, *ho-* | nour, ***laude***, | ***try***-umphe | and ***vic***- | to-*rie* |

adorned by alliteration and Latinate vocabulary as well as, in the prosody, a symmetrically placed inversion in each line and a pitch-prominent monosyllable to open the second; and shortly after descends to the limits of lexical and prosodic simplicity in *Amang the reste, schir, sum thyng for to wryte*. This could, of course, be seen as nothing but another instance of the modesty topos; but the extremity of the contrast, added to the fact that the speaker is the parrot and has been introduced as such in the lines introducing this section, surely implies an ironic twist to the import of that all-too-familiar figure.

In the *Deploratioun*, Lyndsay's most sustained exercise in exploiting the dignity of the pentameter, regular lines abound:

Exemple of our Quene, the flour of France [...] (14)
And left his Realme in greit disesperance [...] (48)

And scho lyke prudent Quene Penelope [...] (50)
The potent Prince, hir lustie lufe and knycht [...] (64)
Sic Banketting, sic sound of Instrumentis. (88)

The name *Magdalene* lends itself to incorporation in "perfect" lines
(as the modern *Madeleine* with its short first syllable would not);
particularly if, as is entirely possible, the most salient syllable in
Lyndsay's pronunciation, owing to both French and Gaelic influence,
was not the first but the last (contrast the Highland and the Lowland
pronunciations of names like MacIntyre and MacIntosh). It is in such
a line that the names of the royal couple are mentioned, for the first
(and in James's case the only) time in the poem:

| As *Iames* | the *Fift*, | and *Mag-* | da-*lene* | of *France* | (40)

and its status is highlighted by its appearing after a sequence of three
slightly "deviant" lines (with trochaic inversions). In the penultimate
stanza another "perfect" line containing the name "Magdalene of
France" likewise follows a sequence of lines with a less emphatic
rhythm.

Small but telling details of prosodic variation appear from the
beginning of this poem. The two opening lines show, at the same
point, a demoted syllable (*to* greit [...] *all* earthlie leuyng thingis),
both words being central to the thought expressed. The stressed
syllable in an inversion in the penultimate line of the stanza, *furth*,
portends the alliterative phrase which opens the next line, *The flour of
France*. A minor lapse occurs at the end of the first verse, where the
rhyme of *land* with *Scotland* necessitates a clumsy distortion of the
natural rhythm of *and comfort of Scotland*; but Lyndsay immediately
recovers his touch: resuming the apostrophe to Adam, with its
necessary trochaic inversion, he underlines its force by using this time
a double trochee (which is, impressionistically, much more than twice
as big a departure from the basic pattern as a single one), *Father
Adam*. Another double trochee, the powerful phrase "*Gredie Gorman*"
by which Death is addressed (26), is followed by a third inverted foot
"*quhy did* [...]", bringing this apostrophe to Death to a striking
metrical climax. And though this is not the only possible reading, it
would be both metrically tenable and dramatically effective to take the
first line of the following section

| O **Dame** | **Na**-ture, | **thow** did | no *di-* | li-*gence* | (29)

as having *Nature* pronounced with its normal stress and pitch pattern, and the resulting trochee inviting a following trochaic pronunciation of *thou did*, suggesting a contrastive stress on *thou* to emphasise that Nature, the new addressee, is as culpable as Death. One of the most sustained passages of unfailingly regular lines is the verse describing the procession of musicians (134–40), the emphatic rhythm (rein- forced by pich prominence on most of the stressed syllables) clearly evoking the spectacle of the march. And in the final verse, the emphatic rise and fall required in the intonation pattern of the phrase *in despyte of the* in the penultimate line is repeated in the following *Keip ay twa realmes* with its demotion on *twa*, forming an intonational contrast with the falling melody of *in Piece and Amitie*. Here, as is not always the case, the rhyming of a syllable taking pitch prominence (as *thee* must in the present context) with one which does not is prosodically an asset, making the poem end on a full close of quiet dignity.

And as his technique with the pentameter visibly improved between the *Dreme* and the *Deploratioun*, Lyndsay's competence in fitting the rhythm of spoken Scots into fluent tetrameters remained on a high level. *The Confessioun of Bagsche* and *In Contemptioun of Syde Taillis* are hardly among the poems on which Lyndsay's reputation rests; but the easy, rapid pulse of the metre carries both along in an appropriately jovial manner. The latter poem even shows a few metrically witty touches: one notes that a polysyllabic rhyme *Supplicatioun – Reformatioun* appears in lines 3–4 and – after the swiftly following *It may nocht haue ane ornate style* – never again; the ungainliness of the lines

| Thocht **Bi-** | schoppis *in* | their pon-*ti* | fi-*callis* |
| Haue **men** | for *to* | **beir** *up* | their **taillis** | (17–18)

with the long sequence of non-prominent syllables, including a hypermetrical one, in the first and the quasi-double iambus in the second, and a rhyme which is not only segmentally false [-kalz -tɛːlz] but prosodically weak in being between a non-prominent and a prominent syllable, immediately preceding a pointed reference to the "dignitie" of their office; and the impudent skip of the final anapaest in the reference to the nun raising her side tail

| Bot *for* | to *schaw* | hir *lil-* | lie quhyte *hois* |.

By the time he came to write *Ane Satyre of the Thrie Estaitis*, therefore, Lyndsay was a practised poet, experienced in writing in various styles and various metres, in exploiting – when he chose – prosodic effects to illustrate or embroider the import of his words, and above all in harnessing the natural rhythms of the Scots tongue. And while it would be absurd to deny that for much, indeed most, of the play his verse technique shows steady competence rather than sustained brilliance, many passages provide clear instances of deliberately contrived prosodic effects. Divine Correctioun's first speech (1572–620) shows the touch of a versifier of more than common skill.

Thir ar	the *words*	*of* the	re-*dout-*	it *Roy*
The *Prince*	of *peace*	a-*bufe*	all *Kingis*	*King*.
Quhilk *hes*	me *sent*	all *cun-*	tries *to*	con-*voye*,
And *all*	mis-*do-*	ars *dour-*	lie to *doun*	*thring*.	(1573–76)

It opens, after the introductory Latin phrase, with a line in which the semantic and prosodic lightness of the first three feet throws the final alliterative phrase into strong relief, and which is immediately followed by a contrasting line where the final monosyllabic foot and sequence of pitch-prominent sylables give a solemn and grandiose effect. The "ordinary" line which follows shows an interesting cadence with the rising pitch-prominence on the syllables in the second and third feet; and the double iambus in line 4 (in association with the reverse rhyme) suggests a decisive finality in *dourlie to doun thring*. Later, a line with a hypermetrical syllable *Till thay be punisched by mee, Correctioun* (1604) pre-echoes the repeated *pum-pa-pa-pum* pattern of the following line, the famous *Quhat is ane King? nocht bot ane officiar*; which shortly afterwards is repeated, as if to ensure that the maxim is not forgotten, at the opening of three successive lines (1613–15).

An obvious difficulty presents itself in discussing the prosody of *Ane Satyre*, namely the existence of two very different early texts. As has often been observed (e.g. McClure 1986; Lyall 1989) the Quarto version is metrically much more regular than that of the Bannatyne MS, in the sense that many lines which are prosodically defective in the MS are regular in the printed edition. (The converse is also true, but not to anything like the same extent.) On the other hand, as Lyall

(1989) has rightly claimed, there is no question of assuming that the Quarto text is in every respect the better one; and a clear illustration of this is the fact that its editor has on some occasions mistaken Lyndsay's metrical intentions and erroneously "regularised" passages by forcing them into a pattern different from that in which they were written. A good example is 489:

| *Kiss* hir and | *clap* her and | *be* nocht af- | *feird* | (B);
| To *kis* | her and *clap* | hir *sir* | be *not* | af-*feard* | (Q)

The Q reading is a perfectly acceptable iambic pentameter line, "deviant" in only one respect (a hypermetrical syllable), like hundreds that appear in the play; the B, taken out of context, would be read as a sequence of dactyls, a very rare metrical formation. Yet a few dactyllic lines *do* occur, as will shortly be shown, and are specifically associated with Sensualitie and the Courtiers; and it is entirely possible that this is one. Further evidence in support of the B reading is that in the same text the following line is a perfect fourteener, but in Q the transposition of the words *hir kiss* to *kis hir* makes for an awkward break in the rhythm. Several further examples can be found in the first part of the Puir Man interlude. The lines in this section of the play are metrically very inconsistent; and this, as will be discussed presently, serves a straightforward dramatic purpose. The Quarto editor, however, has in a few cases (only a few, certainly), altered a line in an evident attempt to make an iambic pentameter out of what was never intended as one.

With-*owt* Ze cum *sone* and *chace* this cairle a-*way*,

a straightforward four-beat line, is altered by the omission of *sone* in the Q text, giving a good "ordinary" iambic pentameter line:

| With-*out* | ze *cum* | and *chace* | this *Carle* | a-*way* | (1936)

(This is a nice illustration of the fact that the number of stresses in a line cannot be predicted from the number of syllables: the line is changed from a tetrameter to a pentameter by *removing* a syllable. The problem in this context is that it would be read with the pattern established by the preceding lines, which is that of a four-beat and not a five-beat rhythm.) In another example, the Q reading differs more radically from the B, but again reads more like an iambic pentameter, this time a slightly "deviant" one:

Quhair *dwellis* thow, *dy*-vour, or *quhat* is thyn en-*tent*?;
| Quhair **deuill** | is *this* | thou **dwels** | or **quhats** | thy in-**tent**? | (1961)

In these and the few other cases, however, the Q editor's regularisation of the metre is almost certainly an error, since the passage is not in iambic pentameters. A modern editor or commentator, therefore, may not assume that either text is correct in any particular reading without examining the entire passage in both versions. In the discussion of the play which follows, I will not devote time and space to justifying my choice between readings. My general principle is to select the more metrically convincing: not (of course) merely on the evidence of single lines, but of lines in the context of the entire passages in which they appear.

The erratic metre in this scene is dramatically a clever stroke, since Lyndsay is suggesting the fiction that the Puir Man is not a character in the play at all but a member of the public who has accidentally wandered into the acting area, and that Diligence is addressing him not as Diligence but as the man playing the part. For this, a prosodic pattern approaching the irregular and unstructured rhythm of common speech is obviously appropriate. The dominant pattern is of a four-beat line with no specified number of syllables or arrangement of stressed and unstressed syllables (interestingly enough, this same line form is later associated with John the Common Weil):

Off Zour *al*-mous, gude *folkis*, for *goddis* luve of *he*-vin;
Ffor I haif *mo*-derles *bairnis* owthir *sex* or *se*-vin.
Gif Ze will *gif* na *gude* for *luive* of sweit *Ie*-sus,
Wiss me the *richt way* to sanct-*an*-drus. (1926–29)

In those lines, only the syllables which I have italicised would be stressed if the lines were read in a manner suggesting a spontaneous, not consciously "dramatic" utterance: that is, a four-beat pattern is the most natural option. Shortly, however, lines begin to appear where the retention of this pattern grows increasingly difficult, either because the words which seem to call for special emphasis exceed four (in my notation of these two lines, the italics indicate only syllables that *could* be stressed: a reading in which they *all* were stressed would sound excessively portentous in the context):

Swyth, furth of the *feild,* thow *fals, rag*-git *loun* (1931);
Ffals hur-sone, *rag*-git *carle,* quhat *is* that thow *ruggis?* (1938)[4]

or because of long strings of unstressed syllables that require an awkwardly rapid declamation:

Quhae *devill* maid Zow a *gen*-tillman wald *nocht* stow Zour *luggis* (1939);
Quhat *now* me think this *cull*-roun *cairle* begynnis to *crak.* (1940)

And soon lines with internal rhymes appear but, unexpectedly, distributed in a random fashion, and not all suggesting the same rhythmic pattern.

Swyth, kerle, a-*way*; or *be* this *day* (^) *I* sall *brek* thy *bak* (1940)

suggests a fourteener; and a still better example is the line printed in Q as *I sall sit heir into this tcheir till I haue tumde the stoup.* (The B version omits *heir*, losing the internal rhyme and the prosodic symmetry with the preceding line, and thus making this a case where the Q reading is the more likely to be correct.) By contrast,

Cum *doun*, or be godis *croun*, theif *loun*, I sall *slay* the (1941)

is a perfectly straightforward four-beat line, and

Sa *sone* thay *leir* to *ban*, to *sweir*, and *trip* on thir *taiss* (1945)

and

Be *sanct* fil-*lane* thow *salt* be *slane*, bot *gife* thow ask *grace* (1947)

suggest, if anything definite, *six*-beat lines. In this context, the one regular – indeed, "perfect" – iambic pentameter line seems almost grotesquely out of place:

---

[4] The *it* silently inserted in this line by Hamer is not in the MS, though it is a reasonable emendation.

| The *diuill* | a *word* | Ze *get* | of *sport* | or *play* | (1937)

(In Q, it is *The Deuill a word ze'is get mair of our play*, which would be a "deviant" iambic pentameter line, but still unique in this passage.) The wildly unstable prosody of this scene is clearly conceived as fitting the pretended breakdown of the dramatic structure, and as appropriate to the knockabout slapstick style in which the scene would be acted. And fittingly, when the mood changes from farce to bitter social criticism with the Puir Man's recital of his injuries, the metre becomes much more regular. Starting with four-beat lines of the type used by the character on his first appearance:

Gude *man*, will Ze *gife* me *of* Zour *chir*-retie,
And *I* sal de-*clair* to Zow the *blak ve*-ritie […]

it modulates, in a most interesting progression, through a series of lines which could be scanned either as lines of this type or as iambic pentameters (albeit in some cases slightly "deviant" ones):

My *fa*-der was an *awld man* and ane *hair*
And was of *aige four*-scoir *Zeiris* and *mair* […]

| My *fa*- | der *was* | an *awld* | *man* and | ane *hair* |
| And *was* | of *aige* | *four*- | scoir *Zeiris* | and *mair* |

– and finally resolves into a sequence of unambiguous and notably regular iambic pentameters:

| My *fa*- | der *was* | sa *waik* | of *bluide* | and *bane* |
| He *dyit*, | quhair-*foir* | my *mo*- | der *maid* | **grit mane** | […]

The impression given by Lyndsay's prosodic developments in this sequence is surely that of first coming back down to earth after the high jinks of the preceding exchange, and then of moving from sobriety to tragedy with the Puir Man's recital of his accumulating misfortunes. It is observable that though the iambic pentameter pattern is resumed for the later comic scene between the Puir Man and the Pardoner, the speeches contain far more "deviant" lines than in the present sequence.

Lyndsay's use of metrical modulations to suggest changes in tone or mood, or developments of the plot, is an instantly recognisable part of his dramatic technique (cf. Bernard 1939: 76–77). In the opening scenes of the play, as briefly discussed by Lyall (1989: xxxii–iv), the trick is applied with a remarkable degree of skill. The first speech of Diligence is couched in alliterative four-beat lines, leading into a two-foot "bob" and a "wheel" of four-beat lines but with a much lower syllable-count. This gives the whole speech a verse structure familiar from non-dramatic poetry, decidedly old-fashioned by Lyndsay's time but providing an imposing and dignified opening to the play. The metrically self-contained nature of this section, and the use of a verse form which never recurs in the play (though four-beat lines *without* the alliteration are of course used in later passages) mark off this opening benediction and call for attention as something separate from the play proper: *Ffor now I begin* is the *last* line of the section; and it is in the next speech, in pentameter lines with alternate rhymes, that Diligence introduces himself and initiates the action of the drama.

Somewhat unexpectedly, Diligence shortly lapses from the pentameter, which Lyndsay generally associates with order and dignity, into the tetrameter quatrains, rhyming *aaab cccb*, soon to be associated with the Courtiers (30–45): the threat of hanging directed to misdoers *in the audience*, and the oath *be him that Iudas sawld*, likewise suggest a more earthy and sardonic tone. The appropriateness of this inheres in the reference to the *trompouris* and *paramouris* – the collocation is emphasised by the rhyme and the ironic association with *flouris* [i.e. early manhood]. Immediately afterwards the formal pentameter is resumed for three eight-line stanzas; and then finally, as if doffing his hat, Diligence steps out of character and out of his dignified lines with a cheerful invitation to the audience to enjoy the play.

The King's speech, which follows, invokes the Deity in an iambic pentameter line "perfect" except for the monosyllabic final foot (78–101): a detail which imparts a slower pace and weightier feel to the phrase *King of Kingis all*. The lines in these three stanzas are predominantly regular: only the short doctrinal passage

| ***Vn***-maid | ***mak***-ar, | quhilk, *hav*- | and ***no*** | **ma**-*teir* |
| Maid ***hevin*** | and ***erth***, | **fyre**, ***air***, | and ***wat***- | ter ***cleir*** |

stands out conspicuously with its opening double trochee and demoted monosyllable in the second line. Perhaps ominously, however, this sequence ends on a metrically ambiguous line *To thy plesour, and to my grit confort*, in which the natural trochaic rhythm of the two key words and the necessity for a contrastive stress on *my* make the line, on any reading, a highly "deviant" iambic pentameter if it can be read as one at all.

The sudden shift into jaunty *rime couée* now signals the change in moral atmosphere with the entry of the Courtiers; and this metre, handled with consistent skill and embodying a notably convincing evocation of colloquial speech, holds the stage for a long time. The King contributes one line, fitting into the metre and rhyme scheme, to the dialogue: *My servand sollace, quhat gart Zow tary?*; but he resumes his pentameter lines, appropriately, when resisting the Courtiers' temptations. The bob-and-wheel with which this speech ends has a sinister significance which it lacked in Diligence's opening proclamation (identical in rhyme pattern and arrangement of long and short lines, though not in actual metre): by this time the aaa^4b^3 pattern has come to be firmly associated with the Courtiers, so that the King's resumption of it signals clearly his entry into their moral world. (Incidentally, Bernard (1939) and Lyall (1989) are mistaken in taking this passage, in which (for once) the B and Q texts are virtually identical except for spelling variations, to be in the same metre as the opening speech of the play. Not only is alliteration absent except for the stock phrase *the prince of parradyiss* and the wholly accidental *Fforswyth, my friend*, but the lines are without exception in perfectly clear iambic pentameters, varied in two cases only by an opening trochaic inversion.) After a speech by Placebo in the same metre, Wantonness unexpectedly assumes pentameters to continue his temptation of the King; but it is observable that whereas Placebo has simply assured him that they have no intention of leading him astray, Wantonness is trying the cleverer and more insidious trick of *arguing* a case for sensual living; and the more formal metre is a guise for his monstrous attempt to impart intellectual respectability to his position. When Solace at the end of his next speech drops the *aaab* rhyme scheme and produces a stanza of ballad meter, the more swiftly changing rhyme pattern suggests the increasing urgency of the Courtiers' moral siege, and the rapid crumbling of the King's resistance:

Schir, knew Ze all the matar thrwch
    To play Ze wald begyn.
Speir at the monkis of balmirrinoch
    Gife lichery be syn. (*Ane Satyre*, 259–62)

Later the same trick is repeated, a similar stanza being linked by an unexpected rhyme to a quatrain in the trimeter lines by then associated with Sensualitie's handmaidens:

Gif it be trew, that Ze me tell,
    I will na langar tary.
I will gang preif that play my sell,
    Howbeid the warld me wary.
Als fast as Ze may cary
    Speid Zow with diligence,
Bring sensualitie
    Fra hand to my presence. (361–68)

The rapid tumble of short lines and tangled rhymes conveys the King's erotic passion to fine comic effect.

The scene with Dame Sensualitie presents some typical examples of editorial puzzles. In her first line, Q's *Luiffers awalk* is more effective, in the context, than B's *O luvaris walk*: the latter would make the line iambic throughout, but the short first syllable of *luvaris* would weaken the auditory effect of the opening. On the other hand, in her last stanza, B's *in ane morrowing* and *with sory hairt* are metrically preferable to Q's *in ane morning* and *with ane sair hart*. Later (435), B has *Ane kiss of Zow into ane morrowing* and Q *Ane kis of zour sweit mow in ane morning*, where the first reading is clearly the better metrically but the second, equally clearly, the more expressive. The task of deciding which text is nearer to what Lyndsay actually wrote is truly daunting. If the Q reading is accepted, Sensualitie opens her speech dramatically with a splendid iambic pentameter line, wielding increased rhetorical force from the opening trochaic inversion and otherwise "perfect". It is surely not an accident, however, that the metre stumbles badly in the next line, another instance of a natural four-beat line forced into a pentameter format by juggling with stress and prominence:

| Be-*hald* | the *na*- | tu-rall *doch*- | ter *of* | Ve-*nus* | (*Ane Satyre*, 272)

The rest of Sensualitie's speech, particularly the second stanza, contains predominantly regular lines; but the impression of an undignified slip puncturing the graceful effect of the opening line is never entirely dispelled. This trick too, of breaking up the relatively smooth flow of Sensualitie's verse, is reprised later: Wantonness's first address to her is in a couplet which, for the first time in the play, requires to be read as a dactyllic tetrameter (with one defective foot):

| *Pas*-tyme with | *ple*-sour and | *grit* pro- | *spe*-ri-tie |
| *Be* to Zow, | *so*-ve-rane | *Sen*-su- | *a*-li-tie |; (*Ane Satyre*, 417–18)

and her reply at first suggests a continuation of the same metre; and though it immediately resolves itself into a pentameter line ending in iambics:

| *Sirs*, Ze are | *wyl*-cum; | **quhair go** | Ze, *eist* | or *west*? | (419)

and her next few speeches are in fairly regular iambic pentameters, her final couplet in this section switches from an "ordinary" iambic pentameter, suggesting a courteous reply, to a skipping dactyllic line which highlights with comic emphasis the force of the words:

| Scho *sal-* | be *at* | com-***mand***, | schir, *quhen* | Ze **will**. |
I | ***trest*** scho sall | ***fynd*** Zow | ***flyng***-ing Zour | ***fill***. | (449–50)

Wantonness's triumphant speech which follows – *Now hay for ioy and mirth I dance* – is metrically impeccable: Lyndsay always handles the *rime couée* with dexterity, but in this passage the iambic feet follow in sequence with scarcely a syllable out of place (in the Q text at least, which in this section is by far the more regular) – until his joyful lowping is interrupted by a sudden breakdown of the iambic sequence:

| A-***lace*** | I haue ***wreis-*** | tit my ***schank*** | ! (469)

And throughout the play, of which clearly time and space do not permit anything like a full examination, similar cases occur of Lyndsay's manipulating the prosody of his lines for effects of varying degrees of subtlety.

A high level of technical skill is necessarily an attribute of any dramatic poet who can sustain a wide variety of contrasting meters, some with intricate and testing rhyme schemes, throughout a long play; and Lyndsay's success in this has never been in question. This is not the limit of his achievement, however: he sometimes, even if not consistently, varies his metres not only to indicate the status and function of the various characters but also to serve as counters in the moral debates which he presents; and his prosodic dexterity extends to exploiting the metre of individual lines for poetic effects of various kinds. J.E. Bernard in his examination of the play comments "Refinement is exquisite in the application of metres if not in the details of their construction". On many occasions Lyndsay's skill in prosodic detail reaches a level which, if not precisely *exquisite*, is at least far higher than has often been recognised.

Bibliography

Aitken, A.J. 1977. "How to Pronounce Older Scots" in Aitken, McDiarmid and
    Thomson (eds) *Bards and* Makars Glasgow: Glasgow University Press. 1–21.
Bernard, J.E. [1939] 1969. *The Prosody of the Tudor Interlude* [Yale Studies in
    English 90]. New Haven Conn and London: Yale University Press.
Black, G.F. (ed.) 1932. *The Seuin Saeges, by John Rolland* [Scottish Text Society 3rd
    Series no. 3.]. Edinburgh: Scottish Text Society.
Hamer, D. (ed.) 1931–36. *The Works of Sir David Lyndsay of the Mount 1490–1555*
    [Scottish Text Society 3rd Series no. 1, 2, 6, 8.]. 4 vols. Edinburgh and London:
    William Blackwood and Sons.
Jespersen, O. 1933. "Notes on Metre" in *Linguistica: Selected Papers in English,
    French and German*. Copenhagen and London: Levin & Munksgaard. 249–74.
Lewis, C.S. 1938. "The Fifteenth-Century Heroic Line" in *Essays and Studies* 24: 28–
    41.
Lyall, R.J. (ed.) 1989. *Ane Satyre of the Thrie Estaitis*. Edinburgh: Canongate.
McClure, J. Derrick. 1986. "A comparison of the Bannatyne MS and Quarto texts of
    Lyndsay's *Ane Satyre of the Thrie Estaitis*" in Strauss, D., and H. Drescher
    (eds) *Proceedings of the Fourth International Conference on Scottish Language
    and Literature, Mediaeval and Renaissance: Germersheim 1984*. Frankfurt:
    Peter Lang. 409–22.
—. 2001. "Dunbar's Metrical Technique" in Mapstone, Sally (ed.) *William Dunbar,
    'The Nobill Poyet': Essays in honour of Priscilla Bawcutt*. East Linton:
    Tuckwell Press. 150–66.
—. 2005. "Blind Hary's Metrics" in Mapstone, Sally (ed.) *Older Scots Literature*.
    Edinburgh: John Donald. 147–64.
MacDonald, A.A. 1996. "William Stewart and the Court Poetry of the Reign of James
    V" in Hadley Williams, J. (ed.) *Stewart Style 1513–1542: Essays on the Court
    of James V*. East Linton: Tuckwell Press. 179–200.
Wittig, K. 1958. *The Scottish Tradition in Literature*. Edinburgh: Oliver and Boyd.

"With Mirth My Corps 3e Sal Convoy": *Squyer Meldrum* and the Work of Mourning

R. James Goldstein

This essay applies Freudian and Lacanian theories of mourning and desire to *The Historie of Squyer Meldrum* and *The Testament of the Nobill and Vail3eand Squyer William Meldrum of the Bynnis*. Such a reading offers a new view of mourning as a consistent theme of Lyndsay's work.
Keywords: Judith Butler; Chivalry; desire; Sigmund Freud; homosociality; James V; Jacques Lacan; Sir David Lyndsay; mourning; *The Historie of Squyer Meldrum*; love; melancholy; mourning; romance; *The Testament of the Nobill and Vail3eand Squyer William Meldrum of the Bynnis*

The following essay explores two closely related poems by Sir David Lyndsay of the Mount, *The Historie of Squyer Meldrum* – a chivalric romance celebrating the life of William Meldrum of Cleish and the Bynnis, a Fife laird who died in 1550 – and its companion piece, *The Testament of the Nobill and Vail3eand Squyer William Meldrum of the Bynnis*. In his often humorous commemoration of his dead friend, Lyndsay was engaged in what Sigmund Freud describes as "the work of mourning", the reparative process in the psyche by which the grieving subject comes to accept the loss of a loved one by gradually withdrawing libidinal attachments to the lost object (Freud 1953–1974: 14: 237–58). Much was at stake in Lyndsay's work of mourning: *Squyer Meldrum* is preoccupied by proper definitions of gender and the regulation of sexual desire. Indeed, Lyndsay's affectionate portrayal of his friend's chivalric career, as we shall see, devotes considerable effort to establishing the heteronormative nature of Meldrum's sexual desire, and to distinguishing his love of women from the love he shared with men. *Squyer Meldrum*, like Lyndsay's other major writings, can therefore be read as a contribution to the early-modern construction of heteronormative desire (Goldstein 1997: 349–65).

Before turning directly to *Squyre Meldrum*, however, we would do well to reflect briefly on how much of Lyndsay's writing is devoted to the themes of loss and reparation (references to Lyndsay's poetry are to Hamer ed. 1931–36, with line numbers given parenthetically). His earliest surviving poetry represents a nostalgic attempt to restore some equilibrium after the factional intrigues that took place during James V's minority. Both *The Complaynt* and *The Dreme* reflect Lyndsay's personal and professional disappointments during his exile from court, and have been recently described as written with a sense of "personal bitterness" (Edington 1994: 75). *The Complaynt and Testament of the Papyngo*, notwithstanding the extravagance of its mock-serious tone, addresses the depredations of history and the poet's anxieties in attempting to redress traumatic loss. Lyndsay explores his vocation through the story of a "woundit Papingo" (63), an obvious figure for the poet, as in John Skelton's *Speke, Parrot*. Lyndsay concludes with a ritual dismemberment of the bird's corpse and an envoy warning the poem not to challenge the authority of true poets. Lyndsay's early fascination with the dismembered corpse of the papyngo takes a grim turn in his account of the ill treatment of Cardinal Beaton's corpse in the *Tragedie* (260–73). The most direct poem of mourning, however, is *The Deploratioun of the Deith of Quene Magdalene*, a highly ceremonious poem in which Lyndsay adopts a public voice of communal grief over the premature death of James V's first queen, who died before she could be triumphantly received by her loving subjects. The poem achieves much of its rhetorical power through its repeated descriptions of what "suld haue been" before death turned the expected joy into sadness. The detailed recollections include a description of the tournament and royal entry that Lyndsay himself was to orchestrate as Lyon King of Arms, the chief heraldic officer of the kingdom. The finely wrought marmoreal stanzas seek to preserve, in the very act of recording it, the memory of the queen who was prematurely lost.

But grief over the queen whom Scotland never came to love was no more than a dress rehearsal for the mourning precipitated by the sudden death of James V himself in 1542, a loss so devastating to the poet that he never fully abandoned his attachment or relinquished his grief (Edington 1994: 56). For the second time in Lyndsay's adult life Scotland was without an adult male monarch, and with Queen Mary but an infant, the prospects were indeed bleak for years to come. Moreover, Lyndsay had also to endure more personal losses. It has been suggested that the death of his wife and younger brother may have closely followed that of the king and that these losses may be connected to the "intensified [...] world-weariness" and "gloomy introspection" of his late works (Edington 1994: 57). Lyndsay's brush with death in a shipwreck in 1549 may have invited the reflections on mortality that surface in his "morbid speculation upon death and its meaning" in *The Monarche* (Edington 1994: 65), his final work, which was written only a few years after *Squyer Meldrum*. *The Monarche* certainly provides rich materials for a study of Lyndsay's poetics of melancholia. The prologue clearly identifies its lost object with the king (10; cf. 17–18), and the narrator describes himself as suffering from "malancolye" (127). Despite the religious consolations the poem later offers, Lyndsay seems unusually haunted by death. "Gretlye it doith perturbe my mynde, / Off dolent Deith the diuers kynd", he observes later in the poem, before unfolding a series of horrid descriptions of the varieties of death through disease, war, judicial violence, murder, accident (5094–5172).

The preceding survey reminds us that a great deal of Lyndsay's work centres on the experience of loss and mourning, and at several stages of his career the poet adopts what we might call a rhetoric of melancholia. It is within this context that we now turn to *Squyer Meldrum* and the work of mourning.

Although there have been too few studies of *Squyer Meldrum* in recent years for us to speak of a critical orthodoxy, the two most rewarding discussions of the poem in the last twenty-five years share some fundamental understandings that are likely to influence future studies of the poem. According to Felicity Riddy, Lyndsay adopted a genre that he "could no longer quite take seriously" because the chivalric ideals implied by that traditional literary form were no longer suited (if they ever were) to the actual conditions of life by the 1550s: "Lyndsay contrives to distance the Squyer from the tradition in which he places him, so that the poem is more than an exercise in nostalgia and Meldrum's life becomes not simply an expression of chivalry in action but a commentary on it as well". The reader is meant to recognise "the simplifications of that poetry for what they are" and to understand "that romance is an imperfect paradigm of life" (Riddy 1974: 26, 29). The dominant mode of the poem, in other words, is self-conscious, distancing, and ironic. Edington agrees with this interpretation: "By emphasising the unbridgeable gap between real life and literature, Lyndsay forcefully suggests that the knightly ideals of love and adventure have no viable place within the context of a real society" (Edington 1994:124).

Although this interpretation calls attention to an important aspect of the poem, the romance is in fact less consistent in its desire to distance itself from chivalric ideology than either of these scholars wishes to acknowledge. It is worth stressing that in calling the poem "more than an exercise in nostalgia", Riddy implies that it is at least *some* form of nostalgia. What I wish to suggest, then, is that Lyndsay's work registers a powerful tension or ambivalence, a double perspective that indicates he was simultaneously *attached* to the traditional chivalric values embodied by his friend and *self-reproachful* for maintaining attachments to values he understood to be moribund. Indeed, in "Mourning and Melancholia", Freud argues that grief is not restricted to the loss of a person but may also be experienced at "the loss of some abstraction which has taken the place of one". Moreover, he notes the tendency in excessive grieving (melancholia) of the critical faculty of the ego to turn against itself in self-reproach (Freud 1953–74: 14: 243, 249). Insofar as Lyndsay is willing to pronounce the old chivalric ideals dead, his ironic distancing suggests an unconscious sense of guilt, a kind of self-directed aggression whose source is located in the superego. Indeed, a psychoanalytic understanding of the subject must call into question the absolute distinction between "real life" and "literature" that Riddy and Edington assume. The following analysis of *Squyer Meldrum* proceeds from the assumption that the poem's surface contradictions are symptoms of the problematic relation of the authorial subject to his desire.

The trajectory of Meldrum's life-story follows the arc of multiple sublimations. In psychoanalytic thought, the term "sublimation" names the process by which the subject obtains satisfaction of the drives by diverting their aim, rather than by seeking a new object (Laplanche and Pontalis 1973: 431–44). This concept is well illustrated in the pattern the Squire's life, with his repeated delay, brief satisfaction, then final turn from the pursuit of heteronormative sexuality. As Freud argues in *Civilisation and Its Discontents*, sublimation is always directed toward a socially useful or valorised aim. Indeed, the Squire spends the first half of the poem diverting the aim of sexual desire in the aggressive pursuit of a socially valorised chivalric honor. After his affair with the Lady of Gleneagles, he spends the rest of his life in acts of self-renunciation useful to the local community, engaged in feudal service to his lord and works of charity to the poor.

But even heterosexual desire poses risks, as Lyndsay's prologue reminds us by referring to the traumatic histories of Troilus and Cressida and Jason and Medea, whose stories remind us of the inter-twined fate of eros and death. Meldrum's life, we are told, deserves to be recorded for posterity because he suffered as much "for his Ladeis sake" (47) as did many other heroes celebrated in poetry. The pro-logue places his sexuality within a strict regulatory matrix: unlike Lancelot, who loved another man's wife, Meldrum was not an adul-terer: "His Ladie luifit him and no mo. / Husband nor Lemman had scho none" (58–59). After Lyndsay establishes Meldrum's noble lineage and legitimates his right to inherit (65–75), we are again told that he "stude for Lufe in monie stour" (76). If the prologue seems somewhat nervous in reassuring us that the Squire's honour in battle has something to do with a fully achieved heterosexuality, we must wait patiently to find out what it might mean to "stand for love" in such a context.

In the first episode, the promise of a lived heterosexuality is only partially fulfilled. In recounting Meldrum's action in the Scottish navy ostensibly fighting the English, the narrative makes little attempt to explain what, politically, is at stake in the destructive Scottish raid on Carrickfergus in Ireland. Against the background of saving all the women and priests he can, Meldrum discovers a fully naked woman under attack by two men. When they refuse his demand to restore her possessions, a fight ensues. He defends himself "manfullie" (145) and slays them both, whereupon the lady recovers her clothing and makes a lucrative offer of marriage. But he refuses to make the desire of this other his own desire because his honour dictates that he must go to France, and that desire takes precedence.

As the narrative continues to unfold, the degree to which he sub-limates his desire seems to correspond to the quantity of chivalric honour he achieves in compensation. The narrator observes:

Because he was sa courageous,
Ladies of him wes amorous.
He was ane Mun 3eoun for ane Dame;
Meik in Chalmer, lyk ane lame:
Bot, in the Field, ane Campioun,
Rampand lyke ane wyld Lyoun. (231–36)

The ladies are not the only ones drawn to him: "because he was weill pruifit, / With euerie man he was weill luifit" (243–44). An under-current of homosocial desire runs throughout the narrative of a highly competitive chivalric masculinity (see Sedgwick 1985).

In the next episode, the Squire answers the challenge of Master Talbart to anyone who will fight "for his Ladies saik" (276), which the Squire will soon equate with the achievement of "honour" (484–88). When the Englishman condescendingly addresses him as "my gude Chyld", and "my barne" (297, 307) and the Squire compares himself to David battling "manfullie" (312) against Goliath, it is not difficult to read the episode as a contest for the possession of the phallic sig-nifier (Lacan 1977). Meldrum courteously declines the spoils of victory: "For I haue gottin that I wald haue" (564) – that is, he has upheld his personal honour and that of his nation. Once again, this episode suggests that Lyndsay continues to take seriously the values of chivalric romance, however idealised or imaginary: courage, martial prowess, honour, and above all, normative definitions of masculinity so naturalised as to seem nearly invisible, but upon which those chivalric virtues are grounded.

After his next increase in honour, when he "sa manfullie" (677) rescues the Scottish lodgers under attack by a band of "Sutheroun" (678), he remains in France "for his plesour, / Weill estemit in greit honour" (681–82), continuing to perform manly deeds. The sublima-tion involved in seeking his satisfaction in honour is underscored when again his hyper-masculinity marks out an erotic position that he continues to refuse: "Quhen Ladies knew his hie courage, / He was desyrit in Mariage / Be ane Ladie of greit Rent" (685–87). But his youth, we are told, made him "insolent" (688), and his desire is to return to Scotland. No sooner than he becomes an object of mourning for the French ladies (691) we are also told that his departure grieves (694) his companions at arms, "For he was luifit with all wichtis, / Quhilk had him sene defend his richtis" (695–96).

In stressing the repeated citation of the ladies' sexual desire in the immediate context of the "love" directed toward the Squire by his brothers-at-arms, I do not mean to suggest that the poet could have drawn a connection between this form of love between men and sexual desire. Indeed, his habit of juxtaposing the two kinds of affective bond is surely evidence that he has foreclosed the possibility of such a thought from occurring to him. Yet it is also worth recalling that Lyndsay's policing of desire in the near-contemporaneous text of *The Monarche* quite clearly suggests that "the problem with sodomy [...] is that anyone, at any time, may be seduced by its pleasures" (Goldstein 1997: 363).

When the Squire finally returns to Scotland, his reputation precedes him and thus as he travels throughout the land, his male hosts "bankettit him fra hand to hand, / With greit solace" (854–55). It is thus in the context of sharing oral pleasures with men that Squire reaches the "lustie Ladie" whose husband, we are told, has recently died (863–65). And thus we reach the pivotal turning point in the poem, where after so many refusals the Squire is finally ready to tell his own story. That is, for the Squire, embracing the position of a heteronormative subject of desire is inseparable from establishing his proper position in the symbolic order of the signifier. When the Squire's "plesant dulce talking" (868) of his adventures attracts the Lady of Gleneagles to him, Lyndsay compares the situation to Dido's reaction to Aeneas's story (875–81). Like Dido, the lady is a grieving widow; unlike Aeneas, however, the Squire has never before answered the call of sexual desire; he has always got his kicks elsewhere, in the company of men.

In this unforgettable scene of seduction, the pleasures of the bed are closely linked with the pleasures of the table. The Squire retires to his private quarters to enjoy the sumptuous feast that has been prepared for him; the lady goes to his chamber "to heir mair of his narratioun" (889). They engage in some symbolic foreplay (the usual games of chess and backgammon). She says goodnight. Left alone, he feels for the first time in his life the "Ioy" and pain left by Cupid's "fyrie dart" (898, 901). Unable to sleep, he engages in a soliloquy about the misfortunes of unrequited love (911–16). But of course he is wrong: the lady overhears the lover's complaint through the wall and determines that he shall have her love so long as she can preserve her "honour" (925).

This need to preserve her honour: there could be no clearer sign that her desire and its prohibition work in conjunction, that desire is subject to the law, or as Lacan explains in Seminar VII, *The Ethics of Psychoanalysis*, the "law is closely tied to the very structure of desire" (Lacan 1992: 76). As Lacan frequently reminds us, Freud's insight into the Oedipus myth was that the incest prohibition is the primordial Law of culture upon which all other laws are founded. In the symbolic

order maintained by the Name-of-the-Father, law and desire are cor-
relatives insofar as the law produces or sets in motion the very desire
it prohibits. What is desired and what is prohibited, in other words, are
the same thing.

The consummation scene in *Squyer Meldrum*, structured on an
oscillation between an opening and a concealment, surely deserves to
be remembered as one of the most remarkable in the history of courtly
romance. On a morning in May the Lady gets up early dressed in
"Kirtill alone, withouttin Clok" (933) and quietly slips into his bedroom, pretending that she needs to retrieve a box from a chest. She
makes a silent spectacle of opening the locks with her keys. But "that
was not hir erand thair" (939), the narrator winks; nor is her true aim
lost upon the Squire. The reader shares the perspective of the "lustie
ȝoung Squyar" (940) who gazes at her standing:

In Kyrtill of fyne Damais broun,
Hir goldin traissis hingand doun.
Hir Pappis wer hard, round, and quhyte,
Quhome to behald wes greit delyte.
Lyke the quhyte lyllie wes hir lyre;
Hir hair was like the reid gold wyre;
Hir schankis quhyte withouttin hois,
Quhairat the Squyer did rejois. (943–50)

The description teasingly both displays and defers desire by figuring
her bodily presence (the firmness of the round breasts, the bare legs
uncovered by hose), and at the same time figuring it in terms of what
it is not (white flower, golden wire). She (and the text) seem to signify
her availability directly by indirection.

But that is enough for the Squire to take the initiative, which he
translates for himself in terms of his military experience, when he
commands himself to make a "sailȝe" upon his lady (952). The
"Courlyke Kirtill was vnlaist, / And sone into his armis hir braist"
(953–54). The unlaced kirtle serves as both a lure and an opening for
his assault, though the syntax leaves the agency ambiguous – she is
braist (embraced) in his arms. Yet the lover appears to be no less
unlaced than the lady, and he calls for her help, "sum remeid" or else
"I am bot deid" (957–58). And so, "he hint hir in his armes, / And
talkit with hir on the flure" before quietly barring the door (960–62;
my emphasis).

Neither the stealthy silence nor the barred door of the bedroom, however, proves sufficient to allow the subject a space of freedom to pursue his *jouissance* or enjoyment without having to pay a certain price. The Lady questions the Squire about his intentions: "quhat is 3our will? / Think 3e my womanheid to spill? / Na, God forbid, it wer greit syn; / My Lord and 3e wes neir of Kyn" (963–96). And thus the law, in its classic formulation as the prohibition against incest, both produces desire and institutes itself as the barrier to full enjoyment. With the Lady's demand that the Squire must obtain a dispensation before he can possess her, the law reveals itself to be capricious and arbitrary. The canon law places them within the forbidden degree because of his relation to her dead *husband*. The lesson of psycho-analysis, as Lacan provocatively concludes, is this:

Sublimate as much as you like; you have to pay for it with something. And this something is called *jouissance* [...] That good which is sacrificed for desire – and you will note that that means the same thing as that desire which is lost for the good – that pound of flesh is precisely the thing that religion undertakes to recuperate. (Lacan 1992: 322)

Meldrum declares it a "greit vexatioun" (981) to wait for a religious dispensation, that is, to postpone his *jouissance* to satisfy the demands of the law, and thus he acts: "in his armis he did hir thrist" (983). The scene, in other words, comes dangerously close to por-traying a rape. But we are not allowed to linger on the implications of the force with which he thrusts her into his arms; instead, the descrip-tion of their lovemaking is calculated to deflect any suggestion that he takes her against her will by offering a series of figures that emphasise both the reciprocal nature of their desire and the naturalness and inevitability of their response:

And aither vther sweitlie kist,
And wame for wame they vther braissit;
With that, hir Kirtill wes vnlaissit.
Than Cupido, with his fyrie dartis,
Inflammit sa thir Luiferis hartis,
Thay mich na maner of way disseuer,
Nor ane micht not part fra ane vther. (984–90)

Notice how the unlacing of the kirtle is again repeated here: if previ-ously the unlaced kirtle was a figure for the lure of desire, here it

serves proleptically as a figure for the sexual act, as does the following simile: "like wodbind, thay wer baith wrappit" (991). Yet after
describing how the Squire lifts her into bed "tenderlie" and "full
softlie" (992–93), the narrator directly addresses the reader in a way
that guiltily reintroduces the question of rape while simultaneously
negating it: "Iudge ȝe gif he hir schankis shed" (994). The Lady, however, doesn't share the narrator's certainty about the status of the act
in progress: "Allace (quod scho) quhat may this mene?" (995), and
with that she covers her eyes with her hair. Again the Lady
simultaneously figures an opening and a concealing, and again the
narrator intrudes to reassure us:

I can not tell how thay did play;
Bot I beleue scho said not nay.
He pleisit hir sa, as I hard sane,
That he was welcum ay agane.
Scho rais, and tenderlie him kist,
And on his hand ane Ring scho thrist. (997–1002)

Significantly, Lyndsay situates *jouissance* on the other side of the signifier, beyond what he translates into discourse.

The odd little quirks and inconsistencies in this narrative – what
Riddy has identified as the episode's "incongruous perspectives"
(Riddy 1974: 33) – perfectly illustrate Lacan's notion of courtly love
as an anamorphosis of "the Thing". To make sense of this claim, it is
necessary to review Lacan's argument in *The Ethics of Psycho-
analysis*. For Lacan "the Thing" (*das Ding*) is a retrospectively constructed precondition of the desiring subject's coming into being.
Serving as a kind of compass in relation to the subject's desire, the
"Thing" locates "points of reference in relation to the world of wishes
and expectations" (1992: 52). The "Thing" marks an aboriginal ex-
terior or Other around which the subject is constituted and functions
as the subject's "central place", as an "intimate exteriority or
'extimacy'" (1992: 139). It is thus "something strange to me, although
it is at the heart of me" (1992: 71). This notion of a strange Other
residing in the subject's very core of being implies that the "Thing" is
foreign, even hostile and thus dooms all of the subject's searches to
failure. In other words, the "Thing" is not only responsible for the
subject's faith that the "object will be there when in the end all

conditions have been fulfilled", it also guarantees that they never will be, that

[...] what is supposed to be found cannot be found again. It is in its nature that the object as such is lost. It will never be found again. Something is there while one waits for something better, or worse, but which one wants. [...] One doesn't find it, but only its pleasurable associations. (1992: 52)

Thus the pleasure principle provides the impetus to the search for the lost object that has never really been lost, and the subject maintains the search "at a certain distance from that which it gravitates around" (1992: 58), seeking "something that is always a certain distance from the Thing, even if it is regulated by the Thing, which is there in a beyond" (1992: 63). And so, "The question of *das Ding* is [...] attached to whatever is open, lacking, or gaping at the center of our desire" (1992: 84).

If my quotations and paraphrases have demonstrated that the Thing is very difficult to talk about, that is precisely Lacan's point, because the Thing is "the beyond-of-the-signified" (1992: 54). This description therefore locates the Thing within the register of the "real" rather than within the symbolic order. In that sense, as Louise Fradenburg explains: "The 'Thing' is that real site of the non-origin of the signifier, constructed retrospectively by the signifier and often fantasised as having been there 'before' the signifier" (Fradenburg 1998: 252 n. 12). Since the Thing lies beyond the signified, it can never be directly apprehended and must always present itself, Lacan suggests, "as a veiled entity" around which our desire hovers (1992: 118). He alludes to the retrospective fashioning of the lost object when he declares that "the Thing is that which in the real [...] suffers from the signifier" (1992: 118, 125). This formulation implies that as the subject's unconscious desire flits metonymically along the signifying chain, each signifier marks the Thing as "the emptiness at the center of the real" so that "the fashioning of the signifier and the introduction of a gap or a hole in the real is identical" (1992: 121). And so the Thing "will always be represented by emptiness" (1992: 129). All approximations of the Thing involve sublimation, which Lacan translates as that which "raises an object [...] to the dignity of the Thing" (1992: 112). For Lacan, the poetry of courtly love is a paradigmatic example of sublimation, which "tends to locate in the place of the Thing certain discontents of the culture" by representing the Lady as inaccessible, distant, even cruel. Emptied of all specific content, therefore, this "feminine object" seems "terrifying" and "inhuman" insofar as she is imagined to possess an absolute authority whose dictates are "as arbitrary as possible" (1992: 150). The figure of the courtly lady is merely a stand-in for the Thing, which presents itself in the unconscious "as that which already makes the law", a law that is "capricious and arbitrary", a "law of signs in which the subject receives no guarantee from anywhere" (1992: 73; cf. Lacan 1998, Kay 1999, Žižek 1994).

In its sublimation of the drive, the discourse of courtly love takes on the structure of an *anamorphosis*. Lacan's famous example of anamorphosis in a painting that happens to be exactly contemporary with Lyndsay is the blurry figure disguising death's head at the bottom of the canvas in Holbein's *The Ambassadors*, which hangs in the National Gallery in London. (In the oral version of this paper I mislocated the painting to Washington, D.C., as Priscilla Bawcutt graciously reminded me. In recapitulating Lacan's error in which he initially placed the painting in the Louvre, my slip uncannily demonstrates his point that owing to the subject's constitution in the symbolic order of language, "the sender [...] receives from the receiver his own message in reverse form", thus guaranteeing that "a letter always arrives at its destination" (Lacan 1972: 72)). In anamorphosis, the Thing can only be apprehended indirectly in the ordinary field of vision; when viewed directly it takes on the appearance of an intrusive stain that seems to have no significance, that seems out of place. When Lacan claims that courtly love is an anamorphosis of the sublimating structure of desire, therefore, he means that it represents, but only obliquely, the fundamental desire – incest. And as we have already seen, what is desired is also that which is prohibited. Lacan explains the moral accounting of "the tight bond between desire and the Law" thus: "Every act of *jouissance* gives rise to something that is inscribed in the Book of debts of the Law" (1992: 176–77). The Law and desire, in other words, are mutually implicated: "Transgression in the direction of *jouissance* only takes place if it is supported by the oppositional principle, by the forms of the Law" (1992: 177).

We are finally ready to return to the fantasy of courtly love in *Squyer Meldrum*, which leaves a blurry residue or remainder through the simultaneous adoption of those "incongruous perspectives" that

Riddy first detected in the consummation scene. The text, in short, represents the Squire pursuing his *jouissance* at precisely the moment the courtly lady reminds him that to do so is to transgress the law, which prohibits them from marrying without dispensation from the church. Yet curiously, it was precisely the transgressive element of the Squire's desire that the prologue took such pains to deny, when Lyndsay insisted that their desire was lawful, unlike that of the famous adulterers of romance, since "His Ladie luifit him and no mo. / Husband nor Lemman had scho none". The Lady's alibi to her maidens re-enacts the same unconscious negation. When they ask where she has been, why she is half undressed, and above all, why she is *sweating* so profusely, her explanation is similar to Freud's joke about the borrowed kettle, which illustrates how the unconscious negates contradictions. When the owner asks the borrower why he returned the kettle damaged, the latter gives three excellent reasons why he is innocent: first, he returned it undamaged; second, it had a hole in it when he borrowed it; and third, because he never borrowed the kettle in the first place (Freud 1953–1974 4: 120). In Lyndsay's case, the lady gives two contradictory reasons why she appears half unclothed and moist: because she "sufferit heit" (which is nicely ambiguous) and because the dew soaked her limbs (1022–26). Thus the sublimating figure of the courtly lady reassembles itself before our eyes into the image of post-coital flush in a moment that may well be unique in the history of courtly literature. In other words, it is impossible to sustain in the same field of vision the image of the ethereal lady of courtly love and a sweaty, sexually satisfied woman.

Having finally taken up his position as a subject of hetero-normative sexuality, Meldrum and his Lady enjoy "Luiferis Chalmer glew" (1040) – glee of the lovers' chamber – in secrecy. This period of satisfaction will be retrospectively identified (and mourned) as the Squire's lost object. Meldrum and the Lady have a daughter, and they console each other as they wait for the dispensation that never comes (1176–78). But here the poem shifts toward tragedy; jealousy and envy lead "ane cruell Knicht" (1191) to ambush Meldrum, which would force the Lady to marry someone else. Yet in retelling what appears to have been (to judge from the fragmentary documentary records) a complex story of her family insisting on a marriage that she opposed, the poem's account of the knight's motivations make little sense and seems highly arbitrary (1195–97; see Lyndsay 3: 221–25; cf. Riddy 1974: 34).

The ambush episode stages what Louise Fradenburg in another context describes as "sacrificial desire", or those "practices of renunciation which seek to recuperate loss by making us choose it" (Fradenburg 1997: 51). Sacrifice is the specific mode of enjoyment that entices us by effectively promising that whatever we voluntarily give up will be amply rewarded eventually. How else might we explain why, when the Lady sensibly advises Meldrum to run away, the only options he sees before him are to defend himself against impossible odds or to die trying? In the Squire's heroic effort against the unchivalric knight, Meldrum advances "his honour" (1321) as much as any of the literary heroes listed by the narrator, who quickly adds: "The quhilk I offer me to preif, / Gif that 3e pleis, Sirs, with 3our leif" (1323–24). In turning combative himself, Lyndsay betrays his imaginary identification with the Squire. Because the enjoyment of sacrificial desire seems so crucially at stake in this episode, it is difficult to believe that he ever fully abandoned his attachment to chivalric ideals or that he is content to let "the facts" of real life "challenge the whole heroic illusion" (Riddy 1974: 34). Rather, his disenchanted ironies are a symptom of his resistance to completing the work of mourning for his lost ideals, since to pronounce dead that which he once loved would be in effect to share the guilt of having killed it.

The assailants inflict "cruell mortall woundis" (1354) and leave him for dead. As the Lady praises her fallen hero, this scene of mourning provides Lyndsay with an occasion to date the event precisely: "Our King was bot fyue 3eiris of age, / That time quhen done wes the outrage" (1389–90). The treacherous knight is never punished, we eventually learn, because the king was so young that "tyrannis rang, into thair rage" (1494). Writing about ten years after the death of James V, it is clear, Lyndsay has yet to abandon his mourning. Yet even though the text has fully prepared the reader for the Squire's death, he recovers with the help of some skilled physicians. What is most remarkable in the abrupt translation of a scene of sacrifice into a mock resurrection is how the poet misses an obvious opportunity to relate the miraculous recovery to a supernatural agency, whether to God or to any big Other that would guarantee that the symbolic order of the law is grounded in an absolute authority, that every sacrifice or renunciation will ultimately be repaid, indeed, that every act of charity will be redeemed.

In the final movement of the poem, the Squire applies the art of medicine to works of charity by healing the poor at his own expense: "Of Money he tuik na regaird" (1454). As deputy sheriff of Fife, he is a refuge to the poor. His self-renunciation obeys the same logic of sacrifice as his chivalric exploits; "charity", as Fradenburg insists, "is not opposed to concupiscence but is itself a passional mode of enjoyment" (Fradenburg 1997: 51). The poem handles the question of guilt by insisting the Lady married "aganis hir will" (1465). Although her "bodie wes absent, / Hir tender hart wes ay present" (1467–68). Now retired from martial activities, he preserves his "honour" (1556) by hosting annual feasts (which the poet tells us he has personally attended): "All this he did for his Ladie, / And, for hir saik, during his lyfe, / Wald neuer be weddit to ane wyfe" (1570–72). In his final sublimation, the aged squire tells "ancient storyis" (1575); his guests partake of his narratives with his food. Meldrum thus becomes a figure for the poet, who inherits the position once occupied by the Squire. But the poet cannot look directly on "dolent deith", which is personified as the figure who arrives at his friend's door and "cruellie, with his mortall dart" strikes "throw the hart" (1584–86); with this conventional figure of mortality, Death's dart replaces Cupid's. When the Squire's soul passes to heaven, the poet leaves the fate of his body untold, promising "3e sall get na mair of me" (1594).

But we do, in fact, get more. In writing *The Testament of Squyer Meldrum* Lyndsay brings his dead friend to life by translating his own voice into that of the Squire. How might we read the work of mourning in this poem, whose main figure hovers eerily between life and death, and who orders an elaborate funeral with a cast of thousands to be arranged by Lyndsay himself? Drawing on the suggestive work of Nicolas Abraham and Maria Torok on fantasies of "encryption", we may interpret Lyndsay's trope of allowing Meldrum to speak through him as a fantasy of keeping his dead friend sealed up inside, of becoming the "carrier of a crypt" through a refusal to mourn that erects "a secret tomb" inside his ego (Abraham and Torok 1994: 131, 130). Henceforth the term "encrypted voice" will signal the borderline status of this fictional voice that speaks through death from inside the poet.

The encrypted voice declares that honour will be the basis of his immortal fame and requests his friends to attend his funeral: "Ʒe knaw how that my fame I haue defendit, / During my life, vnto this latter hour, / Quhilk suld to ʒow be infinit plesour" (47–49). The voice imagines the corpse's disembowelling in preparation for burial and orders an the elaborate marble tomb (50–63). *The Historie* itself – what the voice calls "the legend of my life" (72) – acts as a container for his "honour & renoun" (70). His fame and honor depend on the power of eloquence, figured as the Squire's "toung Rhetoricall" (78), as much as on his martial deeds: "My ornate toung my honour did auance" (84). It is difficult to read these lines without recognising the poet's melancholy identification with his friend, an impression only strengthened when we recall, as we have just learned from *The Historie*, that the Squire was his own original narrator: telling his chivalric history helped win the Lady of Gleneagle's love, and its repeated retelling at the end of his life allowed the local community, including the poet, to love him, that is, symbolically to incorporate him with the food he provided at the annual feast.

The close imaginary proximity of the Squire to the poet is further signalled when the encrypted voice assigns "My freind Sir Dauid Lyndsay of the Mont" responsibility to "put in ordour my Processioun" (92). The undead voice demands that joy predominate at his funeral, which must be a festive occasion with musicians gathered around the bier, dancing and singing "with mirthis Musicall", sending their "plesant sound" skyward (143, 145). The encrypted voice ex-plains: "My spreit [...] salbe with mirth & Ioy; / Quhairfoir, with mirth my corps ʒe shal conuoy" (146–47). The overly exuberant in-sistence on banishing grief, however, suggests that the psychic work of mourning remains incomplete.

Lyndsay's melancholic identification with his friend surfaces again as the Squire orders an "Oratour" to read "Solempnitlie, with ornate eloquence, / At greit laser, the legend of my life; / How I haue stand in monie stalwart strife" (164–68). The periodic syntax attempts to enact this same leisure, to defer the end, and thus masks the grief-stricken desire to keep the lost object alive inside, if only through lan-guage. But all narratives, like the lives they contain, must eventually end. When the orator "hes red my buik fra end till end, / And of my life maid trew narratioun, / All creature, I wait, will me commend, / And pray to God for my saluatioun" (169–72). In Lyndsay's fantasy of a desacralised world of a funeral rite from which all clergy but the priests of Venus have been banished (151–52), the secular legend of the life promises both fame and eternal salvation to the ideal subject of chivalry; the same logic reappears in his epitaph (200–3).

But the final movement of *The Testament*, the Squire's elaborate leave taking from his loved ones, reinstates the grief that the representation of his funeral too insistently foreclosed. The encrypted voice predicts that Lord Lyndsay and his clan "will rew" (210) his departure, and that when "the fair Ladies of France" hear of his death, "Extreme dolour wil change thair countenance" (211–13). Even the ladies of England will "mak dule and drerie cheir" (217) when they learn the news. He expresses deep regret for allowing his "ȝouth and insolence" (224) to prevent him from marrying the lady he saved from dishonour in Ireland. In bidding adieu to the Lady of Gleneagles, he imagines her reading his "legend", where she will note "How, for hir saik, I sufferit mekill sorrow" (234). Abraham and Torok speak of "the crypt of the blameless and guiltless object who left the subject after the idyll for a good reason or [...] in spite of himself" (Abraham and Torok 1994: 154). The poem finally closes the circuits of heterosexual desire when the Squire reserves his final leave-taking for his brothers in arms with whom he hopes to be reunited in heaven. After bidding his brothers adieu, the Squire calls for extreme unction (245), and in a final stanza of prayer commends his spirit into the Lord's hands. Yet Lyndsay cannot bring himself to kill the object of mourning; instead, he encrypts it when the "FINIS" of the printed poem leaves the voice forever frozen in the moment before death.

Although writing about his dead friend in a humorous vein no doubt offered some measure of solace for Lyndsay, there is no reason to think that the work of mourning was completed when he finished the poem. Indeed, Freud eventually became convinced that the work of mourning is never entirely completed, the libidinal attachments never fully withdrawn. When he returns to the subject of mourning in *The Ego and the Id*, Freud suggests that the ego is made up of unresolved grief for a series of objects that were once loved and lost (Freud 1953–74: 19: 29; cf. Butler 1997: 133). More recently, Judith Butler has extended this account by suggesting that the individual's assumption of a gendered subjectivity always involves melancholy, the condition of interminable grief. Heterosexuality, Butler claims, is a "tenuous" accomplishment that enforces the subject's "abandonment of homosexual attachments or, perhaps more trenchantly, *preempt*[s] the possibility of homosexual attachment". In the exclusionary matrix of normative heterosexuality, homosexuality becomes literally unthinkable as the domain of "ungrievable loss" (Butler 1997: 135). In other words,

heterosexual identity is purchased through a melancholic incorporation of the love it disavows: the man who insists upon the coherence of his heterosexuality will claim that he never loved another man, and hence never lost another man. (Butler 1997: 139)

And so we may close these incomplete explorations of what is at stake in the work of mourning in *Squyer Meldrum* with this final suggestion: only by unlacing the intricacies of Lyndsay's passionate attachments might we begin to understand how severe a price must have been exacted in his heteronormative sublimations of the desire of the Other.

Bibliography

Abraham, Nicolas and Maria Torok. 1994. *The Shell and the Kernel: Renewals of Psychoanalysis* (ed. and tr. Nicholas T. Rand). Chicago and London: University of Chicago Press.

Butler, Judith. 1997. *The Psychic Life of Power: Theories in Subjection.* Stanford: Stanford University Press.

Edington, Carol. 1994. *Court and Culture in Renaissance Scotland: Sir David Lindsay of the Mount (1486–1555).* Amherst: University of Massachusetts Press.

Fradenburg, Louise O. 1997. "Sacrificial Desire in Chaucer's *Knight's Tale*" in *Journal of Medieval and Early Modern Studies* 27: 47–75.

—. 1998. "Analytical Survey 2: We are Not Alone: Psychoanalytic Medievalism" in Scase, Wendy, Rita Copeland and David Lawton (eds) *New Medieval Literatures 2.* Oxford and New York: Oxford University Press. 249–76.

Freud, Sigmund. 1953–1974. *The Standard Edition of the Complete Psychological Works of Sigmund Freud* (ed. James Strachey et al.). 24 vols. London: Hogarth Press.

Goldstein, R. James. 1997. "Normative Heterosexuality in History and Theory: The Case of Sir David Lindsay of the Mount" in Cohen, Jeffrey Jerome and Bonnie Wheeler (eds) *Becoming Male in the Middle Ages.* New York and London: Garland. 349–65.

Hamer, D. (ed.) 1931–36. *The Works of Sir David Lindsay of the Mount, 1490–1555* [Scottish Text Society 3rd Series no. 1, 2, 6, 8.]. 4 vols. Edinburgh and London: William Blackwood and Sons.

Kay, Sarah. 1999. "Desire and Subjectivity" in Gaunt, Simon and Sarah Kay (eds) *The Troubadours: An Introduction.* Cambridge: Cambridge University Press. 212–27.

Lacan, Jacques. 1972. "Seminar on 'The Purloined Letter'" (tr. Jeffrey Mehlman) in *Yale French Studies* 48: 39–72.

—. [1966] 1977. "The Signification of the Phallus" in *Écrits: A Selection* (tr. Alan Sheridan). New York and London: W. W. Norton. 281–91.

—. [1986] 1992. *The Seminar of Jacques Lacan: Book VII: The Ethics of Psychoanalysis, 1959–60* (ed. Jacques-Alain Miller, tr. Dennis Porter). New York and London: W. W. Norton.

—. [1975] 1998. *The Seminar of Jacques Lacan: Book XX: Encore: On Feminine Sexuality: The Limits of Love and Knowledge, 1972–73* (ed. Jacques-Alain Miller, tr. Bruce Fink). New York and London: W.W. Norton.

Laplanche, Jean and J.B. Pontalis. [1967] 1973. *The Language of Psycho-analysis* (tr. Donald Nicholson-Smith). New York and London: W.W. Norton.

Riddy, Felicity. 1974. "*Squyer Meldrum* and the Romance of Chivalry" in *Yearbook of English Studies* 4: 26–36.

Sedgwick, Eve Kosofsky. 1985. *Between Men: English Literature and Male Homosocial Desire.* New York: Columbia University Press.

Žižek, Slavoj. 1994. "Courtly Love, or, Woman as Thing" in *Metastases of Enjoyment: Six Essays on Woman and Causality.* London and New York: Verso. 89–112.

The Scottish Sonnet, James VI, and John Stewart of Baldynneis

Katherine McClune

This essay investigates the sonnet form in later sixteenth-century Scottish poetry, with particular emphasis on the sonnets of John Stewart of Baldynneis. The Scottish sonneteers' varied and innovative use of the sonnet form is analysed, incorporating an analysis of the influence of James VI's *Reulis and Cautelis* upon Scottish usage
Keywords: *Amatoria*; Gavin Douglas; *Eneados*; Robert Henryson; James VI; Alexander Montgomerie; *Moral Fabillis*; *Reulis and Cautelis*; sonnets; Scottish sonnet form; Spenserian sonnet form; John Stewart of Baldynneis.

"Only in Scotland before 1603 does love cease to dominate [the sonnet form]" (Jack 1985: 79). Jack's brave assertion identifies a particular feature of Scottish sonneteering – in contemporary Europe, the sonnet was particularly identified with the exposition of love. While love "is not the only occupation of the sonnet", the form is the "commemorator of love [...] [Petrarch's love sonnet] was the glass of fashion and the mould of form for European sonneteers from the Renaissance to the nineteenth century" (Spiller 1992: 1). As used by its most distinguished European exponents, Dante and Petrarch, it was immersed in passion and desire, while the French poets who most influenced the Scots were predisposed also to use the type to examine matters of love.

English sonneteers followed their European influences. *Tottel's Miscellany* shows marked preoccupation with love, with sonnets including "Complaint of the louer disdained", and "Vow to loue faithfully howsoeuer he be rewarded" (Rollins ed. 1928: 1: 9, 11). The first major published sonnet sequence in English, Thomas Watson's *Hekatompathia* (1582) is subtitled "Passionate Centurie of Loue", while John Soowthern's much-maligned *Pandora* sequence (1584) is directed to an audience "that [is] lyke vs amourous" (Klein ed. 1984). The Scots propensity virtually to reject love as a defining topic is thus aberrant within the general European tradition. Lyall's argument that Older Scots texts are inevitably influenced by their participation "in a literary system which is a mechanism both of stability and of change", and by the "sociopolitical environment" (Lyall 1992: 40) within which they are produced, is of significance here. These poems must be viewed both within their context in Scottish literary tradition, and – sociopolitically – in terms of their response to James's *Reulis and Cautelis*, a poetic instruction manual with a double-edged resonance, addressed to reader-poets and authored by a poet-king.

The peculiarly (though not uniquely) Scottish preoccupation with the relationship between authorship, readership, and right judgement is exemplified in a chronologically broad spectrum of work, from James I's *Kingis Quair* to Montgomerie's *The Cherrie and the Slae*. The symbiotic relationship between the ability to "read" or "interpret" accurately – whether reading a literary text or reading oneself – and moral acuity is an important literary conceit, illustrated in the polysemous title of Stewart's poem: "Thir verse disschyphre rycht as I tham bind, / Or than 3e sall no perfyt sentence find" (Crockett ed. 1913: 158. All further references to Stewart's poetry are taken from this edition) where Stewart's usage highlights the shift in meaning of "sentence" from a "rational human observation" to a "grammatical unity making a complete utterance". Spiller suggests that this development is linked to the shifting notion of what eloquence involved, which led to the lessening popularity of the sonnet form. (Spiller 1998: 105). For Scots poets, literature was more than entertainment; it was a moral activity, requiring keen interpretation on the reader's part.

For instance, Robert Henryson's concern with reader perception is evident throughout his work. The *Fables* contain the famous analogy between the hidden educative qualities of the "fen3eit fabill" and "The nuttis schell [which], thocht it be hard and teuch, / Haldis the kirnell, sueit and delectabill" (Fox ed. 1981: 3). In *The Testament of Cresseid*, textual authority is undermined by an unreliable narrator, determined to "excuse" Criseyde, and reliant upon the sensual, epitomised in the revelation that he is Venus's servant (Fox ed. 1981: 111–12). The correspondingly incomplete nature of his "*moralitas*", amounting to a simplistic warning against "fals deceptioun" in love (Fox ed. 1981: 131), obliges the reader to appraise both the "story", and the narrator's ethical judgement thereof. Though the discrete *moralitates* of the *Fables* and *Orpheus* imply more secure interpretative ground, they are often surprisingly inconclusive, requiring the reader to make an evaluation that potentially challenges the authority of the provided moral readings. Twenty-five years later, Gavin Douglas developed this in his *Eneados*, endeavouring to avoid the problems related to the pagan text by framing Virgil's narrative with prologues, or pre-emptive *moralitates*, simultaneously Christianising the books that follow, and colouring the reader's perception of them (Coldwell ed. 1957–64). The amelioration of Virgil's pagan ethical scheme culminate in the addition of the "fift quheill" (Prol.13.118), Mapheus Vegius's thirteenth book of the *Aeneid*, where Aeneas' vulnerability to the amatory (represented by Dido) is neutralised by the containment of passionate forces within marriage (to Lavinia). The extraneous book is the decisive *moralitas*, the final comment upon Virgil's moral input (which consistently troubles the narrator/translator figure). Throughout, via his prologues, Douglas attempts to locate a reading whereby a Christian audience can extract the moral "kirnell"; Mapheus provides this Christianised "schell".

Craigie argues that this literary heritage is not an issue as regards James VI's work, because he "deliberately cut himself off from the older poets, not only of England, but even more of his own country [...] nothing that he wrote is in any way derived from them" (Craigie ed. 1955: 1: xiii. See also Fleming 2002: 125–26). The copy of the *Fables of Æsope in English* in James's library has been identified by Warner as probably "the edition printed by H. Wykes, London, [1570?]", (Warner 1893: lxii) yet James could easily have accessed Henryson's *Fables* and his other poetry. The influential Charteris (1570) and Bassandyne (1571) prints of the fables were circulating; the *Testament* was printed after *Troilus* in Thynne's 1532 edition of Chaucer, and the 1593 Charteris edition was almost certainly based upon an earlier print (Fox ed. 1981: xciv–xcv). The *Eneados'* popularity is testified to by the existence of five manuscripts, and the printed Copland edition of 1553 (potentially indebted to an earlier Scottish version, possibly printed by John Scot).[1] It is unlikely that James VI was unaware of, or deliberately unresponsive to, native literary traditions, since he was clearly familiar with the association between reading and moral examination. Viewed within this ethical framework, his instructions in the *Reulis and Cautelis* regarding the correct usage of the sonnet form take on substantive import.

A form throughout Europe and associated with extreme passion is defined by King James as specifically literary-critical, best used for "compendious praysing of any bukes, or the authoris thairof, or ony

---

[1] These are the Cambridge MS (Trinity College, Cambridge), Elphinstone and Ruthven MSS (both held at Edinburgh University), Lambeth MS (Lambeth Palace), Bath MS (owned by the Marquess of Bath). See Coldwell ed. 1957–64: 1: 101.

argumentis of vther historeis, quhair sindrie sentences and change of purposis are requyrit" (Craigie ed. 1955: 1: 81). He is unique among contemporary authors of poetic treatises in so curtailing the subject matter for particular poetic forms. His *Reulis* mention du Bellay, alongside unnamed "sindrie vtheris" (Craigie ed. 1955: 1: 68), probably including Ronsard and Gascoigne (Craigie ed. 1955: 1: xxxvi–xliv). Du Bellay states "sonne-moy ces beaux sonnets, non moins docte que plaisante invention italienne, conforme de nom à l'ode, et different d'elle seulement, pource que le sonnet a certains vers reiglez et limites [...]" (Humbert ed. 1930: 86); Gascoigne "call[s] those Sonets whiche are of fouretene lynes, every line conteyning tenne syllables" (Cunliffe ed. 1907: 1: 471). Ronsard, Ascham (whose work James possessed), and Thomas Lodge do not mention sonnets (See Laumonier ed. 1949: 14: 3–38; Ryan ed. 1967; Laing ed. 1853). Only James associates the form with textual commentary.

It was a challenge to the received perception of the sonnet as the most suitable vehicle for love verse that simultaneously identified a problem that troubled past poets. The *Reulis* advise the love-poet to use "wilfull reasonis, proceeding rather from passioun, nor reason" (Craigie ed. 1955: 1: 76), that is, base the poem in "passioun". Aspiring poets are counselled to "say, that zour wittis are sa small [...] zour vtterance so barren, that ze can not discryue any part of [the beloved] worthelie" (Craigie ed. 1955: 1: 78). The corollary is that a poem based in passion inevitably results in a poetic utterance of inadequacy – of inarticulacy. James's harnessing of the sonnet, characteristically grounded in extreme passion, and its transformation into a form concerned with notions of readership and authorship is patently an independent development, responsive to the Scottish fixation with reading as a metaphor for moral judgement. The sonnet becomes a suitably ironic vehicle for disseminating questions regarding notions of literary creativity – for the Scots, inevitably bound up with issues of ethical judgement.

James's own poetic meditations are driven by such tension between form and subject matter; the early sonnets in the *Essayes* are more than poetic clichés requesting the divine gift of inspiration. Each is a literary test, examining the reader's interpretative, or moral, strength. Repeatedly, James wishes for dissolution of boundaries between reality and fiction, that the readers' sensual appreciation of the work will be manipulated until they are divested of critical faculties.

They will *"esteme"* Apollo's cart "in their *sight"* (Sonnet 2.4), *"sie* the showris" (Sonnet 3.5) and "think they *fele* the burning heat" (Sonnet 4.4) of summer [my emphasis] (Craigie ed. 1955–58 :1: 9–10; all further references will be made to this edition). This is initially problematic; in desiring the victory of the senses over rational interpretation, James seemingly subverts his poetic predecessors, and their concern with measured judgement. But James develops the familiar topos of the sensually-dependent interpretation by professing desire for a reader subject to the very impulses which so concerned his precursors. In manipulating the concern of earlier poets, James alerts readers to his intention of controlling their response, forcing them into a heightened state of interpretative awareness, and ensuring that the dangers of flawed interpretation will be observed. The final sonnet's evocation of Virgil (implicitly, Douglas) is surely significant, with its promise to the (pagan) gods that "I shall your names eternall euer sing / [...] / I lofty *Virgill* shall to life restoir" (Sonnet 12.10: Craigie ed. 1955: 1: 14).

Like his forerunners, James re-examines excess passion's potential to bestialise man by compromising his power of reason. The subtle interrogation of this danger is refined by using the sonnet, the "love form", to analyse theories of accurate interpretation. He expands upon the issue in his introduction to the *Vranie*, where the address to the reader works on a dual level, recalling Douglas' implicitly instructive prologues. In contrast to the sonnets' archetype of incomplete interpretation, this introduction depicts the perfect reader – James himself, careful and analytical. "Hauing oft reuolued, and red ouer [...] the booke and Poems" of du Bartas, he is "moued by the oft reading & perusing" of them "with a restles and lofty desire, to preas to attaine to the like vertue" (Craigie ed. 1955: 1: 16). "Desire" is sub-dued, channelled into a Christian aim of achieving virtue. Action, however ineffectual, based on such an impulse is infinitely preferable to "vtter dispaire and sleuth" (Craigie ed. 1955: 1: 16). The vocabulary resonates with Christian overtones, citing despair, an offence against God's efficacy, and sloth, a deadly sin, as precarious alternatives to action. The potential for further good from his translation is indicated – some better man may "bee moued to translate it well, and best, where I haue bothe euill, and worse broyled it" (Craigie ed. 1955: 1: 15–16). Literary self-awareness extends to the realisation that readers will reinterpret the text according to their own ethical system, hence James's repeated instructions that they do so intelligently. His determination is reiterated by the inclusion of the French original, necessitating further effort from the reader, who, in comparing two versions, becomes a surrogate editor. It is included

> noght thereby to giue proofe of my iust translating, but by the contrair, to let appeare more plainly to the foresaid reader, wherin *I haue erred*, to the effect, that with lesse difficulty he may *escape those snares* wherin *I haue fallen* [my emphasis]. (Craigie ed. 1955: 1: 17)

James's language is significant – reading is concurrently a moral test, which he has apparently failed, and a hazardous journey, fraught with danger. Other excuses are made for the "innumerable and intolerable faultes" which challenge "my owne treatise" (the *Reulis*) concluding with the hope that the reader will "accept my intention and trauellis in good parte" (Craigie ed. 1955: 1: 17), leading to a paradox in James's polarised depictions of the reading process. Implicitly, the sonnets require an inadequate reader, who contrasts with James's self-portrayal as reader, applying his experience to virtuous activity. The ultimate reader must work to distinguish between exemplar and anti-type. Any apparent abrogation of authorial power in favour of a controlling editor-reader is thus ambivalent, assuming in the first place an audience which will follow the order to read carefully. Such ambiguity is heightened by the "Sonnet of the Authour" (Craigie ed. 1955: 1: 94) which instructs the reader not to be seduced by the author's words, but instead to judge them from an abstract perspective of pure reason, uninfluenced by sensual desire: "loaue my meaning and my panis, / [rather] Then lak my dull ingyne and blunted branis" (lines 13–14).

What might be construed as exceptional is an aspect of the projection of James's poetic concerns, through which he investigates the potential for opposing interpretations. Vital to this is his awareness of poetry as self-conscious literary artefact, seen in the acrostic preface to "The Phoenix" where the first and last letters of each line of the poem spells out ESME STEWART DWIKE (Craigie ed. 1955: 1: 40; see also Dunnigan 1999: 7–28, for perceptive insights into the relationship between literary self-reflexivity and the theme of desire). The metaphor of literary analysis is useful; the repeated indications are that a reader whose rational faculty is outweighed by desire is single-minded, hence incompetent. This conceit is extrapolated onto the poet's role, a preoccupation retained by James throughout his poetic career, culminating in two of his most "literary" sonnets, attributed to him in British Library Add. MS. 24195 under the editorial title *Amatoria*. The poems were written after his arrival in Norway in October 1589, for his fiancée, Anne of Denmark, prior to their marriage in November (Craigie ed. 1958: 2: 226).

"Two Sonnets to her M:^{tie} to show the difference of Stiles" (Craigie ed. 1958: 2: 70) rank as James's most explicit poetic analysis of the equivocalness of literary creation, and were included what was also his closest flirtation with the love sonnet sequence (see Fleming 2002: 141). The apparent intention is to expose the artificial rhetoric comprising the sonneteer's art, undermining the sonnet's ethical system from within. Thus, the inception of both poems is rooted in the Madame's desire for creation of a love poem. The second narrator, following generic convention, does so immediately; but the narrator of the first sonnet refuses, instead detailing the death of his poetic talent.

"Castalias floods" (I.13) have dried up in him, while the "heauenly furious fire" (I.7) of inspiration is "quench'd" by "daylie fascherie" (I.6). (Craigie equates the sonnet narrator with James here, saying that he is referring to the "quarrels which were continually breaking out" amongst his entourage. However, it is by no means certain that James intended the personae in either of these sonnets to be seen as self-representative (Craigie ed. 1958: 2: 226)). The narrator is unmoved by the usual inspirational tropes of the sonnet – his muse has "begunne to tire" (I.5), and he rejects the notion of creating an insincere work. Seemingly, the normal poetic response is acquiescence; creation of dishonest but appreciated work, which could furthermore benefit the poet's romantic suit. James's poem functions as subtle critique, judging harshly those sonneteers who call up their muse dishonestly, using their poetic skills to speed the consummation of their lust. They are tacitly criticised for their intellectual and ethical deceit; their readers for their (intentional?) failure to detect such guile. The traditional, (and for James, challenging) nature of the sonnet scheme is acknowledged via reference to the lover's "desire" in the context of motivating literary creativity, reminding the audience that fulfilment of desire usually involves the defeat of rationality. The poem is a dual rebuke, on a literary level to poets who cheapen their art by creating in proportion to public requests, and more generally, to those who allow their physical desires to overcome their powers of good sense and morality.

The second sonnet depicts the alternative, a poet willingly providing an insincere paean. The vocabulary is metonymic of desire's
overwhelming of reason – the beloved "shall my Muse *inflame*" (II.4).
She becomes an almost occult influence, "inchaunting" (II.5) the
narrator, whose literary integrity and rational powers are influenced by
his feelings for her. James ensures that the reader questions the valid-
ity of the verse with the closing couplet:

[…] since your fame hath made me flie before
Well may your name my verses nou decore. (II.13–14)

Not the sincere declaration of love that might appear in a non-Scots
sonnet, here the beloved is a functional object to whom the poet might
as "well" dedicate his verse.

The conflict established macroscopically between the paired
poems specifically investigates concerns displayed in the *Essayes*
regarding poetic artificiality and the inevitable moral corollary – if the
poet cannot be trusted, but creates work that is insincere, because it
results from passionate excess, then greater pressure is on the reader to
supply the moral dimension. The poems work on two levels, testing
the reader's critical response, and analysing the clash between reason
and desire, and the relationship of this conflict to the poet himself.
Tension is engendered between the first sonnet's refusal to satisfy the
beloved's arbitrary desire, and the pat fulfilment of her demand in the
second. Measured against the standards established in James's "Sonnet decifring the perfyte poete" (Craigie ed. 1955: 1: 69), both demonstrate the necessary attributes: "Ane rype ingyne, ane quick and
vvalkned vvitt, / VVith sommair reasons, suddenlie applyit" (1–2), but
both, consciously or not, are ultimately simply products of
"Madame's" desire to witness poetic output. The *Vranie*'s impulse to
positive action is developed – though the first sonnet is inevitably
based in emotional extreme, the sonnet-narrator's awareness of this
tempers somewhat its dangerous effects.

This possible compromise is inextricably connected with the
sonnet's potential to embody the conflicting relationship between
passion and reason within its status as a limiting form traditionally
used to investigate love. James's restriction of subject matter effectively defined usage of the sonnet as testing the ability and proficiency
of both poet and reader. For one, it served as physical proof of poetic

skill, for the other it tested interpretative and ethical ability. Unsurprisingly, James's poetic contemporaries (and subjects) followed his lead, though, of course, even James himself did not always adhere to the poetic advice of the *Reulis*. Conceivably, the popularity of the self-reflexive sonnet form was due not just to his instruction, but also to recognition of the aptness of analysing excessive desire using consciously literary means. Two other poets stand out for their treatment of the form.

Alexander Montgomerie stretched the sonnet to its limits – indeed, Jack argues he "largely created" the "traditions of Scottish sonneteering" (Jack 1985: 83). He used it to beg for his pension, in insulting enemies, lamenting lost chastity, and – occasionally – for love poems. Stewart of Baldynneis's subject matter is similarly varied, including dedicatory sonnets to James, musings on friendship, betrayal, love and sex, and a group examining the nature of poetic inspiration (Crockett ed. 1913: 189–92: poems 63–66). Their treatments differ, however. More than Montgomerie, Stewart's work is directly related to James's, with recurring themes and motifs. Critically, Stewart's lyric poems have suffered in favour of his "abbregement" of *Orlando Furioso*, "Roland Furiovs", and the Scottish Text Society edition of his work remains incomplete (for studies of his work, see Irving 1861: 466–70; Dunlop 1915; Purves 1946–48; McDiarmid 1948; Nelson 1968; Jack 1972: 42–72; Bell 1995; Dunnigan 1997; Rodger 2001.)

He is seemingly the poet most responsive to James's instructions. James's text is invoked and identified as the inspiration behind Stewart's work: "haifing red ȝour maiesteis maist prudent Precepts in the deuyn art of poesie, I haif assayit my Sempill spreit to becum ȝour hienes scholler" (Crockett ed. 1913: 3). He adopts James's role in the *Reulis*, by designating himself "ane ȝoung and Imperfyt prentes" (Crockett ed. 1913: 3), thus implying that the subsequent poetry accords with the *Reulis*. However, the professed fidelity to James's teachings is undercut by the inclusion of poems with compositional dates which anticipate publication of the *Reulis* (which may have circulated in manuscript, or oral, form prior to publication), e.g. "To His Maiestie The First of Ianvar, 1582", and "To His Maiestie The First of Ianvar Vith Presentation of Ane Lawrell Trie Formit of Gould, 1583". McDiarmid suggests Stewart's manuscript was presented to James in 1586–87 (McDiarmid 1950: 62) (compositional dates of individual poems are more complicated, and yet to be satisfactorily resolved). It contains what appears to be a carefully chosen selection of Stewart's verse, much of which very probably predated the *Reulis'* publication. Physical aspects of the manuscript reinforce this hypothesis: eleven empty leaves between the presentation sonnet "To His Maiestie Vith Presentation of this Volume. Sonnet" and "Ane Schersing" indicate that Stewart included poems according to thematic structure, rather than consecutively, possibly over-estimating the number of poems he would be including. The inference that Stewart chose poems according to a scheme, perhaps connected to their relevance to the *Reulis* means that thematic inclinations take on particular importance.

Stewart's work, like James's, plays with depictions of poetic authority and its relationship to the clash between reason and passion, exploring this within a matrix establishing the dangers of misinterpretation. This fixation leads to literary self-consciousness reinforced by manuscript structure. It opens with the violent extremes of "Roland Furiovs", while the final poem, "Ane Schersing Ovt of Trew Felicitie", at the opposite end of the ethical scale, depicts a narrator immune to temptation, assured of heavenly reward. The lyrics between are imbued with pressure, delineating the conflict inherent in literary attempts to cover the subjects of love and desire. Such careful ordering means that a decontextualised study of Stewart's poems is problematic. The sonnets do not comprise an obvious sequence, but their positioning points to oblique progression, whereby poems become retrospective commentaries on works preceding them in the manuscript, and in literary history. Here I examine a mini-sequence of sonnets, as well as appraising relevant, non-consecutive works.

"To Echo of Invart Havines. Sonnet", is dedicated to Echo, who, like a "poet" without an audience, "dois schout so schill [...] Throch daill, throch vaill, throch forrest, Rock, And hill" (1, 3) (See Lyall 1999: 51–52 for discussion of this poem's mannerist topos). Tragic Echo is emotionally overcome, "consumit" by sorrow. Her attempts to verbalise her grief contrast with the non-creative results of the narrator's "paine" – his lack of subject. He uses Echo's emotional discontent, described as "coequall" to his own, requesting her to "supplie my speitche" (5) with the promise "sum confort" may be gained "be the furthschawing of my painfull part" (7–8). The ramifications of inviting such extreme emotion into the poem are serious. Echo's verbal grief may remedy the narrator's need for a subject, but her vocality results from disproportionate sentiment, and, though heard, is not listened to. Like James's "Sonnets in Two Stiles", the poem's existence depends upon emotional surfeit; raising the problematic question of where poetic inspiration is to come from, if not some extreme. The narrator-poet is aware of this, and though the poetic genesis is identified as absolution of a type, allowing recognition of the futility of his grief, it is of a limited nature. Only a degree of self-knowledge is attained in the revelation that his acute emotional state threatens to "break or birst the boudin brest" (10), that he must "relasche" his "hawie hart" (11). Despite appreciation of the perils of excessive desire, which culminate in "duilfull death" (12), and apparent understanding of how to avert such a fate, the final couplet indicates that his redemption is incomplete. It is impossible for him to completely purge himself, "So reuthfull cryis sum part my cair sall suadge / Quhilk holdin In vold suell me in ane radge" (13–14). Such lack of resolution is an implied result of the poem's rootedness in excess emotion.

"Of Ambitious Men" reinforces the idea that simply recognising the vagaries of fate and desire is insufficient. Here, the untrammelled appetite is for fame and fortune. The arbitrariness of Fortune, and the "feirfull fall" (14) awaiting those who place their faith in her, is juxtaposed with the specificity of the manuscript-given title. Examined in conjunction with the title, the reading of Fortune is diluted by the awareness that the "mortall men" (8) in question are not wholly random, but greedy individuals, whose ambitions "molest" their minds. Consumed by their aspirations, they are inevitably punished, thrown "doune to the ground" (11). The sonnet's similarity to *Ecclesiastes* (compare 1 to Ecc.1.6) adds a Christian dimension, emphasising that Fortune, compared with God's stability, is a fickle mistress, whose "firmtie" few may find. There is a real sense that overt desire for glory and recognition is as dangerous as excessive sexual lust.

"Vpone the Portrait of Cvpid" appositely substitutes arbitrary fate with the equally "vauering" (12) figure of Cupid, while the vocabulary used to describe the painting serves to emphasise the deceptiveness of his wiles. Love is "paintit lyk" (1) a child, "in signe that ȝouth of him hem greatest cuir" (2); he smiles with "semblant sueit" (3). Nothing is real, but rather imitates what is genuine. The embodiment of randomly focused physical desire (exemplified in his blindness), Cupid is depicted as incompetent, even dangerous: "Laik of sycht" (7) denoting corresponding moral blindness, his "Iudgement verray small" (8). Replacing the beloved as the sonnet's subject, he is denounced as "vntrew" (12), while the final couplet emphasises the poem's refraction through an extra layer of artistic interpretation: "Auld painters hes this form for luif prepaird / To lerne ws vit quhan ve do luif regaird" (13–14). The poet-narrator is effectively dissociated from the dubious ethical connotations of a poem inspired by Cupid, while the capriciousness surrounding Cupid is stressed – he is fortuitously depicted as a blind child because artists perceived that that form most appropriately embodied love's irrationality.[2]

Aptly, this theme is developed in the mini-sequence's final poem, "Of the Qvaliteis of Lvif", which begins with the paradoxical description of love as "ane aigre douce delyt and greif" (1). It is the first sonnet to engage specifically with love in its title, indicating progression from the (relatively) abstract to the specific. The most self-consciously literary of the group's sonnets, its use of *vers enchainée* defines it as visual and aural artefact, as well as literary. This is especially pertinent in this ambivalent work; the repetition of the last word of each line at the start of the subsequent line corresponds to the description of the cumulative effects of unmitigated desire, as the dangers of succumbing to uncontrolled passion are depicted: "Mischeif of luif is euirlasting stryf: / Stryf reuling luif, than rancor raidgeis ryf" (4–5).[3] The final line "Men luif obeyis, Gods vill not luif misken" (14) depicts men as slaves to their desires, apparently contrasted to the ability of the gods to "know" or recognise love.

As the manuscript progresses, so the dangers of unbridled passion become more overtly physical. "Of the Assaultis of Luif", depicts a "bodie all in baill" (2) which "laik[s] haill And may find no recuir" (3). Combined with this is a precognition of potential remedy, "In seis I saill *Schersing* remeid thairfor" (6, my emphasis). Apparently, the final poem will contain the means of salvation for a narrative figure who, in his "reuthfull roir" (9), is reminiscent of Roland. Simultaneously though, failure to "lerne" the lesson of the earlier sonnet on Cupid is signalled as the narrator "maist humyllie dois Imploir / The mychtie gloir of the bold blindit boy" (10–11). The "gloir" reminds us of the doomed protagonists of "Of Ambitious Men", while the humble

---

[2] Compare to Montgomerie's sonnet "Against the God of Love", essentially a flyting against Cupid and his arbitrary judgements. Montgomerie's Cupid is more sinister, a "brutal" figure who "abuses" loyal love (Parkinson ed. 2000: 1: 135).
[3] Compare the Henrysonian notion of "repleit" (Fox ed. 1987: 58, 145).

approach contrasts with the attack of the "Portrait" poem. Though the narrator sees Cupid's blindness, stubborn lust means a failure to interpret this as moral blindness. He rejects rational judgement, resulting in the "deedlie dolour" which he endures. Appropriately, it is followed by "Of Deth", which deciphers the results of such worldly lusts, with Death's "deidlie dart" paralleling Cupid's.

"Ane Schersing" embodies a contrastive remedy to the inevitable effects of extreme lust depicted in the "Roland Furiovs", but Stewart also tries to present potential solution in the shorter poems. "Of ane Thochtles and Frie Hart from Vorldlie Cair" advocates a possible compromise position, in which love is tempered with innocence – "Ane giltles hart possessit bot vith luif / Is suir as Rock that storms may not remuif" (13–14). If love is legitimate it serves in itself as protection against extremity's dangers. The poem evokes the "first verses that euer the King made", "Sen thocht is frie", itself a discussion of the importance of "preferring Wisdome to Will", of making the "troublit hairt" subject to self-censorship, as it pragmatically notes that "Thocht vnrevelit can doe na ill" (Craigie 1958: 2: 133; see also Lyall: 200: 55–70, 59–60 for a discussion of the relationship between James VI and Esmé Stewart, for whom the poem may have been written).

Subsequent sonnets retreat into a specifically literary world. "Of Ane Poet" is the only sonnet that provides a variation on the traditional Scottish rhyme scheme, using *abab baba acac dd* – a notable digression, given the overtly self-referential subject matter (Lyall pers. comm. suggests that this is still a form of the Scots sonnet rhyme scheme, but with less variation). The themes of the unfulfilled lover and the search for creative inspiration merge in the depiction of poets, and the "rage [which] rings in thair restles braine" (3), developing the implication in "To Echo" that poets allow their rational impulse to slide. It establishes an opposition to James's list of attributes of the "Perfyte Poete", most of which are attainable rather than intrinsic: "skilfulness [...] pithie vvordis [...] memorie [...] figuris, quilks proceid / From Rhetorique" (4–10). Stewart pre-empts the Romantic notion of the poetic figure, inspired by the ineffable – "All vorldlie velth [...] from tham slyds away" (5) while their "spreit perturbit" (4) seeks a subject. The subtle counterpointing is reinforced by usage of the alternative rhyme scheme, and it is telling that it comes almost at the conclusion of Stewart's poetic endeavour.

Immediately afterwards comes "Againe of Ane Poet", presenting an alternative portrayal. The first sonnet's "solitar and sad" (9) figure is here crowned with "greine triumphall laurell" (2) and blessed with great eloquence. Nail biting and pacing becomes "curious knawledge of [...] hich Ingyn" (13), a poet "be giltit pen expert. / Expert and douce ʒe varpe ʒour vordie verse, / And frilie in ʒour maist sound reherse" (12–14). While the second poet's flowing verse contrasts with the difficulties endured by the earlier poet, his "expertise" recalls Henryson, ensuring the retention of a sense of conflict as the reader reaches "Ane Schersing", the poem that finally attempts to resolve the tension between the amatory and the intellectual.

This search for resolution is characteristic of medieval Scots literature, and – relative to this – the Scots manipulation of the sonnet form, the unique preoccupations of the Scottish sonnet, demand closer study. What might erroneously be identified as aberrances in the sonnet form are, in Scotland, distinctly related to the *ars poetica* out-lined in James's *Reulis*, which were part of a larger endeavour to encourage a more prescriptive, specifically Scottish negotiation of the relationship between reason and desire, incorporating self-referential study of poetic inspiration and its apparent basis in emotional extremes. Stewart's poetry clearly responds to the poetic conundrum identified by James. Shedding more light on this relationship, and that of James and Stewart to their predecessors will lead to a more coher-ent understanding of Scottish literary concerns in the late sixteenth century.

Bibliography

Ascham, Roger. [1570] 1967. *The Schoolmaster* (ed. Lawrence V. Ryan) New York: Cornell University Press.

Bell, Sandra Jane. 1995. *Poetry and Politics in the Scottish Renaissance*. PhD thesis. Queen's University at Kingston.

Bellay, Joachim du. [1549] 1930. *La Défense et Illustration de la Langue Française* (ed. Louis Humbert). Paris: Garnier.

Coldwell, D.C. (ed.) 1957–64. *Virgil's Aeneid Translated into Scottish Verse by Gavin Douglas* [Scottish Text Society 3rd series no. 25, 27, 28, 30.]. 4 vols. Edinburgh and London: William Blackwood and Sons.

Craigie, James (ed.) 1955–58. *The Poems of James VI of Scotland* [Scottish Text Society 3rd series no. 22 and 26.]. 2 vols. Edinburgh and London: William Blackwood and Sons.

Crockett, Thomas (ed.) 1913. *Poems of John Stewart of Baldynneis* [Scottish Text Society new series no. 5.]. Edinburgh and London: William Blackwood and Sons.

Dunlop, Geoffrey. 1915. "John Stewart of Baldynneis, the Scottish Desportes" in *Scottish Historical Review* 12: 303–10.

Dunnigan, Sarah M. 1997. *The Scottish Amatory Lyric 1561–1604*. PhD thesis. University of Edinburgh.

—. 1999. "Poetic Objects of Desire: Rhetorical Culture and Seductive Arts in the Lyrics of John Stewart of Baldynneis" in *Scottish Literary Journal* 26: 7–28.

Fleming, Morna R. 2002. "The *Amatoria* of James VI: Loving by the *Reulis*" in Fischlin, Daniel and Mark Fortier (eds) *Royal Subjects: Essays on the Writings of James VI and* I. Detroit: Wayne State University Press. 124–48.

Gascoigne, George. [1575] 1907. "Certayne Notes of Instruction Concerning the Making of Verse" in Cunliffe, John W. (ed.) *Gascoigne: The Poesies*. 2 vols. Cambridge: University Press.

Goodare, Julian and Michael Lynch (eds). 2000. *The Reign of James VI*. East Linton: Tuckwell Press.

Henryson, Robert. 1981. *The Poems* (ed. Denton Fox). Oxford: Clarendon Press.

The Holy Bible: Authorised Version. 1682. Oxford.

Irving, David. 1861. *The History of Scottish Poetry*. Edinburgh: Edmonston and Douglas.

Jack, R.D.S. 1972. *The Italian Influence on Scottish Literature*. Edinburgh: Edinburgh University Press.

—. 1985. *Alexander Montgomerie*. Edinburgh: Scottish Academic Press.

Klein, Holger M. (ed.) 1984. *English and Scottish Sonnet Sequences of the Renaissance*. 2 vols. Hildesheim and New York: Olms.

Lodge, Thomas. [1579–80] 1853. *A Reply to Stephen Gosson's Schoole of Abuse, in Defence of Poetry, Musick, and Stage Plays* (ed. David Laing). London: Shakespeare Society.

Lyall, R.J. 1992. "Formalist Historicism and Older Scots Poetry" in *Études Écossaises* 1: 39–48.

—. 1999. "Montgomerie and the Moment of Mannerism" in *Scottish Literary Journal* 26: 41–58.

Mapstone, Sally and Juliette Wood (eds). 1998. *The Rose and the Thistle: Essays on the Culture of Late Medieval and Renaissance Scotland*. East Linton: Tuckwell Press.

McDiarmid, Matthew P. 1948: "Notes on the Poems of John Stewart of Baldynneis" in *Review of English Studies* 24: 12–18.

—. 1950. "John Stewart of Baldynneis" in *Scottish Historical Review* 29: 52–63.

Nelson, Timothy. 1968. "John Stewart of Baldynneis and *Orlando Furioso*" in *Studies in Scottish Literature* 6(2): 105–14.

Parkinson, David (ed.) 2000. *Alexander Montgomerie: Poems* [Scottish Text Society 4th series no. 28, 29.]. 2 vols. Edinburgh: Scottish Text Society.

Purves, John. 1946–48. "The *Abbregement of Roland Furious,* by John Stewart of Baldynneis, and the Early Knowledge of Ariosto in England" in *Italian Studies* 3: 65–82.

Rodger, Donna. 2001. *A critical edition of John Stewart of Baldynneis' "Roland Furious", with a critical introduction, appendix of proper names, notes, and a full glossary*. PhD thesis. University of Edinburgh.

Rollins, Edward Hyder (ed.) 1928. *Tottel's Miscellany (1557–87)*. 2 vols. Oxford and Cambridge Mass.: Harvard University Press.

Ronsard, Pierre de. [1565] 1949. "Abbregé de l'art poëtique François", in Laumonier, Paul (ed.) *Pierre de Ronsard: Œuvres Complètes*. 22 vols. Paris: Hachette.

—. 1998. Smith, Malcolm (ed.) *Sonnets pour Helene*. Geneva: Droz.

Spiller, Michael R.G. 1992. *The Development of the Sonnet: an Introduction*. London and New York: Routledge.

—. 1998. "The Scottish Court and the Scottish Sonnet at the Union of the Crowns" in Mapstone, Sally and Juliette Wood (eds) *The Rose and the Thistle: Essays on the Culture of Late Medieval and Renaissance Scotland*. East Linton: Tuckwell Press. 101–15.

Warner, George F. 1893. *The Library of James VI: 1573–88*. Edinburgh: T. and A. Constable.

Flowres of Sion: The Spiritual and Meditative Journey of William Drummond

David Atkinson

This essay examines the religious feeling expressed in the *Flowres of Sion* by William Drummond. It argues that the consistent critical attention to Drummond's borrowings from European literature has hidden the depth and sincerity of this collection, and demonstrates its mediation between rival Protestant and Catholic theologies.
Keywords: Catholicism; derivativeness; William Drummond; *The Cypress Grove; Flowres of Sion*; *memento mori*; Protestantism; Reformation; religious verse; sonnets

The poetry of William Drummond of Hawthornden (1585–1649) has often been criticized for its derivative nature, and certainly there is evidence that Drummond draws on all manner of sources, both European and English. Kurt Wittig, for example, disparagingly refers to Drummond's "largely imitative poetry" (Wittig 1958: 129), while Matthew McDiarmid writes about Drummond's "literary plunder" (McDiarmid 1949: 2). This is, however, to diminish Drummond's accomplishment as a poet. Despite accusations of slavish imitation, he has retained his reputation as one of Scotland's pre-eminent seventeenth-century "English" poets, and in this context deserves recognition for his own particular contribution to Scottish poetry.

Drummond is generally characterized as living a retiring life removed from the political and religious activities of Scotland. Not surprisingly, then, Drummond's poetry is characterized by a quiet but intensely personal voice, which reveals much about his own particular attitudes and values. While the speaker in Drummond's poems is rarely identified, there are sufficient personal references to suggest that the *Flowres of Sion* is intended as an expression of Drummond's own meditative reflections on the Christian process of resurrection and Christian hope. Comprised of sonnets, shorter madrigals, and longer, more discursive hymns, the *Flowres* exhibit a tension that comes from seeing what the goal is and knowing the difficulties standing in the way of its achievement.

The first eight poems of the *Flowres* seem little more than an uneventful iteration of the commonplaces of the *memento mori*. Drummond concentrates on the insubstantiality of life, on how "All onely constant is in constant Change" (MacDonald ed. 1976: 88),[1] on the misery of a world in which "all good had left" (Sonnet vii, 5) and on the rigours of time and how life "with swifter speede declines than earst it spred" (Sonnet iii, 7). But putting aside possible "borrowing", and the commonplace sentiments of these poems, there is a power in the simplicity of Drummond's writing, reinforcing as it does the unpredictable ephemerality of life:

Life a right shadow is
For if it long appeare,
Then is it spent, and Deathes long Night drawes neare;
Shadowes are moving, light,
And is there ought so moving as is this?
When it is most in Sight,
It steales away, and none can tell how, where,
So neere our Cradles to our Coffines are. (Madrigal i, 1–8)

The juxtaposition of life to "Deathes long Night", and the conflation of time so that cradles and "coffines" become one, reinforces our obliviousness to time and mutability; we simply have no sense that life is truly being "stolen" from us. Ostensibly, the Christian message is intended to fortify us against this insecurity and to give meaning to our earthly trials. But for Drummond this is just a little too pat, a little too convenient, denying as it does the simple joys of life. In Sonnet iii, "No Trust in Tyme", the concluding Christian message is not an altogether satisfactory one, reduced as it is to an uninspired declaration. We are initially reminded of how "the Flowre", the "Mornings Darling late, the Summers Queene" (2) "lingringlie doth fade" (1). But as with time itself, what is once slow "With swifter speede declines than earst it spred" (7). And while there is consolation in dwelling on "thy Home (my Soule) and thinke aright, / Of what yet restes thee of Lifes wasting Day" (11–12), there is a hollow emptiness in the bluntness of the concluding couplet, "Thy Sunne postes Westward, passed is thy Morne, / And twice it is not given thee to bee borne" (13–14).

One finds the same sort of contradiction in Sonnet V, "Nature Must Yeelde to Grace". Here, too, Drummond muses on the emptiness of earthly things –

---

[1] All quotations from Drummond's verse are taken from MacDonald (ed.) 1976, and will hereafter be referenced by poem and line number.

Too long I followed have on fond Desire,
And too long painted on deluding Streames,
Too long refreshment sought in burning Fire,
Runne after Joyes which to my Soule were Blames; (Sonnet v, 1–4)

– as well as on the solace of Christian faith:

Hence-foorth on Thee (mine onelie Good) I thinke,
For onelie Thou canst grant what I doe crave
Thy Nailes my Pennes shall bee, thy Blood mine Inke,
Thy winding-sheete my Paper, Studie Grave. (9–12)

The second intervening quatrain, however, gives room for pause. While the speaker has "prov'd of Lifes delightes the last extreames" (6) only to find "a Rose hedg'd with a Bryer" (7), there is a wistful regret in his description of it as "a show of golden Dreames" (8), that are not real but nonetheless of priceless value.

To counter the world's inescapable attractiveness, Drummond in Sonnet vii writes with a heavy, unrelenting voice that broods over the darkness and corruption of the world:

The Griefe was common, common were the Cryes,
Teares, Sobbes, and Groanes of that afflicted Traine,
Which of Gods chosen did the Summe containe
And Earth rebounded with them, pierc'd were Skies;
All good had left the World, each Vice did raigne,
In the most hideous shapes Hell could devise. (1–6)

But the clumsiness of the final couplet is troubling: "When (pittying Man) God of a Virgines wombe / Was borne, and those false Deities strooke dombe" (Sonnet vii, 13–14). The point is that nothing is ever simple. Yes, the world is a place of temptation, and yes, it is to be set aside in hope of something better. But it is not exclusively a place of darkness, a place of *vanitas*, where nothing redeeming is to be found. Drummond allows that there is no one simple answer. Drummond is a man of fundamental piety, but he is not willing to set aside completely a world which he knows to be a place of joyful loveliness. In this tentativeness is the understanding of one who cares little for false piety or religious correctness and who only knows what he sees and experiences. Religious life is not straightforward; put another way, we know and give voice to knowing God in many ways.

The second group of poems in the *Flowres of Sion* stands in dramatic contrast to the first. Gone is any sort of tentativeness, as the focus shifts to the sacrifice of the crucifixion and the gift of the resurrection. Thus is expressed the joyful celebration of the first quatrain of his Sonnet ix, "For the Nativitie of Our Lord":

O than the fairest Day, thrice fairer Night!
Night to best Dayes in which a Sunne doth rise,
Of which that golden Eye, which cleares the Skies,
Is but a sparkling Ray, a Shadow light. (Sonnet ix, 1–4)

Or, along similar lines, in the first quatrain of Sonnet x, which asserts the glory and power of God:

To spread the azure Canopie of Heaven,
And make it twinkle with those spangs of Gold,
To stay this weightie masse of Earth so even,
That it should all, and nought should it up-hold. (Sonnet x, 1–4)

Drummond provides a convincing alternative to earthly life, although his purpose is not so much to praise God, as to bring attention to the extraordinary gift of God's grace:

LORD, to thy Wisedome nought is, nor thy Might;
But that thou shouldst (thy Glorie laid aside)
Come meanelie in mortalitie to bide,
And die for those deserv'd eternall plight. (Sonnet x, 9–12)

In humanising Christ, Drummond makes real His suffering, and thereby fixes the devotional commitment of the believer. At the same time, the poem retains a cosmic significance, as the hands so cruelly nailed to the cross become the hands that hold the world and draw us to God in a caring embrace, as shown in Hymne i:

And thou (my Soule) let nought thy Griefe relent.
Those Hands, those sacred Hands which hold the raines
  Of this great All, and kept from mutuall warres
  The Elements, beare rent from thee their Veines. (Hymne i, 33–36)

It is the reality of Christ's suffering which has a profound impact on one's capacity to believe. Emphasis is no longer on the world, but on the all-consuming, unconditional love of God: "His armes (loe) stretched are you to embrace" (Hymne i, 75), and "All that is from you crav'd from this great King / Is to beleeve, a pure Heart Incense is" (Hymne i, 67–68).

Much the same thing can be said about the "Hymn of the Ascension", whose punctuated, staccato-like rhythm asserts the reality and significance of Christ's ascension to heaven:

> Bright Portalles of the Skie,
>   Emboss'd with sparkling Starres
>   Doores of Eternitie,
>   With diamantine barres
>   Your Arras rich up-hold,
>   Loose all your bolts and Springs,
>   Ope wyde your Leaves of gold;
>   That in your Roofes may come the King of kings. (Hymne iii, 1–8)

The poem's assertiveness underlines how everything is subservient to Christ's glory. Satan is reduced to a mere inconvenience; his crimes are little more than "mischiefe" (Hymne iii, 58). In an odd reversal, Satan becomes Christ's victim: "His spoyles are made thy pray, / His Phanes are sackt and torne, / His Altars raz'd away" (Hymne iii, 61–63).

There is no denying that this emphasis on the passion and resurrection of Christ has a Catholic quality about it, which stands in contrast to the more Protestant viewpoint focusing on faith as a sign of divine favour, to which, from time to time, Drummond also alludes. In Sonnet xxvi, for example,

> Let us each day enure our selves to dye,
> If this (and not our Feares) be truely Death
> Above the Circles both of Hope and Faith
> With faire immortal pinniones to flie? (Sonnet xxvi, 1–4)

And in Sonnet xvi, focus is not so much on the physical reality of Christ's crucifixion, as on its significance for salvation:

> Life to give life deprived is of *Life*,
> And Death displai'd hath ensigne against *Death*;
> So violent the Rigour was of *Death*,
> That nought could daunt it but the Life of *Life*:
> No Power had Pow'r to thrall Lifes pow'r to *Death*,
> But willingly Life hath abandon'd *Life*.

Love gave the wound which wrought this work of *Death*, […]
Dead JESUS lies, who Death hath kill'd by *Death*,
His Tombe no Tombe is, but new Source of *Life*. (Sonnet xvi, 1–7, 13–14)

The thrust of the poem is obvious: that through Christ's death comes
life; that such life is really the death of life; and that one must die to
life in order to live. One should not, however, make too much about
what might seem "Catholic" or "Protestant" in Drummond's poetry.
While Drummond makes clear that salvation extends from divine
mercy, the poem is without theological bias, as Drummond exhibits
the same ecumenical emphasis on Christian fundamentals expressed in
his prose, perhaps most notably, *Irene: or A Remonstrance for
Concord, Amity, and Love amongst His Majesty's Subjects*.

Never far away in Drummond is the poet who produced *The Cypress Grove*, the bookish recluse who is given to meditative reflection,
an image to which we have become accustomed and indeed perhaps a
bit too fond. While there is comfort in the recognizable details of
Christ's life, and the spiritual comfort they bring, Drummond seems
inevitably swayed by the ultimate incomprehensibility of God, and the
anxiety this creates. The Old Testament echoes are obvious in Sonnet
xvii. God purposefully keeps himself hidden and punishes those who
presume to know too much. God exists "beneath a sable vaile, and
Shadowes deepe, / Of Unaccessible and dimming light" (Sonnet xvii,
1–2). "This great King naill'd to an abject Tree" as in Hymne i
(Hymne i, 23) has become the "Sunne invisible that dost abide /
Within thy bright abysmes, most faire, most darke" (Sonnet xvii, 9–
10). The oxymoron at the end of this line ("most faire, most darke")
reinforces the incomprehensibility of the divine mystery. It also anticipates the inevitable conclusion of the poem, "The more I search of
thee, The lesse I know" (Sonnet xvii, 14), which voices a fundamental
paradox of religious experience, that the divine is found, not so much
in grasping, but in letting go, in acceptance rather than in possession,
in allowing that God is found when one recognizes the impossibility
of the task. It is what Drummond calls, very simply, "a quiet Peace"
(Madrigal iii, 9). What remains clear, though, is Drummond's interest
in relationship with God; his is not an abstract theological position,
even though his language sometimes has this quality. Rather Drummond experiences God deeply, even if this experience remains unex-
plained; what he does know is that it is truly transformative and that
how one views life as a consequence will never be the same.

Indirectly, Drummond's desire to avoid the world is really an expression of the theme of the *ars moriendi* – that we must get past our concern with the world, or, as he says in Sonnet xxvi: "Let us each day enure our selves to dye" (Sonnet xxvi, 1). It is on this message that Drummond concentrates in a third group of poems, which connects the transience of life with the permanent, transcendent glory of God, although he never quite gives up on the appeal of the solitary life, not only for how it anticipates the peace of eternity, but also as a thing in itself. "The World is full of Horrours, Troubles, Slights", he writes, but "Woods harmelesse Shades have only true Delightes" (Sonnet xxii, 13–14). There is something self-serving about this helpless romanticising of the solitary life, even if we are inclined to forgive Drummond his indulgence:

Thrice happie hee, who by some shadie Grove,
Farre from the clamorous World, doth live his owne,
Though solitarie, who is not alone,
But doth converse with that Eternall Love (Sonnet xxii, 1–4)

There is no doubting his feelings when he writes that the "Sobbings of the widow'd Dove" are more sweet than "the smooth whisperings neere a Princes Throne", and, similarly, "how more sweet is Zephires wholesome Breath" than "that applause vaine Honour doth bequeath" (Sonnet xxii, 6, 7, 9).

Sometimes, as in the following madrigals, Drummond's verse is unadorned and to-the-point. The first of these reads:

The world a Hunting is,
The Pray poore Man, the Nimrod fierce is Death,
His speedie Grei-hounds are,
Lust, sickness, Envie, Care,
Strife that neere falles amisse,
With all those ills which haunt us while wee breath. (Madrigal iv, 1–6)

Death will inevitably catch us up, making all that we achieve in life of little, if any, consequence. The rhythmic momentum of the abbreviated lines make the bluntness of the final line especially apt: "Old Age with stealing Pace, / Castes up his Nets, and there wee panting die" (Madrigal iv, 9–10). The second of these madrigals has much the same message, as it captures an all-too-human sense of loss, and manages to incorporate a dramatic urgency about what it all means:

New doth the Sunne appeare,
The Mountaines Snowes decay,
Crown'd with fraile Flowres foorth comes the Babye yeare.
My Soule, Time postes away,
And thou yet in that Frost
Which Flowre and fruit hath lost,
As if all heere immortall were, dost stay:
For shame thy Powers awake,
Looke to that Heaven which never Night makes blacke,
And there, at that immortall Sunnes bright Rayes,
Decke thee with Flowres which feare not rage of Dayes. (Madrigal v, 1–12)

There is a nervous fear here, which in some ways is an extension of the overall tentativeness of Drummond's belief. It might be right and proper to talk of death as a gateway to something better, but at a human level, death remains a frightening unknown that no faith can totally allay. Sonnet xxv is that much more effective because it portrays death as at once an intimate, as someone who wants to do us a favour, and as someone who does not care, who relies on threats, the great leveller from which no one can escape. There is truly a visceral chill when Drummond writes:

More oft than once, Death whisper'd in mine Eare
Grave what thou heares in Diamond and Gold,
I am that Monarch whom all Monarches feare,
Who hath in Dust their farre-stretc'd Pride uproll'd. (Sonnet xxv, 1–4)

It is perhaps this real and abiding fear that generates the human need for an antidote in Christian faith, although Drummond still calls on what is at best a rather tired commonplace in the seventeenth century: "Trust flattering Life no more, Redeeme Time past, / And Live each Day as if it were thy Last" (Sonnet xxv, 13–14). This is really only possible if one looks past death to something new. In this regard, Hymne iv is one of the most accomplished poems in the collection, juxtaposing as it does the strife of life and the bliss of heaven. While we cannot ever forget that "Swift is [...] [the] mortall Race", and that "Vaste are Desires not limited by Grace" (Hymne iv, 109, 111), the nymph who speaks voices comfort and hope. The motivation is not fear but peace and security, how "From Toyle and pressing Cares / How yee may respit finde, / A Sanctuarie from Soule-thralling Snares" (Hymne iv, 25–27).

If there are poems out of place in the *Flowres of Sion*, they are the concluding two poems, "An Hymne of the Fairest Fair: An Hymne of the Nature, Atributes, and Workes of God", and "A Prayer for Mankind", if for no other reason than both have a bookish pretension about them, as Drummond aspires to an epic style which really does not work for him. The "Hymne of the Nature, Attributes, and Workes of God" is about as muddled as its title suggests. At once an allegorical representation of creation, a theological treatise on the one and the many, an account of the chain of being, and a meditative reflection on the nature of Godhead, the Hymne is grossly inflated with overblown language that seems to trip over itself:

Whole and entire all in thy Selfe thou art,
All-where diffus'd, yet of this *All* no part,
For infinite, in making this faire Frame,
(Great without quantitie) in all thou came,
And filling all, how can thy State admit,
Or Place or Substance to be voide of it? (Hymne v, 285–90)

One can make the same observations about "A Prayer for Mankinde", which has much the same sort of exaggerated expression:

Great GOD, whom wee with humble Thoughts adore,
Eternall, infinite, Almightie King,
Whose Dwellings Heaven transcend, whose Throne before
Archangells serve, and Seraphines doe sing;
Of nought who wrought all that With wondring Eyes
Wee doe behold within this spacious Round (Hymne vi, 1–6)

Drummond struggles in both poems to convey his sense of God; everything is "great", or "boundless" or "numberless". The result is a lack of conviction, which his more personal poems carry. On the one hand, we might express regret that Drummond included these poems in the *Flowres*, because it means the collection concludes on less than a satisfactory note. On the other, their very presence points not only to Drummond's limitations as a poet, but also highlights the achievements of his shorter devotional poems. The genuineness that Drummond exhibits elsewhere is drawn from his own personal religious experience, and has, as a result, a resonance with his readers. The exaggeration of his two concluding hymns has a sense of Drummond trying to fulfil expectations, that these kinds of poems are expected of one noted for his meditative and reflective bent. At the same time, the final two poems reaffirm the fundamental simplicity of belief and faith. While theology might constitute the intellectual foundation of belief, it does not give voice to it.

What, then, can one conclude about Drummond as a religious poet? In the bigger picture, his poetry exhibits a creative tension not unlike that which characterized the general state of affairs in Protestant Scotland, or even England for that matter. There still had not occurred an effective transition from the Catholic emphasis on the Incarnation, Passion, and Resurrection to a Protestant emphasis on sin, calling, and righteousness, as even Drummond's poetry signifies. There was a sense of wanting the best of both worlds. Similarly, the medieval residue of the *memento mori* still held sway, in the face of a world to be viewed as an expression of both divine glory and divine mystery. If nothing else, Drummond's "Hymne of the Fairest Fair" struggles to reconcile these opposites. While this tension might generate the artistic inspiration for Drummond, along with any number of other poets, it can only be resolved with a simplicity of expression and belief which matches that of scripture itself. If there is, then, a motivating force behind Drummond's poetry, it is this, and in this regard he exhibits a moving, if not entirely original, expression of seventeenth-century religiosity.

Bibliography

Atkinson, David W. 1986. "The Religious Voices of Drummond of Hawthornden" in *Studies in Scottish Literature* 21: 197–209.

Fogle, French Rowe. 1952. *A Critical Study of William Drummond of Hawthornden.* New York: King's Crown Press.

Jack, R.D.S. 1968. "Drummond of Hawthornden: The Major Scottish Sources" in *Studies in Scottish Literature* 6(1): 36–46.

Kastner, L.E. (ed.) 1913. *The Poetical Works of William Drummond of Hawthornden, With "A Cypresse Grove".* Edinburgh: William Blackwood and Sons.

MacDonald, R.H. 1969. "Amendments to L.E. Kastner's Edition of Drummond's Poems" in *Studies in Scottish Literature* 7 (1–2):102–22.

—. 1971. *The Library of Drummond of Hawthornden.* Edinburgh: Edinburgh University Press.

—. (ed.) 1976. *William Drummond of Hawthornden: Poems and Prose.* Edinburgh and London: Scottish Academic Press for the Association for Scottish Literary Studies.

Masson, David. 1969. *Drummond of Hawthornden: The Story of His Life and Writings.* New York: Haskell House.

McDiarmid, M.P. 1949. "The Spanish Plunder of William Drummond of Hawthornden" in *Modern Language Review* 44: 17–25.

Rae, Thomas I. 1975. "The Historical Writing of Drummond of Hawthornden" in *The Scottish Historical Review* 54(147): 22–62.

Reid, David. 1987. "Royalty and Self-Absorption in Drummond's Poetry" in *Studies in Scottish Literature* 22: 115–31.

Severance, Sibyl Lutz. 1981. "'Some Other Figure': The Vision of Change in *Flowres of Sion*, 1612" in *Spenser Studies* 2: 217–28.

Wallerstein, Ruth C. 1933. "The Style of Drummond of Hawthornden in its Relation to his Translations" in *Publication of the Modern Language Association* 48(4): 1090–107.

Wittig, K. 1958. *The Scottish Tradition in Literature.* Edinburgh and London: Oliver and Boyd.

"Quintessencing in the Finest Substance": the Sonnets of William Drummond

Michael Spiller

William Drummond's remarks on contemporaneous Petrarchan writing, made between 1609 and 1617 and uniquely preserved in the 1711 *Works*, are analysed to suggest reasons for the very considerable alterations made between the 1614 and 1616 printings of his *Poems*.
Keywords: William Alexander; William Drummond; *Tears on the Death of Moeliades; Works of William Drummond*; madrigal; Francesco Petrarcha, *Rime*; Petrarchanism; John Sage; Sir Philip Sidney; song; sonnet; Edmund Spenser; Thomas Ruddiman; James Watson.

The phrase in the title of this article is adapted slightly from a comment made by William Drummond about Petrarchan imitation in the context of a series of remarks on contemporary writers, from Sidney and Spenser in the 1590s to Joshua Sylvester's *Tobacco Battr'd* of 1617. These remarks can be found in the *Works of William Drummond* edited by John Sage and Thomas Ruddiman, and published in Edinburgh by James Watson in 1711, under the heading "Characters of Several Authors" printed immediately after the "Heads of a Conversation betwixt Ben Johnson and William Drummond" (Sage and Ruddiman eds 1711: 226–27). When they undertook their edition, Sage and Ruddiman received the manuscripts and correspondence then in the possession of Drummond's son and heir, Sir William Drummond (1636–1713), which were subsequently returned to the family. These, or most of these, reappeared in 1782, when they were donated to the Scottish Society of Antiquaries by Bishop Abernethy-Drummond, husband of Drummond's only surviving descendant, Barbara Mary (d. 1789). These then passed through the hands of David Laing, who rearranged and indexed them (Laing 1857a; 1857b) and they are now in the National Library of Scotland. Probably in the eighteenth century, items used by Sage and Ruddiman had gone missing, and one such item is the manuscript of "Characters of Authors".

In associating these "Characters" with Drummond's publication of his sonnets in his *Poems* of 1616, it is necessary to point out that, though we do not have Drummond's original manuscript, internal evidence shows that what Sage and Ruddiman printed as a single piece must have been jotted down, and perhaps interpolated, at various times from 1610 to 1617. They print it in discrete paragraphs, and three of these have dateable references, one to Shakespeare's *Sonnets* of 1609, one to Sir David Murray's *Caelia* of 1611, and the last to Joshua Sylvester's *Tobacco Battr'd* of 1617. This tells us that the lost ms. was used by Drummond between 1609 and 1617 – he often recurred to sheets of paper written on earlier.

What Drummond has to say about Petrarchanism in English in these notes is of particular interest for the progress of his own Petrarchan sonnet sequence, due to appear in 1616 as *Poems by William Drummond of Hawthorne-denne*. Kastner's thorough biblio-graphical account of this printing revealed that there was a previous undated edition, surviving in two issues, evidence of Drummond's fondness (as he said in an undated letter) for "having caused print only some coppies equaling the number of my friends" (Kastner ed. 1913: 1: xlv–lxxix; Laing 1857a: 57). But at least one of these pre-publication proofs had a more definite purpose, because his friend Sir William Alexander of Menstrie wrote to him in April 1615 from London (the letter is quoted below) to say that he was checking his proofs and making suggestions. The pre-publication copies, then, must have been being printed before 1615, probably in the year before; and thus his remarks in the "Characters of Several Authors" may be taken as representing his opinions around the time that his own poems were being written and assembled for printing.

The interest of these opinions for this article is that what Drummond thought he was doing, as a Scots Petrarchist, as he wrote and assembled his poems, may explain why he made so many and such considerable alterations between what I shall now call the 1614 printing (Pollard et al. 1976–91: STC 7253–56) and the 1616 printing. He altered so much that his printer, Andro Hart, was obliged to redis-tribute the 1614 type and reset the 1616 volume entire. Drummond, however, made very few substantial alterations to his *words;* what he altered massively was the order of the poems, and as this must have been inconvenient and expensive for himself and Andro Hart, it must have mattered to him.

What I may call his quintessencing remarks, as the 1711 *Works* presents them, constitute the longest piece of literary comment on adapting Petrarch that I know of in British literature of Drummond's time; it is remarkable that for all the adulation and imitation of

Petrarch in Britain, there was no English version of Petrarch's sonnets, and hardly any criticism of his writing, so that Drummond's brief reflections actually lead the field. His comments are playing the familiar Renaissance game of comparing foreign authors to native ones, and he begins with conventional homage:

> The best and most exquisite Poet of this subject [love], by consent of the whole Senate of Poets, is Petrarch. S. W[alter]. R[aleigh] in an epitaph on Sidney, calleth him our English Petrarch; and Daniel regrets he was no Petrarch, though his Delia be a Laura: so Sidney, in his Ast. and Stell. telleth of Petrarch, You that pure [sic: Scots "puir"] Petrarchs long deceased woes with new born Sighs.

But looking abroad, he notes that

> The French have also set Petrarch before them as a Paragon, whereof we shall find, that those your English poets who have approached nearest to him, are the most exquisite on the subject. When I say, approach him, I mean not in following his invention, but in forging as good; and when one matter cometh to them all at once, who quintessenceth it in the finest substance. (Sage and Ruddiman eds 1711: 226)

Now Drummond was in his own poetry an inveterate imitator, translator and paraphraser of other European poets, and it must be supposed that when he defined imitation, as here, he reflected his own practice and aims. "Approaching near" to someone is clearly a term of praise and a criterion of merit, and "exquisite" (used twice), carries a sense of "a full and satisfactory treatment", but this praise is earned, it would seem, not by slavishly using the same rhetorical images and tropes (invention), but by making one's own just as effectively. The point of particular relevance to Drummond's own writing then follows: when the situation arises that a Petrarchan subject has been or is being handled by a lot of poets, as happened routinely all over Europe, then the prize for national achievement, as it were, goes to the poet who gives, in his carefully crafted words, the most concentrated and pure sense of the Petrarchan experience. (Note that it is almost impossible to explain Drummond's terse and clever alchemical metaphor without using distillation imagery oneself).

Generalised though all this is, it seems clear that it does not apply to simple translation or paraphrase of Petrarch, which Drummond often did, but it might, I suggest, apply to sonnet 44 in Drummond's 1616 volume, not noted by Kastner as a Petrarchan inspiration, but certainly starting from Petrarch's *Rime* 100:

Quella fenestra, ove l'un sol si vede
quando a lui piace, e l'altro in sù la nona,
et quella, dove l'aere freddo suona
ne' brevi giorni, quando Borea l'fiede;

e 'l sasso ove a gran dì pensosa siede
Madonna, et sola seco si ragiona,
con quanti luoghi sua bella persona
coprì mai d'ombra, o disegnò col piede

e 'l fiero passo ove m'aggiunse Amore,
et la nova stagion che d'anno in anno
mi rinfresca in quel dì l'antiche piaghe,
e 'l volto e le parole che mi stanno
altamente confitte in mezzo 'l core:
fanno le luci mie di pianger vaghe. (Petrarch 1976: 203)

[That window where one sun appears
when she chooses, and the other at noon,
and the one where the cold air whistles
in the short days when the North Wind hits it;

and the stone where in the long days my lady
sits, and communes with herself;
and all the places that her lovely form ever
cast its shadow on or marked with a footstep;

and the cruel pass where Love assailed me,
and the new season that yearly
opens up, on that day, the old wounds in me;
and the face and the words that are set
deeply embedded in my heart of hearts –
these make my eyes desire to weep.]

Thou Window, once which served for a Spheare
To that deare Planet of my Heart, whose Light
Made often blush the glorious Queene of Night,
While Shee in thee more beautious did appeare,
What mourning Weedes (alas) now do'st thou weare?
How loathsome to mine Eyes is thy sad Sight?
How poorely look'st thou, with what heauie cheare,
Since that Sunne set, which made thee shine so bright?
Vnhappie now thee close, for as of late
To wondring Eyes thou wast a Paradise,
Bereft of Her who made thee fortunate,
A Gulfe thou art, whence Cloudes of Sighes arise:
  But unto none so noysome as to mee,
  Who hourly see my murth'red Ioyes in thee. (Drummond 1616: Sonnet 44)

Drummond has used Sidney's trick of apostrophising an object connected with Stella as a starting point, but has thereafter lost, or
deliberately avoided, Petrarch's hard particularity in favour of an
ingenious elaboration of the idea of the single window, first as a frame
or "sphere", then a black shape of mourning, then a gateway to
Paradise, and then (until the gates close) a sort of Dantesque gulf into
darkness. I hesitate to say that he has done better than Petrarch, but
this is a more focused and metaphorically more coherent sonnet,
which in its elaboration of Petrarch's opening image could be said to
"quintessence" in fine (i.e. detailed and elaborate) "substance".

But this is of course just a single sonnet – what might one say
about the quintessencing of a whole sequence? Here again, Drummond's critical comments are suggestive:

Among our English Poets, Petrarch is imitated, nay surpast in some things, in Matter
and Manner: In Matter, none approach him to [*sic*: Scots "nearer than"] Sidney, who
hath Songs and Sonnats in Matter intermingled: In Manner, the nearest I find to him is
W. Alexander; who, insisting in these same steps, hath Sextains, Madrigals and
Songs, Echoes and Equivoques, which he hath not; whereby, as the one hath surpast
him in Matter, so the other in manner of writing, or Form. (Sage and Ruddiman eds
1711: 226)

We would now think Drummond over-partial to his good friend Sir
William Alexander, but the point has a certain force. Alexander's
sonnet sequence, *Aurora* (1604), which Drummond read in 1606, is
the only British sequence, apart from Drummond's own, to do what
Petrarch had done, that is, mingle longer serious poems apparently at
random among the sonnets. Petrarch has 317 sonnets, 29 canzoni of
varying lengths and subject matter, 11 ballads and madrigals, and 9
sestinas. Alexander has 105 sonnets, 10 songs, 3 elegies, and 6
madrigals and short poems. (Drummond, to anticipate a little, has 68
sonnets, 4 songs, 2 sestinas and 15 madrigals.) Thus Alexander, writing about a third as much, has songs and madrigals in about the same
proportion as Petrarch; but Drummond clearly thinks that by using one
or two verse forms that Petrarch did not use, Alexander had gone one
better, and for him variety of forms is a criterion of excellence.

The comment on Sidney is less clear. It is true that the formal
variety of Sidney's *Astrophel and Stella* is not nearly as great as that
of Petrarch's *Rime*; it is also true, and this is probably what
Drummond is getting at, that the tone or register of Sidney's lyrics is

much more variable, ranging from the wanton, as Puttenham might have said, to the high-minded, and with constantly varying topics ("in matter intermingled"). Drummond imitated Sidney so much that he obviously approved of this. Yet, if this is what he meant, when Drummond came to assemble his own sequence, he did not, other than very briefly in particular sonnets, try to catch Sidney's intermingling of *matter*. He did his best to surpass Petrarch in *manner* by following Alexander's example, and varying his forms: he has 68 sonnets, 4 songs, 13 madrigals (a huge number in proportion to Petrarch's) and 2 sestinas. But in the songs, as if to strike out deliberately on his own, he takes quite the opposite rhetorical direction from Sidney. Instead of going down to the folksong or ballad or lute song register, he goes up to the dream vision register of high romance, and writes two enormously long songs, one near the beginning of the first part of the sequence, a spring song of love of 252 lines ("It was the time"), and the other at the end of the second part, an apparently symmetrical autumn song of death and loss of 248 lines ("It Autumn was"). The other two songs also balance: "Phoebus arise" in the first part is a song in irregular couplets welcoming love and the sunrise; "Sad Damon being come" is a song likewise in irregular couplets, lamenting the death of his mistress, though it is about twice the length of its opposite number in the first part.

Drummond's pre-publication "issues" of his poems, already referred to, may have been designed to sound out his friends and elicit their criticisms: certainly Sir William Alexander obliged him:

To his very worthy Friend Mr William Drummond of Hawthornden

Brother,
I have perused those Pieces, which you sent me, but in such Haste, that I have rather marked the Faults than mended them; which are very few, some of the Printer, some of the Accent, and others in the Congruity according to the phrase here. This is only in a few particulars, but the whole is good, especially your Song.
I may have mistaken some Defects which I find; but I am too free a Friend not to be a Critick at such Times.
Be plain with me again, for no Fortune can change me from what I am to you. Yesterday M. John Murray dies. Eight Days ago I wrote a Sonnet, divining his Death, which you shall receive here: The King commended it much, but thought that I gave him too much Praise, at least it was a generous Error. I envy no man, and shall never be a Niggard to any Mans Worth in that which I can afford. It may be I come to Scotland the [sic] Year for a Forth-night; if I do, I will forwarn you to be where we

may meet, and I shall be loath to want you all the time. Commend me to Scots-Tarbet. So continues

Your loving Brother, W. Alexander
London 12 of April 1615

This (Sage and Ruddiman 1711: 150) tells us, not just that Alexander was trying to bring Drummond's Scots grammar and stress into line with English usage, but that what Drummond had sent him was printed material, and only a portion of his *Poems* – at least, if the word "Song" is to be trusted in the singular (the reader is reminded of the Affair of the Missing Manuscripts – we are dependent upon the accuracy of Sage and Ruddiman's transcription, and *Songs* is easily to be misread as *Song)*. If the singular is correct, the Poems were evidently going through the press in the first quarter of 1615, and Drummond had peeled off the sheets as far as the portion before the second Song to send to his friend. (It is of course not clear which Song of the four Drummond wrote is being referred to, but Alexander's letter does not suggest that this was the second or third time he had done this for Drummond).

We do not know what detailed comments Alexander (and Drummond's other friends) sent back to him, but he decided, it seems, not just to correct misprints and Scotticisms but also to rearrange the order of the poems throughout, take out a couple and add about twenty new ones. As said earlier, all this took so much time that his printer, Andro Hart, broke up and redistributed his type, and the 1616 *Poems* are a new edition. (There were actually two impressions of that edition, but these were textually identical.) The pre-publication edition, if I can call it that, is usually assigned to 1614, mainly because it includes translations and adaptations of poems by Giambattista Marino, whom Drummond read in 1613; but the 1616 edition includes extra translations and adaptations from Marino, suggesting that Drummond was still absorbing Marino's poetry in the period between the two editions. If what Drummond sent to Alexander in early 1615 was only the first Song and its preceding and following sonnets, then Hart had probably started resetting for the 1616 *Poems*.

Now if Drummond was thinking, as he rearranged his material for the new edition, of quintessencing Petrarch, the rearrangements that he made might give some clues. At this point, it is relevant to recall that since the discovery in 1957 of the unique copy of

Drummond's broadside sonnet on the death of "the right Worthie and Vertuous Euphemia Kyninghame" with the date of death on it, 23 July 1616 (STC 7252.3), and R.H. Macdonald's masterly article in 1965 (Macdonald 1965), the idea that Drummond wrote the second part of his sonnet sequence, containing the poems on his mistress's death, in response to Miss Cunningham's death, is not accepted now. Nearly all the poems *in morte* were in the prepublication edition, and even the 1616 edition must have been well through the typesetting stage, if not actually finished, by July 1616. To explain the earlier writing of the poems *in morte*, we have Drummond's comment that "this one thing which is followed by the Italians, as of Sanazarius and others is, that none celebrateth their mistres after her death, which Ronsard hath imitated" (Sage and Ruddiman 1711: 226). If he was indeed trying to improve on the Petrarchan template, then what he had noted there would supply him with a motive for writing a set of sonnets on his mistress's death.

Some of the other changes between 1614 and 1616 then begin to make sense. It is impossible in the space of this article, to describe all the rearrangements he made, but the two editions can be schematised as follows:

[1614]
The First Part

12 sonnets
Song I ("It was the time")
20 sonnets, 1 madrigal, 1 sextain
Song II ("Phoebus arise")
12 sonnets, 4 madrigals
Sextain ii Sextain ii
8 sonnets, 1 madrigal

The Second Part

10 sonnets, 2 madrigals
Song I ("Sad Damon being come")
2 sonnets, 2 madrigals
Song II ("It Autumn was")
----
3 miscellaneous sonnets, 1 madrigal

Urania: 4 sonnets

[1616]
The First Part

11 sonnets
Song I ("It was the time")
24 sonnets, 3 madrigals, 1 sextain
Song II ("Phoebus arise")
8 sonnets, 3 madrigals

12 sonnets, 4 madrigals

The Second Part

7 sonnets, 1 madrigal
Song I ("Sad Damon being come")
6 sonnets, 4 madrigals
Song II ("It Autumn was")

Teares on the Death of Moeliades

Urania or Spirituall Poems
9 sonnets, 3 madrigals

Song I ("Great God")

4 complimentary sonnets to the author   1 complimentary sonnet

----

Tears on the Death of Moeliades.

--------------------   --------------------

Madrigals and Epigrammes   *Madrigals and Epigrammes*

(It is notable that while in 1614 there is a type ornament separating "The Second Part" from the 3 miscellaneous sonnets, and while *Tears on the death of Moeliades* and *Madrigals and Epigrammes* have their own title pages, in 1616 "The Second Part" has its running title continued right on to the last complimentary sonnet.)

We may notice that the long 248-line poem "It Autumn was" which ends the second part of the sonnet sequence in both editions seems to have been modelled on a long poem by Petrarch towards the end of his *Rime*, the poem "Quando il soave mio fido conforto" in which he imagines Laura appearing at his bedside in a vision and consoling him with a gentle rebuke. After this Petrarch puts five spiritual sonnets, and then a long poem to the Blessed Virgin, which ends the sequence. Now in Drummond's 1614 volume, "It Autumn was" is followed by a group of miscellaneous poems: three complimentary sonnets, four semi-religious sonnets entitled "Urania", four poems by friends of Drummond's praising him, and then a reprint of his 1613 poem on the death of Prince Henry, *Tears on the Death of Moeliades*, with its own title page dated 1614. In 1616 this order changes: after "It Autumn was", comes *Teares on the Death of Moeliades*, completely reset, without its title page but with a new fly-title, showing the Drummond was thinking of it as subsidiary to his sonnets, not an independent work; then comes "Urania, or Spirituall Poems", again with its own fly-title, consisting of the four spiritual poems from 1614 plus eight other lyrics and a long devotional poem of 68 lines in quatrains, "Great God, whom we with humble thoughts adore". And all this material, including the "Tears on the Death of Moeliades", has the same running title, "The Second Part", which it didn't have in 1614.

So we have an intensification of the Petrarchan template: a bedside consolation poem, and then after that a group of poems of spiritual resignation, followed by a long prayer poem, not to the Virgin Mary, but to God. The joker in this Second Part pack is of course the poem on Prince Henry; but again there is a parallel.

Immediately after "Quando il mio soave conforto" Petrarch placed
another long poem ("Qual antiquo il mio dolce empio signore") in
which he complains against Love for destroying his life – a plaint
poem. If Drummond saw this, in one or other of the two editions of
Petrarch that he owned (Petrarch 1598; Petrarch 1600; Macdonald
1971: 1135, 1261), he might well have felt that his lament for Prince
Henry would fit: it does not break the mood of lamentation, it is a
complaint against death, and it is of course a poem which Drummond
already had, which he was proud of and wished to publish again. He
would also know, I suppose, that there are quite a number of long
poems and short ones, in Petrarch's *Rime* directed to or about persons
other than Laura.

This is pure hypothesis, but it is backed up by something else one
can see in the rearrangement of sonnets within the two parts (Drummond and his printer did not number the 1616 sonnets, so all numbers
are mine, ignoring all non-sonnets.) More than seventy-five percent of
the poems in the 1614 volume have been moved about in 1616, and
though I have no space to detail all those shifts of sonnets and songs,
they can be summed up by saying that in the short Second Part, the
sonnets apparently written after his mistress's death, Drummond just
extends what he already had. In the First Part, it looks as though he
grouped his sonnets in thematic groups: he opens (in 1616) with three
sonnets about writing poetry, very much in Sidney's manner [1–3],
and then moves into a group of sonnets about light and dark and sleep
[4–11]: one sonnet, "When Nature now had wonderfully wrought",
which was in that group in 1614 and didn't fit was shifted out to become no. 18. Then after the Song "It was the time" we have a small
group of sonnets about rivers and floods [14–17]. After that come ten
rather miscellaneous sonnets, mostly in praise of the mistress [18–27],
which finish with an epilogue sonnet about writing poetry [27], again
shifted down from an earlier place in 1614 where it did not fit.

Then in both editions comes a group of lamentation sonnets
[1616: 28–35], finished with a Song, "Phoebus arise" which is a call
for spring love, leading into five sonnets and a madrigal about the
fairness of the earth [36–40]. It is the next section, from 41 through to
55, that is the most thoroughly rearranged from the 1614 edition, with
two new poems added, and the old ones shuffled about quite a lot. The
effect of the rearrangement is to put first the very Petrarchan poems
about the absence of the mistress from the places where he used to see

her [41–48], and then after them, in a gradually intensifying sequence, the poems of grief over her continuing absence (the madrigal "Unhappy light", 49–54 and 3 other madrigals). The two new sonnets that he added [51, 53] were poems of that kind Finally, he had finished Part One in 1614 with a sonnet to Fame, inviting Fame to keep Auristella's name alive ("Fame, who with golden pennes"); now he moved it up [52] and brought down to the end his own reworking of Petrarch's "Place me whereas the sun doth parch the green" sonnet 55, thus finishing his lamentation sequence with a declaration of constancy. This makes a very neat transition into Part Two, where the speaker then has to be constant in the face of the mistress's death.

It makes a kind of sense, and moreover it does something that Petrarch did not obviously do. Allowing for the fact that Drummond is working at less than a quarter of Petrarch's length – 89 poems in all as compared with Petrarch's 366 – Petrarch's ordering in his first part, that is, the sonnets *In vita di Madonna Laura,* is pretty miscellaneous, and Drummond, if he was really grouping thematically and in a kind of emotional progression, might well have thought he was quintessencing Petrarch in a more refined substance – missing out, for example, the political and occasional sonnets that Petrarch inserted, and giving some kind of intensifying movement to the whole, particularly by punctuating the sonnets with songs and madrigals which, unlike Petrarch's canzoni and sestinas, always correspond to the mood of the sonnets around them.

If so, then we may read the remaining changes as in some way climactic: the very miscellaneous poems which came after the Song "It Autumn was" in 1614 have been edited and rearranged, and formally reassembled under a new running-title "The Second Part", which did not exist in 1614. Sir David Murray's complimentary sonnet shifts to the end of the whole Second Part, and "Teares on the Death of Moeliades", with its 1614 title page now removed, stands before the "Urania" group of spiritual sonnets, now extended with five new sonnets and three madrigals. Then at the end Drummond placed his hymn, "Great God whom we with humble thoughts adore", a final, penitential song which if different in religious sentiment is not so very different in effect from Petrarch's "Vergine bella" at the end of the *Rime Sparse*. Drummond was no doubt loth to omit his elegy on Prince Henry, and was prepared to shoehorn it into place under the running-title: that he did not leave it with its previous title page as an independent work is probably the clearest indication of his unifying intentions – not always successful – in rearranging and augmenting the contents of the 1614 prepublication edition for what was to be his poetic debut in 1616.

Bibliography

Drummond of Hawthornden, William. 1969. *Poems by William Drummond of Hawthornden*. Menston, England: The Scolar Press.

—. 1616. *Poems by William Drummond, of Hawthorn-denne*. Edinburgh: Andro Hart.

Kastner, L.E. (ed.) 1913. *The Poetical Works of William Drummond of Hawthornden*. 2 vols. Manchester: University Victoria Press.

Laing, David. 1857a. "A Brief Account of the Hawthornden Manuscripts" in *Archaeologia Scotica or Transactions of the Society of Antiquaries of Scotland*. 5 vols. Edinburgh: for the Society. IV: 57–116.

—. 1857b. "Extracts from the Hawthornden Manuscripts" in *Archaeologia Scotica or Transactions of the Society of Antiquaries of Scotland*. 5 vols. Edinburgh: for the Society. IV: 241–270.

MacDonald, R.H. 1965. "Drummond, Miss Euphemia Kyninghame and the poems" in *Modern Language Review* 60: 494–99.

—. 1971. *The Library of Drummond of Hawthornden*. Edinburgh: Edinburgh University Press.

Petrarch, Francis. 1598. *Il Petrarcha di nuovo ristampato e diligentemente corretto*. Venice: N. Misserino.

—. 1600. *Le Petrarque en Rime Francoise avecq ses Commentaires, traduict par Philippe de Maldeghem, Seigneur de Leyschoot*. Bruxelles: R. Velpius.

—. 1976. *Petrarch's Lyric Poems* (ed. and tr. Robert M. Durling). Cambridge, Mass. and London, England: Harvard University Press.

Pollard, A.W. et al. 1976–91. *Short-Title Catalogue of Books printed in England, Scotland and Ireland: and of English Books printed abroad: 1475–1640*. 3 vols. London: Bibliographical Society.

Sage, John, and Thomas Ruddiman (eds). 1711. *The Works of William Drummond*. Edinburgh: James Watson.

Afterword

Sally Mapstone

Keywords: John Barbour; Robert Bruce; William Drummond; Patrick Gordon; historiography; history; kings; James I; James IV; James V; James VI; Arthur Johnston; reading and writing; relationships between Scottish and English literature;

Up to the nineteenth century one of the caves close to William Drummond's castle at Hawthornden was known as Bruce's Library, "on the supposition that the square-holed stone shelving must have served admirably for the numerous books and parchments with which that scholarly hero may have solaced himself in the hard time of his skulking and probationary fighting for the Scottish kingdom" (Masson 1873: 4).[1] Despite the intrinsic unlikelihood of this appealing idea, it does, of course, receive some support from Barbour's *Bruce*, where during a crossing of Loch Lomond, "The king [...] meryly / Red to thaim that war him by / Romanys of worthi Ferambrace" (McDiarmid and Stevenson 1980–85: 2: 61: II, ll. 435–37), that is from a (probably English) version of the Charlemagne romance of *Fierabras* (for its transmission in England and Scotland see Ailes 2003 and Knott 2003). And in Barbour's poem the king also cites other references which suggest his familiarity with historical and classical literature (for the examples of Hannibal and Caesar, see McDiarmid and Stevenson 1980-85: 2: 52-56, III, 188-298). Bruce thus seems to have sustained some reputation as a king with literary inclinations from at least the late fourteenth century onwards.

William Drummond of Hawthornden was himself interested in monarchs as readers. His *History of Scotland, From the Year 1423, to the Year 1542*, composed c.1633–44 and first published posthumously (in London; see Rae 1975: 23–25), assessed the varying degrees of

---

[1] The caves are thought to go back to Pictish times. By the 1960s the "Library" had lost precedence to other designations: "In the cliffs beneath the house are numerous caves and passages carved out of the solid rock which are traditionally associated with Robert the Bruce and the Wars of Independence. These are known as the King's Gallery, the King's Dining room and the King's Bedchamber" (Tranter 1962:106). There is no mention of "Bruce's Library" in the standard Buildings of Scotland volume; rather, "In one of them a COLUMBARIUM of about 370 compartments, cut from the rock": (McWilliam 1980: 248).

literacy of the first five James. James I seemed "rather born to letters than instructed. He wrote verses, both *Latine* and *English*, of which many yet are extant" (Drummond 1655: 31). This image of James was founded in Bower's *Scotichronicon* (Watt 1987; 308-9, ll. 3-4 and Watt et al. 1998: 128-31, Perth MS epitaph), and heightened by the transmission of the *Kingis Quair*, and by John Mair's *Historia Maioris Britanniae* (Mapstone 1997: 66-68). James IV, on the other hand, "delighted more in War than the Arts" (Drummond 1655: 152; in later editions this is revised to "delighted more in Mars than the Muses"). Drummond started his *History* with the reign of James I, and thus did not address in any detail the reign of Bruce;[2] nor is Bruce treated at any length in his poetry. There is no record that his extensive library contained a printed edition of Barbour's poem.[3] And when Drummond did express views on the Bruce and the *Bruce* he did so with a whimsy that twice exposes some of the ideological complications of what it meant to be a Scots royalist in the post-Union of the Crowns era.

The brief "Bibliotheca Imaginaria" that Drummond compiled c.1611[4] concluded with *The Battle of Banoch-burne*. His bibliographer thought this title "pointless" as far as any kind of literary joke was concerned (MacDonald 1971: 228) but Drummond was surely positing a work along the lines of his friend and correspondent Michael Drayton's celebrated "Battle of Agincourt". That poem had appeared in 1606 to considerable acclaim in Drayton's *Poemes Lyrick and Pastorall*, of which Drummond possessed a copy (MacDonald 1971: 191, item 761); and it remains one of Drayton's best-known works. The battle of Bannockburn is, of course, a highpoint of Barbour's *Bruce*. The humorous tenor of the invented titles in Drummond's

---

[2] The 1655 edition, printed in London by Henry Hall, contained (doubtless for the benefit of English readers) a prefatory account, by Christopher Irwin, of Scottish history from the Great Cause, up to the reign of James I.

[3] Those available to him would have included the Charteris edition of 1571, and (probably too late for influence on his imaginary library mentioned below) the editions printed by Hart in 1616 and in 1620.

[4] MacDonald (1971: 228) suggests that "Drummond must have meant to compile a list of joke titles (on the lines of John Donne's imaginary library), but ran out of wit". Donne's *Catalogus Librorum Aulicorum* ...was not, however, published until 1650, and it more likely that Drummond had in mind the imaginary library at St Victor spoofed in Rabelais' *Pantagruel* (chapter 7), of which he owned a copy (MacDonald 1971: 213, item 1137); see also Screech (1979: 60–63). For Donne's imaginary library, see Simpson: 1930.

"Bibliotheca Imaginaria" suggests that Drummond did not envisage himself as competing seriously with Drayton's poem or Barbour's *Bruce* itself, nor would he necessarily have wished to. That there was a continuing market for Bruceian materials in the two decades after the Union was borne out in 1615 by the publication (in Dordrecht) of Patrick Gordon of Ruthven's poem, the *Famous Historie of [...] ROBERT, surnamed the BRUCE*,[5] and Barbour's poem was reprinted by Andro Hart in 1616 and 1620. But for the royalist Drummond, engagement with the nationalistic epics of a time of conflict between England and Scotland may not have appealed. This is certainly the tenor of his approach later in life, when he returned to the issue of the publication of the *Bruce* in his *Considerations to the Parliament, September 1639*. Opposed to the radicalism of the Covenanting Parliament of that year, Drummond satirised its pretensions by setting out 59 measures which the Parliament should pass. These included

That the Books of *Wallace* and King *Robert* the *Bruce* be printed over again, against our old Enemies of *England*, and Pensions be given to some learned Rhimers, to write XII. Books of our Expedition and Victory at *Dunslaw*, or *DUNSLAIDOS*, Libri 12. (Drummond 1711: 186; see Kerrigan 2001: 174-5)

From this satirical perspective, the *Bruce*, a poem that originally emerged from a context of Stewart support, if not Stewart patronage, has become an inflammatory and anti-(Charles) Stewart poem.

Barbour's *Bruce* and Drummond's poetic writings are the book-ends of this volume. Its two hundred and fifty year span covers the major period in which Older Scots literature defined itself. Poetry, the major focus of this volume, was a key element throughout. And across this period many Scottish writers, from Barbour himself onwards, pursued a continuous dialogue with their source material. For reasons undoubtedly connected with the complex political course of its history, Older Scots literature is a highly interrogatory medium. It is enquiring of itself, and of the consonance of its own literary history with the present day, as we have already seen in Drummond's

---

[5] It had been licensed for publication in December 1613 (Brunsden, 1999: 90–91); see also Spiller (1998: 154–55); and Stevenson (1996: 175–87). Drummond cannot be shown to have possessed a copy of this poem, but he is likely to have known it, given that he contributed commendatory verses to another of Gordon's works *The first book of the famous historie of Penardo and Laissa*, published again in Dordrecht in 1615 (MacDonald: 1971: 50).

reactions to the *Bruce*. But it is equally enquiring, as the essays in this volume have delineated, of materials it inherits from England, from the Continent, and from Gaelic tradition.

Andrew Taylor's fascinating analysis of the role of the Giles D'Argentan episode in Barbour's *Bruce* and its relation to other accounts in English and continental sources, focuses on a part of the poem that equally preoccupied a poet of whom we have already heard, Patrick Gordon of Ruthven. His *Famous History* of Bruce indeed concludes with a lengthy and flamboyant account of the encounter between Bruce and Giles D'Argentan at Bannockburn. For Gordon this is the highpoint of the Bruceian story. The attention that his account accords to the English knight, Argentan, may represent a diplomatic restyling of Anglo-Scottish relations in the post-Union era; but Argentan still dies at Bruce's hands. Equally intriguing is the way in which in his prose preface to his poem Gordon posits Bruce as a man of letters who would "always repeat these werses following: Ni me Scotorum Libertas prisca moveret/Non mala tot paterer orbis, ob imperium", verses which were said to be "written and subscribed with his owin hand in his Manuall book which he always careed about with him [and] was extant within thes few years" (Gordon 1615: sig. ii^v). These verses have a distinguished history, as they are included in chapter 11 of Book XII of Bower's *Scotichronicon*, having first appeared in annal 118 of the *Gesta Annalia* often attached to Fordun's Chronicle (Watt 1991: 324, 424). However, Gordon's attribution marks another significant contribution to the image of Bruce as a man of letters. The D'Argentan episode and the image of the literate and literary Bruce look of course like creative responses to Barbour's poem, but Gordon's discussion of his source materials is at once obscure and fascinatingly provocative. He does not name the *Bruce*, but initially suggests that he struggled creatively with an unnamed "old printid book" (Barbour's poem had been printed by Robert Lekprevik for Henry Charteris in 1571), which "besyds the owtworne barborous speiches was so evill composd that I culd bring it to no good method" (Gordon 1615: sig. ii^v). This situation was resolved,

Gordon claims, by his friend Donald Farquharson,[6] providing him with "a book of virgine parchement, which he hade found amongst the rest of his books":

> [...] it was old and torne and almost inlegeable in manie places vanting leaves yet hade it the beginning and hade bein sett doune by a monk in the abbey of melro*s*, called *Peter Fenton* in the year of god/one thousand thrie hundredth sixtie nyne, [...] it was in old ryme like to Chaucer, but vanting in manie parts and in especial from the field of *Bannochburne* forth it wanted all the rest almost, so that it could not be gotten to the press. (Gordon 1615: sigs ii^v–iii^r)

This supplementary but fragmentary text sounds perhaps more like Barbour's *Bruce* than the "old printed book", but Gordon distances it from Barbour's poem by attributing it to the Melrose monk Fenton. Given that the Latin quotation he ascribes to Bruce suggests that Gordon may have seen Fordun or Bower's chronicles in manuscript, one should not too rapidly treat this reference to a source manuscript as a convenient invention. But as far as I am aware, no record of a Melrose monk called Peter Fenton in this period survives, and the Melrose allusion rather suggests that Gordon knew something of the Melrose chronicle and thought this a plausible location with which to link his "source".[7] His debt to Barbour's poem seems one he is rather more concerned to disguise than to identify; seventeenth-century royalist writers like Drummond and Gordon seem thus to have had a far from straightforward relationship with the earlier Scots literature of the independent kingdom.

As Nicola Royan's admirable introduction to this volume makes clear, in Older Scots literature, the political is rarely far from the poetic. This comes across especially strongly in the essays by Joanna Martin, Rosemary Greentree, and Thomas Rutledge. Joanna Martin's important placing of the *Kingis Quair* against a backdrop of English

---

[6] Possibly his neighbour Donald Farquharson of Monaltrie, who figures with distinction on the royalist side in the Civil War in Gordon's later historical work, *A Short Abridgement of Britane's Distemper*; this was completed c.1650, but not printed until the Spalding Club edition of 1844 (110–12). For discussion of Farquharson's role in the war, as treated by Gordon see Cowan: 1977.

[7] I am grateful to Stephen Boardman and to Dauvit Broun for discussion of this point. One of the first commentators to treat this issue in Gordon's work was David Irving (1861: 109–10). He took Fenton's work as a reality; Matthew McDiarmid, in the Scottish Text Society edition of *Bruce*, is clear that it is a "seventeenth-century fiction" (McDiarmid and Stevenson 1980–85: 1: 15).

"Lancastrian" texts takes even further than Taylor's a sustained analysis of how Scottish texts both adopt and critique English material. Martin's adept scrutiny of the workings of the amatory and the political in the *Kingis Quair* sets up a paradigm that could so usefully be extended to a book-length study of the interaction of these themes in Scottish writing of both the fifteenth and the sixteenth centuries. This is borne out in this volume itself by the way in which Rosemary Greentree's study of Dunbar's "This hyndir nycht in Dunfermeling" connects back to Martin's in its uncovering of the theme of unbridled kingly desire in the poem's probable allusions to James IV. Greentree's essay also looks forward to Thomas Rutledge's study of Bellenden's *Proheme of the Cosmographe*, an advice to princes poem to the young James V that again focuses its admonitory message through contrasting the dangers of desire and "delite" with the values of reason and virtue. Strikingly, related subject matter surfaces again in this collection, in essays focusing on the poetry of the middle and the latter parts of the sixteenth century. R. James Goldstein's discussion of Lyndsay's two "Squyer Meldrum" poems, points up their complex lineaments of desire, but also their crucial connection to a period characterised by the absence of kingly authority, "Our King was bot fyue yeiris of age, / That time quhen done wes the outrage" (Hadley Williams 2000: 168, ll. 1389–90) – of the attack on Meldrum. But one also wonders whether the absence of a dominant kingly figure is not felt to increase the sense of sexual licence and its consequences that these poems explore. In Katherine McClune's study of the sonnets of James VI of Scotland and John Stewart of Baldynneis, the tensions between amatory desire and reasoned self-governance that feature in the work of the king and his distant relative are seen to emerge from an Older Scots tradition of some age and substance. New the sonnet may have been to post-Reformation Scotland; but the use to which it was put had its roots in the pre-Reformation period. These various essays show up this theme; a more extended study would do so even more strongly.

Equally valuable too for Older Scots literature would be a wider exploration of the associative vocabulary of texts concerned with both the royal body and the body politic. This kind of work is being done very effectively in relation to Middle English literature. Paul Strohm's challenging analysis of the competition amongst different political factions for mastery of the lexical hierarchy of English political discourse in the mid-late fifteenth century (Strohm: 2005) maps a mode of approach that could be usefully appropriated in relation to Scottish writing of the same period, and beyond; Brown (1996) offers the beginnings of a related analysis of the lexical connotations of "tyranny" in the pre-1450 period. Nicole Meier's essay in this collection, however, also reminds us of the crucial importance of keeping in view the Gaelic or Celtic context for Older Scots literature – reading across from the Dunbar and Kennedy *Flyting* to its (at the least) analogues in Scots Gaelic and Irish literature, offers an insight into Dunbar's own poetic strategies concerning his Highland opponent in this poem (for comparable examples of reading across Scots and Gaelic literature in the later sixteenth century, see Hadley Williams 2005 and Gillies 2005).

In the 1970s and early 1980s the area of main focus in Older Scots literary study was the second half of the fifteenth century and the beginning of the sixteenth (major events here were Fox 1981 and Gray 1981, and seminal articles included Lyall 1976). From the second half of the 1980s, through the 1990s and into the first decade of the new millennium, literature of the second half of the sixteenth century and the early seventeenth century has come to dominate the focus, particularly through the excellent work that has been done on Alexander Montgomerie and James VI and I (for example, Lyall 2005 and Fischlin and Fortier 2001). Periods that now deserve comparable attention are that between Flodden and the Reformation,[8] and the seventeenth century. Both receive impetus in essays in this collection. Thomas Rutledge's intriguing analysis of Bellenden's self-fashioning as Gavin Douglas's heir is part of a spate of recent work on this yet still neglected poet and prose-writer. J.Derrick McClure's essay on Lyndsay treats another neglected area of the writing of this period, though it is one which McClure's recent set of essays (including McClure 2001 and 2005) on this subject is doing much to repair, that of prosody. The consonances he finds between moral state or subject and metrical consonance in Lyndsay's poetic and dramatic advisory works dovetail suggestively with the kinds of ideological and thematic analysis pursued in other essays in this book, especially those by

---

[8] Much of the most valuable cultural criticism of the literature of the 1520s–40s, especially on David Lyndsay, has been written by Janet Hadley Williams. See, for example, Hadley Williams (2003). Another significant contributor in this period is A.A. MacDonald; see for instance, MacDonald (1996).

Martin and Rutledge. The advantage of following through from
Lyndsay's earlier poetry to *Ane Satyre* illustrates once more the value
of "joined up thinking" in relation to the study of Older Scots
literature. Our field is one which attracts the essayist; it needs to do
more to cultivate the monograph.

The seventeenth century is represented in this volume by the two
essays by Michael Spiller and by David W. Atkinson. Both deal with
William Drummond. As my own comments on Patrick Gordon of
Ruthven have sought to show, there is much more in the seventeenth
century than Drummond, especially in the post-Jacobean era; but it is
nonetheless the case that Drummond's works themselves call out for
more sustained scrutiny by literary scholars. Drummond has been well
treated by bibliographers; although ground-breaking work has been
done on his historical and poetic output, there is still much more to be
undertaken. These two essays, on two different though related aspects
of Drummond's poetic writing (his Petrarchanism and his religiosity),
are good markers of the kinds of enquiry his work needs. Spiller's
engagement with the publication history of Drummond's 1614 and
1616 *Poems* is especially telling. His essay also shows up another way
in which currents were significantly changing in post-Union poetry.
The kind of Petrarchanism Drummond goes in for has its precedents
in Scottish writing, especially in William Alexander's *Aurora* (1604).
But its Scottish (as opposed to English or continental) analogues are
primarily in post-Union of the Crowns writing. The tension between
the amatory and the political, so evident, as we have seen, in so much
pre-1603 Scottish poetry does continue in the post-Union era, notably,
for instance, in Alexander's *Monarchicke Tragedies*; but this period
also sees the release of a quantity of amatory writing that feels less
need to engage with that particular area of conflict. This phenomenon,
too, is worthy of greater study.

Drummond's *Flowres of Sion* (discussed here by David W.
Atkinson) was published a couple of years before James I's death; the
poet himself living on for another quarter century. For scholars of
Older Scots the end of the Jacobean era often seems to mark a staging
post beyond which relatively few critics keenly venture (for notable
exceptions, see Spiller 1998: 154-55; Bawcutt 1994 and 2005). This
should not continue to be the case – not least because so many Scottish writers, especially Hary and Lyndsay, went on being published in
the post-Jacobean era, as Scotland continued the interrogation of its

native literary culture (Brunsden 1999, also Parkinson 2002 on the transmission of Montgomerie's poetry).

In his *Epigrammata*, published in Aberdeen in 1630, the Scots Latin poet Arthur Johnston, compared Buchanan and William Drummond. Buchanan had rejected the idiom of his native land for Latin. Drummond, though he could have challenged Buchanan in Latin, preferred the language of his native land:

Maior uter? Primas huic defert Scotia, vates
Vix inter Latios ille secundus erat. (Geddes 1895: 47)

[Which is the greater? Scotia gives first place to the latter [Drummond], the other poet [Buchanan] was scarcely second among the Latin [writers].]

Drummond is ostensibly the beneficiary of Johnston's praise, as the poet given prime billing by the nation's symbolic mother-figure. But for Buchanan to be a narrow second amongst all Latin writers is, surely, an accolade indeed. And Johnston himself is, as customarily, writing in Latin. Drummond is venerated as the poet of Scotland's vernacular – but the vernacular that Drummond commonly wrote in was English rather than Scots (see MacQueen 1990: 29-30). Johnston personifies the nation as *Scotia*, a name traditionally said to derive from the female figure in the Scots origin myth (*"A muliere Scota vocitatur Scocia tota"*, Watt 1991: 142; see Broun 1999: 120–21), and has that personification endorse a poet who writes in the English vernacular. In so doing he shows how far attitudes to Anglicisation had moved in the one hundred and fifty odd years since Walter Kennedy was claiming in the *Flyting* that Gaelic, or "Irische" was "the gud langage of this land, / And Scota it causit to multiply and sprede" (Bawcutt 1998: I, 311). The relationship between the use of Scots and the articulation of nationalistic conviction had in the course of the sixteenth century become a still more contentious matter (McClure 1981). Johnston thus not only communicates here how Latin continued for many Scots writers to be a thriving medium of poetic expression; he also show that to write in English in the post-Union of the Crowns era, was not necessarily to be seen as to have lost one's sense of Scottish nationhood. To observe the continuation of this argument past the watershed of the death of James VI and I in 1625, is to recognise how Scottish writers continued that interrogation of their literary past that we have seen to be an abiding feature of Older Scots literary culture. Johnston's generous but politically nuanced remarks on Drummond's poetry (at a time when Drummond was of course still alive and writing) are a telling reminder of how our own understanding of Older Scots writing is enhanced by reading around and beyond its standard parameters. That must be one of the major challenges for the next generation of Older Scots criticism.

Bibliography

Ailes, Marianne. 2003. "La réception de *Fierabras* en Angleterre" in Le Person, Marc (ed.) *Le Rayonnement de Fierabras dans la Littérature Européenne*. Lyon: Centre d'Etudes des Interactions Culturelles de l'Université de Lyon. 177–89.

Bawcutt, Priscilla. 1994. "The Mystery of *The Spyte of Spaine* (Heirs of Andro Hart, 1628)" in *The Bibliotheck* 19: 5–22.

—. (ed.) 1998. *The Poems of William Dunbar*. 2 vols. Glasgow: Association for Scottish Literary Studies.

—. 2005. "Manuscript Miscellanies in Scotland from the Fifteenth to the Sixteenth Century" in Sally Mapstone (ed.), *Older Scots Literature*. Edinburgh: John Donald. 189–210.

Broun, Dauvit. 1999. *The Irish Identity of the Kingdom of the Scots in the Twelfth and Thirteenth Centuries*. Woodbridge: the Boydell Press.

Brown, Michael. 1996. "'I have thus slain a tyrant': *The Dethe of the Kynge of Scotis* and the right to resist in early fifteenth-century Scotland" in *Innes Review* 47: 24–44.

Brunsden, George M. 1999. "Aspects of Scotland's Social, Political and Cultural Scene in the Late 17th and Early 18th Centuries, as Mirrored in the Wallace and Bruce Traditions" in Cowan, Edward J. and Douglas Gifford (eds) *The Polar Twins*. Edinburgh: John Donald. 75–113.

Cowan, Edward J. 1977. *Montrose: for Covenant and King*. London: Weidenfeld and Nicolson.

Drummond, William of Hawthornden. 1655. *The History of Scotland from the Year 1423 until the Year 1542*. London. Henry Hall.

—. 1711. *The Works of William Drummond of Hawthornden*. 1711. Edinburgh: James Watson. Reprinted 1970. Hildesheim and New York: Georg Olms.

Fischlin, Daniel and Mark Fortier (eds). 2001. *Royal Subjects: Essays on the Writings of James VI and I*. Detroit: Wayne State University Press.

Fox, Denton (ed.) 1981. *The Poems of Robert Henryson*. Oxford: Clarendon Press.

Geddes, Sir W.D. 1895. *Musa Latina Aberdonensis*, vol. 2. Aberdeen: New Spalding Club.

Gillies, William. 2005. "*Gun ann ach an ceò*, Nothing Left but their Mist: Farewell and Elegy in Gaelic Poetry" in Mapstone, Sally (ed.) *Older Scots Literature*. Edinburgh: John Donald. 370–96.

Gordon, Patrick [of Ruthven]. 1615. *The Famous Historie of the Renouned and Valiant Prince ROBERT surnamed the BRUCE king of SCOTLAND &c*. Dordrecht: George Waters.

Gordon, Patrick. 1844. *A Short Abridgement of Britane's Distemper..from M.DC. XXXIX to M.DC. XLIX* (ed. J. Dunn). Aberdeen: Spalding Club.

Gray, Douglas. 1981. *Robert Henryson*. Leiden: E.J. Brill.

Hadley Williams, Janet (ed.) 2000. *Sir David Lyndsay: Selected Poems*. Glasgow: Association for Scottish Literary Studies.

—. 2003. "James V as a Literary Patron" in Gosman, M. A. MacDonald, and A. Vanderjagt (eds) *Princes and Princely Culture 1450–1650, vol. I*. Leiden: E.J. Brill. 173–98.

—. 2005. "'We had the ky and thai gat bot the glaikis': Catching the Echoes in *Duncan Laideus' Testament*" in Mapstone, Sally (ed.) *Older Scots Literature*. Edinburgh: John Donald. 346–69.

Irving, David. 1861. *The History of Scottish Poetry*. Ed. John Aitken Carlyle. Edinburgh: Edmonston and Douglas.

Kerrigan, John. 2001. *On Shakespeare and Early Modern Literature*. Oxford: Oxford University Press.

Knott, Gordon. 2003. "De l'Espagne à l'Écosse (via Maltrible)" in Le Person, Marc (ed.) *Le Rayonnement de Fierabras dans la Littérature Européenne*. Lyon: Centre d'Etudes des Interactions Culturelles de l'Université de Lyon. 191–200.

Lyall, R.J. 1976. "Politics and Poetry in Fifteenth and Sixteenth Century Scotland" in *Scottish Literary Journal* 3: 5–29.

—. 2005. *Alexander Montgomerie: poetry, politics, and cultural change in Jacobean Scotland*. Tempe, AR: University of Arizona Press.

McClure, J. Derrick. 1981. "Scottis, Inglis, Suddroun: Language, Labels and Language Attitudes" in Lyall, Roderick J. and Felicity Riddy (eds) *Proceedings of the Third International Conference on Scottish Language and Literature (Mediaeval and Renaissance)*. Stirling and Glasgow. 52–59.

McDiarmid, M.P. and J.A.C. Stevenson (eds). 1980–85. *The Bruce* [Scottish Text Society 4th series no. 12, 13, 15.]. 3 vols. Edinburgh.

MacDonald, A.A. 1996. "William Stewart and the Court Poetry of the Reign of King James V" in Hadley Williams, Janet (ed.) *Stewart Style 1513–1542, Essays on the Court of James V*. East Linton: Tuckwell Press. 179–200.

MacDonald, Robert H. (ed.) 1971. *The Library of Drummond of Hawthornden*. Edinburgh: Edinburgh University Press.

MacQueen, John. 1990. "Humanism in Sixteenth- and Seventeenth-Century Literature" in MacQueen, J. (ed.) *Humanism in Renaissance Scotland*. Edinburgh: Edinburgh University Press. 10–31.

McWilliam, Colin. 1980. *Lothian, except Edinburgh (Buildings of Scotland)*. Harmondsworth: Penguin.

Mapstone, Sally. 1997. "Kingship and the *Kingis Quair*" in Cooper, Helen and Sally Mapstone (eds) *The Long Fifteenth Century*. Oxford: Oxford University Press. 51–69.

Masson, David. 1873. *Drummond of Hawthornden: The Story of his Life and Writings*. London: Macmillan.

Parkinson, David J. 2002. "Dreams in the Clear Light of Day: Older Scots Poetry in Modern Scotland" in van Heijnsbergen, Theo and Nicola Royan (eds) *Literature, Letters and the Canonical in Early Modern Scotland*. East Linton: Tuckwell Press. 138–50.

Rae, Thomas I. 1975. "The Historical Writing of Drummond of Hawthornden" in *SHR* 54: 22–62.

Screech, M.A. 1979. *Rabelais*. London: Duckworth.

Simpson, Evelyn Mary (ed.) 1930. *The Courtier's Library*. London: Nonesuch Press.

Tranter, Nigel. 1962. *The Fortified House in Scotland*. Vol. I. Edinburgh and London: Oliver and Boyd.

Spiller, Michael. 1998. "Poetry after the Union 1603–1660" in Jack, R.D.S. (ed.) *The History of Scottish Literature, Origins to 1660*. Aberdeen: Aberdeen University Press.141–62.

Stevenson, David. 1996. *King or Covenant? Voices from the Civil War.* East Linton: Tuckwell Press.

Strohm, Paul. 2005. *Politique: Languages of Statecraft between Chaucer and Shakespeare:* Notre Dame: University of Notre Dame Press.

Watt. D.E.R. et al. (eds). 1991. *Scotichronicon by Walter Bower.* Volume 6. Aberdeen: Aberdeen University Press.

—. (ed.) 1987. *Scotichronicon by Walter Bower.* Volume 8. Aberdeen: Aberdeen University Press.

—. et al. (eds). 1998. *Scotichronicon by Walter Bower.* Volume 9. Edinburgh: Mercat Press.

Index